RHETORIC AT THE MARGINS

RHETORIC AT THE MARGINS

Revising the

History of

Writing

Instruction

in American

Colleges,

1873–1947

DAVID GOLD

SOUTHERN ILLINOIS UNIVERSITY PRESS / *CARBONDALE*

11 10 09 08   4 3 2 1

Library of Congress Cataloging-in-Publication Data
Gold, David, date.
  Rhetoric at the margins : revising the history of
writing instruction in American colleges, 1873–1947 /
David Gold.
      p. cm.
  Includes bibliographical references and index.
  ISBN-13: 978-0-8093-2834-5 (pbk. : alk. paper)
  ISBN-10: 0-8093-2834-8 (pbk. : alk. paper)
  1. English language—Rhetoric—Study and teaching—
United States—History—19th century. 2. English
language—Rhetoric—Study and teaching—United
States—History—20th century. 3. Report writing—
Study and teaching (Higher)—United States—History.
4. Education, Higher—United States—History. I. Title.

PE1405.U6G65 2008
808'.042071173—dc22   2007025438

Printed on recycled paper. ♻
The paper used in this publication meets the minimum
requirements of American National Standard for Information Sciences—Permanence of Paper for Printed
Library Materials, ANSI Z39.48-1992. ∞

FOR SARAH AND NATHAN

CONTENTS

Preface: Revisioning History ix
Acknowledgments xiii

Introduction: Beyond Ideology in Rhetoric and Composition
    Historiography 1
1. Integrating Traditions at a Private Black College 14
2. Balancing Tensions at a Public Women's University 63
3. Challenging Orthodoxies at a Rural Normal College 113
Conclusion: History Matters 152

Chronology 159
Notes 163
Bibliography 173
Index 191

PREFACE: REVISIONING HISTORY

All politics, Tip O'Neill famously declared, is local. The same might be said for history. National trends intersect with and often emerge from local communities and constituencies, whose experiences can complicate and confound received historical narratives. Unfortunately, local histories often get erased in the process of history making. In rhetoric and composition studies, recent historical scholarship has begun to reverse this trend. Yet what John C. Brereton acknowledged over a decade ago in his introduction to *The Origins of Composition Studies* remains true today; we still know too little about the classroom experiences of students and educators at Southern, religious, women's, working-class, and historically black colleges. More troublingly, our knowledge has often been filtered through a myth of rhetorical decline, an assumption that innovation begins at elite institutions, and a too-strict adherence to an epistemological taxonomy that does not do full justice to the range of pedagogical practices in diverse institutions.

The stories of such schools need to be told and not simply to represent the experiences of once-neglected communities or to satisfy a sense of historical injustice but to offer a more nuanced and representative picture of the past. Though at the margins of historical consciousness, these schools are far from marginal. In the late nineteenth and early twentieth centuries, significant numbers of rural, working-class, female, and black students were attending college. In 1920, 47% of college students were women (Newcomer 46), a figure that would not again be equaled until 1976. By 1900, over twenty-two hundred black students had received college degrees (*Negro Year Book, 1941–46* 299); by 1937 over thirty-five thousand black students were enrolled in black colleges and universities (Jenkins 118), creating the core of a new black middle class that would lay the groundwork for the civil rights era. Under the auspices of the Morrill Acts, dozens of state universities and industrial colleges were created throughout the South and the West, greatly expanding opportunities for higher education to white and black students of both sexes, while numerous normal schools, both public and private, brought higher education to rural communities throughout the nation. The histories of these schools are our own, and they deserve detailed examination.

This book examines rhetorical education—reading, writing, and speaking instruction—at three institutions neglected by previous historical study: Wiley College in Marshall, Texas (1873), a classically based, private, black liberal arts college; the public Texas Woman's University in Denton (1901), at one time the nation's largest residential college for women; and East Texas Normal College in Commerce (1889), an independent teacher-training school and at one time home to the state's largest summer teachers' program. Each represents an important source of information about the development of higher education in America. All are in the same state, and all were founded to serve disenfranchised communities, yet they display a remarkable range of diversity in faculties, student bodies, institutional missions, and curricula and thus are perfect testing grounds for extant historical claims about the development of rhetoric and writing instruction in American colleges. I chose these schools both because they provide a cross-section of the range of institutions that served American students in the late nineteenth and early twentieth centuries and because each had archival resources substantial enough to sustain in-depth inquiry.

Each of these schools speaks to an important emerging area of research in rhetoric and composition historiography—historically black colleges and universities and African American education, women's colleges and women's education, and normal schools—and, as I hope this study demonstrates, these traditions speak in turn to each other. Though each of these schools offered its students singular, locally enacted experiences, each also belonged to a rich, alternative tradition of rhetorical education in America. Black colleges, women's colleges, teacher-training colleges, and other institutions did not simply adopt, respond to, or even transform pedagogies practiced elsewhere; they created their own.

I have three main goals: (1) to recover important histories that would otherwise be lost and give voice to the experiences of students and educators of a diverse past; (2) to complicate and challenge the master narratives of rhetoric and composition history and the ideological assumptions that underlie them; and (3) to demonstrate persistent connections between the past and the present in order to help develop richer pedagogies for diverse bodies of students. I argue that each of the schools in this study championed intellectual and pedagogical traditions that diverged from the Eastern liberal arts model that often serves as the standard bearer for the development of English studies and rhetorical education. Furthermore, by emphasizing community uplift and civic responsibility and by validating local institutional and demographic realities, these schools created contexts in which otherwise moribund curricular features of the era—such as strict classroom discipline and an emphasis on prescription—took on new possibilities. Indeed, I suggest that the epistemological schema that have long been applied to pedagogical practices may actually limit understanding of those practices.

At Wiley, poet and civil rights activist Melvin Tolson combined African American and classical rhetoric to produce a critical pedagogy that honored students' home voices and fostered progressive political action. At Texas Woman's University, gender-based vocational education served progressive ends; unlike their peers at many contemporary private women's colleges, students were encouraged to participate in public discourse and professional life. At East Texas, founder William Mayo held that each student had a sacred dignity that schools must honor and that practical, universal education was the basis for a democratic society. Together, these schools demonstrate the impressive diversity of rhetorical practices to be found not only in a single geographical region but also in a single classroom. The instructors in these institutions did not enact clearly delineated ideologies or easily identifiable epistemologies but made use of a wide range of practices. Moreover, each school's pedagogical approach was developed with local needs in mind, demonstrating the importance of taking local cultural and historical circumstances into context when developing pedagogies—and writing histories.

The diverse practices at these three institutions in Texas tell us not only about Texas but about emergent trends changing the shape of rhetorical education throughout the country; each college was but one of many nationwide struggling to educate previously disenfranchised communities. These histories also remind us that the history of writing instruction cannot be reduced to simple binary oppositions and epistemological classifications, nor can any given historical period be treated monolithically, nor can any one college—or type of college—serve metaphorically for all. By looking to the margins of rhetorical history, we may find a new center.

ACKNOWLEDGMENTS

I would foremost like to thank my friend and mentor Linda Ferreira-Buckley for her guidance and support. She is the model of professional deportment for more scholars and teachers than she knows. Davida Charney offered early encouragement for the project, and Kate Adams, Trish Roberts-Miller, John Ruszkiewicz, and Helena Woodard provided expert readings and advice. I am particularly grateful to Southern Illinois University Press reviewers Lucille Schultz and Susan Kates for their insightful feedback; this work is richer because of their guidance. My editor, Karl Kageff, was a calm and steady presence throughout. The Spencer Foundation, the East Texas Historical Association, and California State University, Los Angeles, provided generous financial assistance.

Without librarians and archivists, archival historians would not exist. Jim Conrad of Texas A&M University–Commerce and Ann Barton and the library staff of Texas Woman's University guided me through their collections and undoubtedly undercharged me for the many pounds of photocopies they patiently made and mailed. The archival staff of the Library of Congress assisted me in examining the Melvin B. Tolson Papers, and Christina Wolf at Oklahoma City University and Cindy Von Elling at Kansas State University helped me track down important source material.

Over the years, many friends and colleagues have offered advice and support, including Hema Chari, Sharan Daniel, Marilyn Elkins, Jan Fernheimer, Julie Garbus, Catherine Hobbs, Lynda Nuss, Liz Rohan, and Lisa Wittenberg Hillyard. My mother, Sarah Gold, taught me how to read when I was four years old, and I haven't stopped since. Both she and my sister, Paula Gold, have encouraged me throughout my professional career. Priscilla Hohmann has supported me through two years of writing and revision, celebrating every step forward. Her faith, generosity of spirit, and genuine joy on my behalf have made the last part of the journey possible.

Earlier versions of portions of this book were previously published in *College English* ("'Where Brains Had a Chance': William Mayo and Rhetorical Instruction at East Texas Normal College, 1889–1917," copyright 2005 by the National Council of Teachers of English, reprinted with permission); *College Composition and Communication* ("'Nothing Educates Us Like a Shock': The Integrated Rhetoric of Melvin Tolson," copyright 2003 by the National Council of Teachers of English, reprinted with permission); and *Rhetoric Review* ("Beyond the Classroom Walls: Student Writing at Texas Woman's University, 1901–1939," copyright 2003 by David Gold, reproduced by permission of Taylor & Francis Group, LLC, http://www.taylorandfrancis.com). Archival materials appear courtesy the Melvin B. Tolson Papers, Library of Congress; the Woman's Collection, Texas Woman's University; and the Texas A&M University–Commerce Archives.

RHETORIC AT THE MARGINS

INTRODUCTION

Beyond Ideology in Rhetoric and Composition Historiography

In rhetoric and composition studies, historical inquiry has long been driven by a desire not to repeat the pedagogical mistakes of the past. And those mistakes, under the rubric of what is now called current-traditional rhetoric, have been well documented by scholars from Albert R. Kitzhaber in *Rhetoric in American Colleges* to James A. Berlin in *Rhetoric and Reality* and *Writing Instruction* to Sharon Crowley in *Composition in the University* and *Methodical Memory*. Indeed, current-traditional rhetoric has become a convenient catchphrase and catchall for whatever historical pedagogical practices we have deemed reductive, impolitic, or inelegant. As Robert J. Connors summed it up: "Got a contemporary problem? Blame it on that darn old current-traditional rhetoric" (*Composition-Rhetoric* 5).

Despite scholarship that has challenged Berlin's taxonomies—indeed, despite Berlin's own acknowledgement of the limitations of his taxonomies—a tendency remains in the field to rely on epistemological labels to define pedagogical approaches and to see a direct line between ideology and pedagogy, treating the latter as an enactment of the former. In their 2005 study of nineteenth-century textbooks, *Archives of Instruction*, Jean Ferguson Carr, Stephen L. Carr, and Lucille M. Schultz note both the "still common tendency to treat the period dismissively" (3) and the "simplification of varied instructional traditions as 'current-traditional'" (208). The narrative of decline not only persists, it continues to distort attempts at historical inquiry and interpretation. While contemporary rhetoric, writing, and composition instructors have been rightly concerned with the legacy of institutional practices that traditionally limited opportunities for minorities, women, and working-class students, we have too often seen students as helpless victims of instructional ideology, leading us to dismiss or misread historical practices that do not fit easily into contemporary notions of critical, liberatory, or student-centered pedagogy. We have been especially wary of agonistic or prescriptivist language instruction and thus have ignored the potential value of such instruction for empowering students as rhetors and inspiring civic participation. In this chapter, I describe current tensions in the practice of rhetoric and composition historiography, locate my work within emerging trends in the field, and argue for the value of diverse, institutional microhistories that assume a fluid relationship between ideology and pedagogy.

The Roots of Reductive Rhetoric

The story often told of the origins of the field of rhetoric and composition in the late-nineteenth-century academy is a troubled one. Increasing industrialization, a shift from oral to print culture, the advent of institutions of higher learning for black, female, and working-class citizens, and the rise of progressive educational ideals created new constituencies of students, new institutions, and new curricula that challenged long-standing pedagogical traditions. Where students once declaimed in Latin or Greek, they now wrote essays in English. Where a thorough grounding in the classics had once been the mark of a gentleman, a new professional class of businesspeople, engineers, agronomists, health practitioners, home economists, and teachers now demanded practical training in the communicative arts. Where colleges could once be assured of a relatively homogenous group of students, about whom familiarity with canonical texts and a shared oral and written dialect had been assumed, they now faced the task of teaching reading and writing to students of differing social, economic, regional, ethnic, and linguistic backgrounds.

It was within this setting that the first courses in freshman composition were created, born out of the traditional course in rhetoric. These early freshman English courses naturally reflected the dominant institutional concerns of the era. The need to justify coursework in English to an academy that still valued the rigors of Latin and Greek grammars and was suspicious of upstart English departments, the influence of science, scientism, and the Germanic research model, and an increasingly narrowing conception of rhetoric within the academy gave rise to a system of instruction in writing that narrowly construed the possibilities for public discourse and emphasized grammatical correctness over nearly all other rhetorical features.

Scholars have argued that current-traditional rhetoric, as this system has since been labeled,[1] was dominant in American colleges from the late nineteenth century through most of the twentieth, and many maintain it remains the dominant form of writing instruction today. Current-traditional rhetoric has come to embody a number of academic misdeeds. It was positivistic and foundationalist. The truth was "out there"; thus, invention was no longer a knowledge-making process as it ideally was in classical rhetoric but simply a matter of figuring out how to say what one had already concluded. Epistemologically compromised and severed from its classical roots, current-traditional rhetoric, so we are told, stifled students' political participation, perpetuated class inequities, erased or supplanted students' home voices, and was found dull by students and instructors alike. The prevailing attitude of the time was summed up in Harvard University's 1892 *Report of the Committee on Composition and Rhetoric* (Adams, Godkin, and Quincy), which decried the lack of basic writing skills amongst the school's freshmen, setting off a widely reported literacy crisis that further helped institutionalize the teaching of composition. Current-traditional rhetoric has been especially indicted for the contempt with which its practitioners held their students and their use of language. Reading Harvard admissions essays in 1888, Le Baron Russell Briggs complained, "More than all, I am discouraged by wooden unintelligence. . . . Dulness is the substance of scores of themes, and inaccurate dulness at that: there is neither a boy's sprightliness, nor a man's maturity, nor a scholar's refinement, nor yet a reporter's smartness. The average theme seems the work of a rather vulgar youth with his light gone out" (30).

But a turn-of-the-twentieth-century, elite liberal arts college—where what a student learned in the classroom was perhaps less important to his future socioeconomic status than his simple presence—may not necessarily be the place to look for innovative, student-centered English pedagogy. Throughout the last half of the nineteenth century and into the twentieth, traditional liberal arts colleges resisted the systematic changes taking place in American education, often reluctantly incorporating new fields of professional, technical, and scientific training into their curricula only after such programs had been established elsewhere. As Thomas P. Miller has noted, if we were to write the history of rhetoric and composition through the lens of "the most prestigious universities," we would "conclude that there was no such field" ("Where" 66).

The Revisionist Turn

Recently, scholars have begun to complicate the narrative of reductivism and decline associated with rhetorical instruction in the late nineteenth and early twentieth centuries through both a reexamination of traditional sites of historiographical inquiry and an exploration of new ones. Robin Varnum has reminded us of the presence of varied, competing pedagogies—and robust debates about them—in what we have come to call the current-traditional era, and Charles Paine has demonstrated that seemingly Ur-current-traditionalists such as Adams Sherman Hill and Edward T. Channing saw themselves as engaged in cultural critique, hoping to help students resist what we today might call crass commercial or market culture. Susan Kates has demonstrated the presence of activist rhetorics at multiple sites of rhetorical instruction, while Lucille Schultz has pointed out the heretofore forgotten importance of Pestalozzian influences on nineteenth-century composition textbooks.

Thanks to these and other studies, a richer picture of the history of rhetorical instruction in American colleges is beginning to emerge. At literally hundreds of sites of instruction throughout the country—private black colleges, public women's colleges, A&M and engineering schools, labor colleges, and public and private normal schools (teacher-training colleges)—students were being taught that writing and speaking were fundamental to public and professional life. Oratory and public speaking, discontinued or truncated elsewhere, were often integrated into the curriculum, while reductive rhetoric handbooks frequently played only limited roles in writing instruction. Rather than rely on imported philosophical and pedagogical practices, these schools developed their curricula to meet local needs. English instructors stressed the rhetorical components of writing; introduced politics and discourses of power into the classroom; encouraged both self-expression and participation in public discourse; took great personal interest in their students' emotional, academic, and social development; and tried to develop dynamic, useful, locally responsive classroom methods and materials. They introduced innovative pedagogies such as peer review, student grading, portfolios, proposal arguments, and group work. Some even rejected the teaching of "technical" or "formal" grammar. Normal schools in particular stressed the dignity and individuality of each student. While many instructors frequently insisted upon a strict classroom rigor and a disciplinary approach to language instruction that may look suspect today—and resemble what has come to be called current-traditional practice—they did so with a belief it would be valuable to their students' lives. The testimony of their students suggests that they agreed.

   This book extends the dialogue begun by Varnum, Kates, Paine, Schultz, and others through an examination of three sites of rhetorical education at the margins of previous scholarly inquiry: a private black liberal arts college, a public women's college, and an independent normal college. By treating institutions traditionally underexamined by curricular histories, I hope to show the diversity and complexity of rhetorical practices in American colleges in the late nineteenth and early twentieth centuries. While each site in this study displays elements of what Kates has called activist rhetorics—instruction that encouraged students to interrogate their social and political roles through writing and speaking—I am less interested in demonstrating the presence of specifically *activist* rhetorics than in locating the broad confluences of competing and complementary rhetorical traditions within individual sites. Indeed, I argue that the epistemological schema that we have long applied to pedagogical practices may actually limit our understanding of those practices. What we have dismissed as current-traditional rhetoric often represents a complex of interwoven practices, both conservative and radical, liberatory and disciplining, and subject to wide-ranging local and institutional variations.

   As a historian of rhetoric, I set my research within the context of disciplinary histories of rhetorical education, which are entering a new phase of inquiry, both in subject matter and historiographical assumptions. Robert Connors ("Writing the History") and Nan Johnson have described two waves of historical scholarship on the development of rhetoric in American colleges. The first, beginning in the 1930s and extending through the 1950s, was written by speech communication scholars interested in the relationship between classical rhetoric and the development of oratory, and the second was written largely by English department scholars interested in the development of rhetoric and composition. Johnson notes that while first-wave histories tend to be celebratory, second-wave histories assess the era as the period "most responsible for the theoretical impoverishment of the rhetoric of composition and the academic marginalization of rhetoric studies in modern English studies" (11). These second-wave works have brought critical theory and self-reflectiveness to rhetoric and composition historiography. As Stephen M. North has stated, if the first generation of scholars was interested primarily in "the recovery and preservation of teaching practices from the past," the second, "instead of treating historical materials as sources of potentially useful practices . . . [has] begun to try to account for the political, economic, educational, and other forces that have affected writing instruction" (66–67).

   Even as they have done so, however, second-wave historians have tended to be suspicious of the motives of the actors they have studied, often situating themselves within a Marxist-influenced discourse that sees institutional knowledge-making as in the service of illegitimate power structures. Sharon Crowley is one of the most vocal critics of current-traditional rhetoric and institutionalized writing instruction:

> The myth of the academic essay . . . fosters and supports the persistent American belief that universal standards of literacy exist, and it legitimizes and covers over the social and institutional functions of Freshman English (*Composition* 233). . . . [D]o we want to equip students to succeed in a culture that is devastating its natural environment, that fails to care for children, elderly, and poor people, that subjects people to verbal or physical abuse on the basis of gender, ethnicity, or sexual behavior, and that wages war on other peoples for self-serving reasons? Do we want to force students to take a course whose traditional practices aim at making them oblivious to all of this? (*Composition* 248)

James Berlin's histories of rhetoric and writing instruction in American colleges, while offering a groundbreaking taxonomy of the epistemological foundations of rhetorical practices, also grant great cultural power to the work of elite theorists and to institutional artifacts, such as textbooks, in promulgating problematic ideologies.

But literacy, argues Charles Paine, "is neither wholly hegemonic nor wholly subversive; rather, diversity and consolidation are always in tension" (41). Taking note of recent scholarship that rejects "the nice, clean cause-and-effect relationship between ideology and practice" (40), Paine describes three periods in the history of literacy and education. In the first, scholars are not overly concerned with ideology, in the second, they view it as dominant, while in the third, they seek a less monolithic, more divergent understanding of the complex interaction between individuals and cultural forces: "[H]istorians of literacy have gone from viewing literacy unproblematically, to viewing it as dominant-class hegemonic imposition, to viewing literacy as a complex factor in a vast web of social relations that cut across class lines, institutions, and time periods" (40). In describing this trend, Paine specifically refers to scholars in literacy studies, such as Carl Kaestle. However, his description also points toward a complex of increasingly shared—though not always articulated—emergent trends in rhetoric and composition historiography. Reviewing Paine's *Resistant Writer* and other recent works in rhetoric and composition history that offer "more multifaceted readings of the people or movements they describe," Julie Garbus suggests calling this revisionist turn a "third wave" in historical scholarship (120).

Historiographical Assumptions, Pedagogical Implications

This book is thus informed by several assumptions about the practice of historiography in the field. First, we cannot make broad claims about the development of rhetorical education without examining the diverse range of student bodies and institutions that participated in such education, including those previously underrepresented or neglected by earlier scholarship. In this regard, I am influenced not only by recent work recovering the rhetorical practices of women, African Americans, and working-class Americans both inside and outside of formal educational settings but also by Winifred Horner, Robert Crawford, and Thomas Miller's (*Formation*) groundbreaking work on the development of English studies at Scottish public universities, which reminds us that it is often in provincial regions where demographic and social changes are first felt and where innovation and progressive change may first take place. An examination of instructional practices at institutions outside the traditional circles of political and academic power not only expands our understanding of rhetorical traditions at these institutions but illuminates the development of rhetoric and writing instruction in America as a whole. Indeed, when it comes to rhetoric and composition studies, schools that have traditionally formed the basis for historical study may be among the least productive places to look.

We must also continue to complement broadly drawn, comprehensive master narratives with finely-grained local and institutional microhistories. Historian Giovanni Levi describes microhistory as "essentially based on the reduction of the scale of observation, on a microscopic analysis and an intensive study of the documentary material. . . . The unifying principle of all microhistorical research is the belief that microscopic observation will reveal factors previously unobserved" (95, 97). Such small-scale, local histories can illuminate, inform, challenge, and inspire larger histories. By setting the two modes in tension, we can best develop a corpus of work that will illuminate the past with a minimum of narrative distortion. Taking note of this historiographical trend in rhetoric and composition, Janet Carey Eldred and Peter Mortensen have express concern that it might lead to a fragmenting of both histories and the audience for them, thus replicating "a nineteenth-century legacy of separate political, racial, and gendered spheres. . . . Will the compositionists reading about Paine's Harvard also read about Logan's church-women and Mattingly's temperance advocates?" (754–55). While I share their desire that the field not be fragmented by a politics of identity or overly narrow scholarly interest, higher education in America unfortunately *has* been fragmented by politics, race, and gender; indeed, its history cannot be understood but through the sometimes divergent, sometimes intertwined experiences of students from each sphere. I hope this work will demonstrate the value of setting seemingly disparate institutions and rhetorical traditions in dialogue, as well as the scholars who study them.

Too often, progressive-minded scholars do a disservice to the agency of their subjects by presuming them to be helpless victims of social forces beyond their control. "A revised account" of composition history, argues Susan Miller, "requires that we endow agency and dignity on its protagonists by making them 'relevant' to contexts we already find greater than the sum of their parts" (*Textual* 3). Unlike scholars such as Berlin and Crowley, who have indicted current-traditional rhetoric for reducing the possibilities for public discourse and fostering class inequities, I am not convinced of the hegemonic determinism of institutional practices and dominant-class ideology in rhetorical instruction. Rather, I follow Charles Paine in assuming a more fluid interaction between ideology and practice, teacher and student. I also reject the sometimes tacit assumption in the field that institutional and social hierarchies in themselves are de facto problematic or that our first job as English and composition instructors is to liberate our students from false, capitalistic, or masculinist ideologies. Gary A. Olson, for example, critiques what he terms the "rhetoric of assertion" as being "masculinist, phallogocentric, foundationalist, often essentialist, and, at the very least, limiting," inhibiting our efforts to help students become "more dialogic and less monologic, more sophistic and less Aristotelian, more exploratory and less argumentative, more personal and less academic" ("Toward" 9). For Donna Haraway, even the traditional "injunction to be clear is a very strange goal" (qtd. in Olson, "Writing" 49). Robert Connors, himself a thoughtful critic of the current-traditional paradigm, critiques the agonistic rhetoric of the nineteenth-century classroom for being too masculine while lauding female rhetoric as irenic (*Composition-Rhetoric*, "Women's Reclamation"). I do not question the common assertion that the rhetoric and composition classroom is an ideal place to interrogate received assumptions and ideologies. Yet I believe we are sometimes too quick to draw clean causal lines between conservative practices and conservative ideology, classroom discipline and disciplinary epistemology. As Raúl Sánchez points out, rhetoric is not "merely the distributor of hegemonic goods" (753), and we do ourselves and our students a disservice if we treat it as such. What may ultimately serve to liberate and empower students may simply be the ability to write with confidence to contemporary rhetorical norms, goals shared—and to a large degree achieved—by the schools and students in this study.

Though this book covers nearly a seventy-five-year span, from 1873–1947, each chapter focuses on a narrower period of time. In addition to detailing rhetorical instruction at each college, I link that instruction to relevant contemporary classroom debates about the teaching of writing. Chapter 1, "Integrating Traditions," examines Wiley College, a classically based, black liberal arts school in rural East Texas, where Melvin B. Tolson, the black modernist poet and civil rights activist, taught English, debate, and drama for over twenty years. While I concentrate on the years of Tolson's tenure at Wiley, 1923 to 1947, I trace the history of Wiley from its founding by the Methodist Episcopal Church in 1873 in order to provide the background for understanding Tolson's roots in the black liberal arts college tradition. Tolson's complex classroom style mixed elements of classical and African American rhetorical traditions to produce a pedagogy that was at once conservative, progressive, and radical, inspiring his students to academic achievement and social action. His race-aware critical pedagogy demonstrates that it is possible to instruct students in the norms of the academy without sacrificing their home voices or identities. Using personal interviews, written testimony, Tolson's published writings, and his papers at the Library of Congress, I set his work within the context of rhetorical education in early-twentieth-century black liberal arts colleges and capture the classroom and extracurricular practices that made him a powerful teacher.

Chapter 2, "Balancing Tensions," examines the public Texas Woman's University (TWU), at one time the nation's largest residential college for women, where Victorian- and progressive-era politics and pedagogies mixed freely. I trace the history of the college from its founding in 1901 through World War II, focusing on its first quarter century. TWU was one of eight public colleges for women established in the South after the Civil War. Founded as a vocational and industrial college, it became an important center of education for women in the state. Though working within a social structure that acknowledged limits on women's public roles, students, faculty, and founders actively promoted women's education, professional development, and political rights. Both literary and vocational courses were featured prominently in the curriculum, playing important roles in developing students' identities and professional opportunities and contributing to a textually rich environment that valued both language reception and production. Unlike their peers at many private women's colleges who were expected to be "a lady first and a college girl afterwards" (Ruth Bradford, qtd. in J. Campbell, "Freshman" 117), TWU students were encouraged to participate in public discourse as rhetors. Using the university's extensive archives, which contain student and teacher diaries and class notes, complete collections of the student newspaper, literary journal, and yearbook, and records of the Texas Federation of Women's Clubs and the Southern Association of Colleges for Women, I depict how students made wide use of their rhetorical education when writing and speaking in a variety of public forums.

Chapter 3, "Challenging Orthodoxies," examines East Texas Normal College, an independent teachers' college founded by maverick educator William Mayo, who offered open admissions, minimal tuition, and ten-week, year-round terms, allowing students to come and go as finances and farm work allowed. I cover the period from the founding of the college in 1889 to Mayo's death in 1917. Despite his iconoclasm and independence, Mayo was in the forefront of contemporary normal school practice, which held that students' practical needs should drive curricula, that each student had a sacred dignity that schools must uphold, and that universal education was the basis for a democratic society. While faculty at East Texas maintained a rigorous, disciplinary approach to instruction in the "fundamentals" of English, they also sought to spark student interest and achievement. This blending of teacher- and student-centered pedagogies both encourages a reconceptualization of the history of rhetoric and composition and offers lessons for contemporary practice. Using oral, local, and institutional histories, I describe both how Mayo put national curricular trends to local use and describes the important role the college played in student, community, and regional life.

In addition to complementing and challenging previous histories, these studies offer lessons that address current concerns in rhetoric and composition history and pedagogy. Educators in this era were faced with many of the same challenges as those of today, including increasingly diverse student bodies and ranges of academic preparation, cultural pressures at odds with institutional goals, the desire to teach practical literacy skills without forsaking a humanistic education, and a conscious awareness of the need to address students in their own language while acknowledging the language of power. Although limited by social and political inequities, students at these schools received a rhetorical education that was geared to their needs and was, in many ways, superior to what they likely would have received at more elite, coeducational, or integrated institutions. Furthermore, students took their rhetorical training outside of the classroom, demonstrating that progressive educational goals are not necessarily incompatible with conservative pedagogical techniques.

Following the Archives

The histories in this book are from a wide variety of archival sources, including catalogues, course descriptions, student and faculty class notes and essays, contemporary newspaper and governmental reports, letters and diaries, and interviews and oral histories. Throughout I have sought to recover the voices of students and instructors engaged in the daily practice of rhetorical instruction and production, in order to explore more fully the complex, two-way relationship between culture and composition. My work has been informed both by Linda Ferreira-Buckley's insistence on the value of archives in illuminating the past and by Alison Elizabeth Regan's stressing of the importance of looking outside of departments of English and composition classes for evidence of rhetorical practices. In her dissertation on the development of English studies at the University of Texas, Regan finds that while current-traditional rhetorical practice was dominant in the department of English, the department of speech, under the direction of Edwin DuBois Shurter, had a robust program of instruction that "encourag[ed] students to exercise social responsibility through academic discourse" (18). Notes Regan, "When we examine the history of college English studies, we must look beyond the boundaries of departments of English in order to gain a fuller understanding of institutional practices; if we cannot find evidence of certain kinds of practices in departments of English, we should not automatically assume that such practices did not exist" (15). I have thus looked at the broad range of rhetorical instruction and practice at each school, considering not only classes in English and rhetoric and composition but also oratory, elocution, and public writing as well as extracurricular activities.

While my use of archival sources has been driven by a desire to write rich histories, it has also been shaped—and therefore limited—by what sources have been available. Because of the small size of these schools, their limited financial resources, and previous scholarly inattention, the archival materials available have often been limited or haphazard. Unlike Harvard University, Wiley College has no archive of nineteenth-century student papers or self-published histories of its writing program. William Mayo's personal papers were destroyed in one of East Texas Normal's three fires. Texas Woman's University, while having a rich repository of published student writing, has a less systematic collection of classroom documents. In some cases, I have had to work backwards, extrapolating from what students produced to determine what instructors valued. These are histories based less on textbooks than testimony.

I realize of course that it is easy for historians to fall into the trap of making qualitative judgments about their subjects, especially when writing from within their own disciplines. Disciplinary histories, notes Peter Novick, tend to be "celebratory" or "denunciatory," singing praises or "settling scores" (12). Hayden V. White describes the dilemma:

> [I]t is difficult to get an objective history of a scholarly discipline, because if the historian is himself a practitioner of it, he is likely to be a devotee of one or another of its sects and hence biased; and if he is not a practitioner, he is unlikely to have the expertise necessary to distinguish between the significant and insignificant events of the field's development. (*Tropics* 81)

Indeed, White claims it is impossible to write any history without falling into a distorting narrative mode and that the only way of honestly writing history is to confront and admit one's selective biases. Even then, the results will be somewhat fictive (*Metahistory*). So let me state my biases here. I am interested in the institutions in this study because I am convinced they have something to teach us, something that broad, general curricular histories have missed. Now, as in the progressive era, access to and diversity in education remain important questions. Can we recover the sense of community and community building that black, women's, and normal colleges fostered without reverting to institutional segregation and separatism? Can we join the study of the liberal arts with professional training? Can we foster civic values and participation in social discourse through rhetorical education? Can we instruct students in dominant discourse norms while still respecting the voices and experiences they bring to our classrooms? As writing teachers and writing-program administrators regularly use history to make policy and curriculum decisions, it is essential that our understanding of the past be as comprehensive as possible.

In addition to recovering a richer, more nuanced past, I also hope to extract lessons from the past that will assist in developing more effective pedagogies that aid rhetorical instruction today, thus helping students become better writers, more effective participants in civic discourse, and more active citizens. The late-nineteenth- and early-twentieth-century concern with increasing educational opportunities for all citizens mirrors today's. While we would not wish to return to a time of institutional segregation and widely unequal educational funding, many segregated, underfunded institutions achieved remarkable results with limited resources and often underprepared students. As Lynn D. Gordon notes, despite the era's institutional and curricular deficiencies, students and teachers "worked together for the good of the campus community and viewed higher education as intimately connected with larger social issues" (11). If we can recover the public spirit of the past while maintaining a commitment to the diversity of the present, the promise of progressive education may yet be fulfilled.

1
_____

Integrating Traditions at a Private Black College

The banquet of my Wiley years was the tutelage of Tolson. A scholar without cre-
dentials . . . a poet and dramatist who had not yet published, Tolson taught English,
but that was the least of the things he taught. He stretched the minds of all whose
minds would be stretched.—James Farmer

He excluded nothing, nobody, / Except the repeatedly vain, repeatedly foolish, / And
told them, excluding them, how to know better.—Thomas Whitbread

The University of Texas at Austin in the early 1940s was no place for a liberal
academic. For several years, the school's board of regents, fearing com-
munism and President Franklin D. Roosevelt in seemingly equal measure,
waged a bitter campaign against academic freedom and left-leaning faculty;
they attempted to abolish tenure and cut the university's budget, eliminated
research funds for the social sciences, fired untenured economics instructors who had publicly protested in support of federal labor laws, and, after
unsuccessfully attempting to find and fire the English professor who had
placed a book from John Dos Passos's *USA* trilogy on a sophomore-class
reading list, banned the book from the university. In 1944, when President
Homer Rainey protested these and other actions, he himself was fired, an
act that caused thousands of students to march on the capitol and helped
earn the university a seven-year censure by the American Association of
University Professors (A. Cox).

While the controversy in Austin attracted national attention, at Wiley
College, a small, black liberal arts school in Marshall, Texas, in the state's

rural northeastern corner, openly liberal professors flourished: theologian James Leonard Farmer, who preached the social gospel; sociologist Oliver Cromwell Cox, who argued that race was a social construct and a function of capitalist exploitation; and poet, activist, and self-professed socialist Melvin Beaunoris Tolson, who blended conservative language instruction with race pride and radical politics.

That two schools in the same state and era could have such different campus environments suggests the importance of examining diverse local histories in order to build a better understanding of the development of rhetorical instruction in American colleges. UT and Wiley were each set up for different purposes to serve different constituencies. As a state institution, UT was checked by a legislature and governing body recognizing the need for higher education but also highly suspicious of it. Wiley, in contrast, was founded by the Freedmen's Aid Society of the Methodist Episcopal Church, with the express goal of creating black leaders.

As a private black liberal arts college, Wiley represents an important site of inquiry for historians of rhetoric and composition. Although a number of scholars, such as Jacqueline Bacon, Shirley Wilson Logan, Elizabeth McHenry, and Jacqueline Jones Royster, have called our attention to rich African American rhetorical practices outside of formal educational settings, the wide-ranging diversity of practices within diverse *institutional* settings of higher learning has only just begun to be explored.[1] We need curricular histories as rich as those community histories to fully trace the development and impact of African American rhetorical traditions. Moreover, an examination of historically black colleges and universities, such as Wiley, reveals a fascinating counterstory to received rhetoric and composition histories. At many private black liberal arts colleges, the classical liberal arts tradition persisted well into the 1920s, with Latin and Greek retained as requirements long after such courses had become electives at elite white schools. Oratory, moved to the periphery of the curriculum elsewhere,[2] continued to play an important role; speechwriting was frequently incorporated into freshman composition courses, and debate and drama were enormously popular campus activities.

The role of what is now called current-traditional rhetoric was also complicated by both the unique mission of private black colleges and the constituencies they served. These schools were frequently hierarchical and authoritarian, with what might be regarded as a foundationalist grounding in Christian ethics and social mores. Yet they were also set up to serve explicitly civic purposes, building on long-standing tropes in African American political discourse that emphasized the role of education and literacy in promoting citizenship and community strength. Strict classroom and campus discipline and prescriptivist language instruction, elsewhere criticized for their association with positivist epistemologies and homogenizing or even deracializing effects, in private black colleges served curricular and community ends.

In this chapter, I examine the pedagogical practices of perhaps Wiley's most famous professor, Melvin Tolson, through the lens of both African American educational history and Wiley's own unique institutional circumstances. Tolson's style of instruction, which integrated wide-ranging rhetorical traditions, challenges and enriches our understanding of the development of English studies and offers lessons for developing rich, responsive classroom practices of our own. I hope not only to recover and describe the pedagogy of this important figure in American letters but to explain why it succeeded—and what that suggests for the contemporary composition classroom.

Best known today as a poet, Tolson first gained recognition as a lecturer, newspaper columnist, and college debate coach. By the time of the publication in 1944 of his first book of poems, *Rendezvous with America*, Tolson had been teaching at Wiley for over twenty years; the man who left indelible portraits of urban black life in *Harlem Gallery* lived most of his life in rural Texas and Oklahoma. A highly complex figure, Tolson embraced the contradictions and controversies of his era. A staunch integrationist, he taught at separatist institutions his entire career. An outspoken socialist and the son of a Methodist preacher, he invoked Jesus and Marx in equal measure in his public demands for social justice. A celebratory chronicler of the black experience, he reserved his harshest political criticism for the black elite. An infamously strict prescriptive grammarian, he continually stressed the social role of rhetoric in his classroom. A grandiloquent church-influenced orator, he was a relentlessly experimental writer and a master of mixing both the high and the low.[3] At the time of his death in 1966, Tolson was a nationally known figure, lauded by poets from Gwendolyn Brooks to William Carlos Williams. Recently, his poetry and criticism have received a well-deserved revisiting, including an extensive treatment by Michael Bérubé in *Marginal Forces: Cultural Centers*, a critical edition of his poems by Raymond Nelson with an introduction by Rita Dove in *Harlem Gallery*, and the publication of his master's thesis on Harlem Renaissance writers, edited by Edward J. Mullen, in *The Harlem Group*. Outside of two biographies, however, the last published in 1984, scholars have paid little attention to his teaching.

Tolson promulgated an embodied, epistemic, activist rhetoric, in which knowledge was crafted through agonistic, often confrontational dialogue.

He closely involved himself in the lives of his students, serving as a mentor and role model. At the same time, he also promoted a highly prescriptive and disciplinary approach to language instruction and classroom behavior and engaged in pedagogical practices, such as shaming and bullying his students into action, that may look to the contemporary eye as a misuse of his authority. Yet in and out of the classroom, his blend of racial pride, radical Christianity, philological rigor, and liberatory rhetoric changed students' lives; several went on to become key figures in the struggle for black civil rights, and forty years after his death, his former students still speak of him with reverence and awe.

Tolson's teaching speaks to several concerns of central importance to contemporary rhetoric and composition scholars and teachers. First, it demonstrates the limitations of traditional taxonomies in describing rhetorical instruction. While James Berlin's descriptions of epistemological differences have been immensely useful to our understanding of the development of rhetorical instruction in American colleges, his categories have sometimes been treated as mutually exclusive and discrete—one is either epistemic or current-traditional in pedagogical practice and never the twain shall meet. Melvin Tolson's rhetorical practices, however, fit into no simple category; rather, he combined elements of classical, current-traditional, liberal, social-epistemic, and African American rhetoric as he saw fit. His teaching also calls into question our understanding of the functions and effects of current-traditional rhetoric. As Charles Paine points out, we have often been too quick to join ideology to pedagogy. By classifying current-traditional rhetoric and its attendant pedagogical techniques as both positivist and hegemonic, we have allowed ourselves to ignore the potential value of disciplinary, prescriptivist, or agonistic language instruction. And by focusing on the experiences of students at elite white liberal arts colleges—or even large, public research institutions—we have paid too little attention to how students in other environments might have welcomed instruction in speaking and writing that gave them access to the language of power. Tolson demonstrates that it is possible to join both conservative and radical practices into a pedagogy that serves both students and society.

Of course, Tolson did not teach in a vacuum. Indeed, he embraced what Susan Kates, in writing of Hallie Quinn Brown, calls an embodied rhetoric, "located within, and generated for, the African American community" (54). Therefore, before discussing Tolson's pedagogy, this chapter describes the aims and curricula of private black liberal arts colleges and details the founding and development of the school at which he taught for over twenty years. Wiley College's history illuminates not only trends in African American higher education in the late nineteenth and early twentieth centuries but also differences among black colleges and the importance of individual actors in determining an institution's development. Wiley's association with the Methodist Episcopal Church contributed greatly to the college's self-determination as a black-run school with a race-conscious mission, as did its long, stable tenure under President Matthew Dogan. Dogan, who led the school from 1896 to 1942, provided an atmosphere in which faculty such as Tolson could thrive, despite the external pressures of racism and segregation that marked life in a small Texas town in the first half of the twentieth century. Dogan's careful stewardship of Wiley speaks to the tensions that black colleges, faculty, and students in the South had to negotiate in order to survive—and thrive.

Classics and Citizenship at Private Black Colleges

The history of higher education for African Americans in the segregated South is the history of African American educational institutions, particularly private ones. In the decades following the Civil War, dozens of private black colleges were started throughout the South by both white and black religious bodies. These schools were commonly established as classically based liberal arts colleges, in contrast to the industrial model for black education established by Samuel Chapman Armstrong's Hampton Institute (1868) and Booker T. Washington's Tuskegee Institute (1881). Until World War II, black higher education in the South was primarily in the hands of these private, predominantly church- or mission-supported institutions (Heintze; Anderson). Although a number of public black colleges were established in the South, these were slower to develop and offer college-level work. Texas closely mirrored this national pattern. The first black college in Texas, Paul Quinn College, was established in 1872 by the African Methodist Episcopal Church. By 1915, eleven denominational private schools were in operation in Texas, with six offering college-level work, enrolling a total of 132 students (T. Jones 59, 567–606; Heintze 69).[4] In contrast, the state's first public black college, Prairie View A&M, opened in 1878, did not permanently institute a four-year program until 1919. Texas did not obtain its second public black senior college until Houston Colored Junior College (now Texas Southern University), established in 1927, added an upper division in 1934. Through the end of World War II, over half of black college students in Texas were at private denominational colleges. Table 1.1 traces these enrollment trends.

The split between public and private black colleges in Texas is not merely one of financial support but is representative of differing goals of their

Table 1.1. College-level enrollment at black public and private colleges,
Texas, 1915–45

	1915		1921		1927		1935		1945	
	Number of students	%	Number of students	%	Number of students	%	Number of students	%	Number of students	%
Private	132	100.0	362	72.4	1,219	68.6	1,837	61.4	2,932	53.2
Public	0	0.0	138	27.6	559	31.4	1,153	38.6	2,579	46.8
Total	132		500		1,778		2,990		5,511	

Source: Data from 1915: T. Jones 567–606; 1921: *Negro Year Book, 1921–22* 269–74; 1927: Heintze 73; 1935: Anderson 275; 1945: *Negro Year Book, 1941–46* 88–89.

founding bodies. In the post-Reconstruction era, black public colleges and those founded and funded by Northern industrial philanthropists tended to be established as industrial, agricultural, and normal schools, following the Hampton-Tuskegee model. While such schools served an important function, they were sometimes formed with little regard for the needs of local black communities. Prairie View A&M was established as an agricultural training college, but the first year only six potential students expressed interest. As one early-twentieth-century commentator somewhat grudgingly conceded, "The Negroes could not understand the need of studying something that they already knew how to do and the agricultural institution failed completely" (Todd 28). Prairie View was quickly reorganized as a normal school the following year and added an industrial curriculum soon thereafter. It flourished under this organization, eventually becoming the largest teacher-training college for blacks in the nation (Todd 29).

In contrast, black private schools founded by religious bodies and mission societies were almost universally established as classically based liberal arts colleges. The institutional goals and curricula of these institutions are of special significance to historians of rhetoric and composition, as they challenge many of the generalizations made about the development of rhetorical instruction in American colleges. While the traditional classical course of study began to erode at elite white institutions in the 1870s, at black colleges, Latin, Greek, and other elements of the classical liberal arts curriculum remained in force as required courses well into the 1920s. (Historians of education have noted the persistence of the classical tradition in black colleges, but we have not often been sensitive to this distinction in rhetoric and composition and English studies.) Although black colleges were criticized in their day by the white educational establishment for offering what was widely perceived to be either an outdated or unnecessary curriculum, for

black educational and religious leaders and their white missionary counterparts, classics had both powerful symbolic and practical value. While many
American schools struggled to deal with changing conceptions of higher
education and the rise of mass education in the post–Civil War industrial
boom, for black colleges this challenge was doubly felt. Schools had to
negotiate between the practical needs of a population left largely illiterate
by slavery and the widely expressed desire by African American leaders
to uplift the race through education. For black colleges, the promotion of
liberal arts education often represented a conscious struggle against white
definitions of what black educational institutions should be.

   The role of oratory at private black colleges also differs from that at many
white liberal arts colleges. Scholars of rhetoric generally concur that by the
last quarter of the nineteenth century, written composition had replaced
oratory as the center of rhetorical instruction. By 1871, Yale graduate Lyman
Bagg could declare that at his alma mater "a declamation prize counts for
but little" in comparison to a prize-winning essay: "[E]ven a successful
speaker in prize debate cannot be sure of his reputation as a 'literary man,'
until he has strengthened it by winning a prize composition" (619). While
black colleges established courses in written composition that mirrored
those offered at white institutions, oratory remained an integral part of
rhetorical instruction and campus activity through the 1930s, long after
it had moved to the periphery of instruction elsewhere or had become the
province of departments of speech. The University of Texas, for example,
had one of the nation's earliest and most progressive speech programs under
the direction of Edwin Shurter, but it enrolled far fewer students than the
school's current-traditional required course in freshman English (Regan
37–38). In contrast, at black colleges, students frequently did extensive
practice in declamation in their composition classes, and oratory and debate
remained the province of English departments. In a 1940 survey of debate
at thirty black colleges, John W. Parker found that at half of them, debate
was led by an English-department instructor ("Current Debate Practices"
34). Oratory also remained an enormously popular campus activity, with
oratorical competitions prominently featured in school publications. Of the
five "Annual Events" listed in the 1914 Samuel Huston College *Catalogue*,[5]
three promoted oratorical/rhetorical competitions: the Oratorical Contest, the Histrionic Exercises, and the Temperance Declamation Contest,
sponsored by the Women's Christian Temperance Union (12). From at least
1915 to 1921, the college offered two prizes for public speaking, one for "best
orator" and one for the winner of the Temperance Declamation Contest, and
commonly featured pictures of the winners in their catalogues. At Wiley,

the debate team under Tolson became nationally known and one of the school's main points of pride.

But perhaps the most distinguishing feature of black colleges was their relationship with the populations they served. Black schools expressed their mission in explicitly communitarian terms.

> We must have prophets, priests, seers, historians, poets, philosophers, artists, physicians, orators. These men must be profound in thought, sane and courageous. We must have inspirers, leaders. We must have men with insight and foresight. . . . We must have a few men who are able to stand the test of these new and exciting times. Brains rule. Mere physical force can take its place only with the ox. And shall we not do a man's full part of the world's work? It is not only best for us as individuals, it is best for the South and the Nation. . . . In higher education there is peace and harmony. In ignorance there is turmoil and hatred. (Samuel Huston College, *Catalogue 1914* 39–40)

What James Berlin has called the old "elitist" enterprise of educating students "of means and status for the three major professions" of law, medicine, and the church (*Rhetoric and Reality* 21), black colleges saw as a progressive, community enterprise. Few of the black students in the South preparing for professional careers at this time would have come from economically or socially privileged backgrounds; moreover, African American political rhetoric explicitly marked these professions as ones of service. Indeed, in a time when black literacy was still largely suppressed, college graduates, whatever their profession, played an important social role in helping communities negotiate the demands of a culture in which print literacy was becoming ever more important. Upon moving back to her hometown of Taylor, Texas, Ilah Wright, who graduated from Austin's Tillotson Institute in 1915, served as an informal community liaison, reading and writing letters and checking contracts and government documents for neighbors. Her daughter Etta Robinson recalls, "[A]nything anybody had to do, any papers that needed to be filled out, they would come to my mother. . . . She was very happy that she went to school there" (qtd. in Thatcher).

Private black colleges in Texas were publicly committed to the communities in which they operated. To financially strapped parents, they promoted their low costs. "Samuel Huston College will take any student for the entire year and give him good treatment for the sum of $90 cash in advance," announced the 1914 *Catalogue*. "This is just about the worth of one good bale of cotton" (18). Black campuses often served as de facto community centers, running everything from day care to health-education programs. In 1942,

Texas's black colleges, public and private, began a program of cooperative community education workshops, designed to train primary and secondary schoolteachers in skills appropriate to their communities' local needs. Most importantly, perhaps, these colleges formed key links in the process of increasing black literacy. In 1890, black literacy in Texas was 47.5% (United States Bureau of the Census, *Twelfth Census* cxi). By 1920, it had increased to 82.2% (United States Bureau of the Census, *Fifteenth Census* 946), the fourth highest of seventeen Southern states (D. Taylor 11). This was due largely to the increase in the number of black primary and secondary schools and the number of students attending them. But black high schools and colleges had a symbiotic relationship. Although only a small percentage of black students finished high school, those who did frequently received a solid liberal arts education. High schools, both white and black, of the period molded their curricula to college entrance requirements; as black colleges especially placed a heavy emphasis on classics and English education, so did black high schools—and black students. In 1925, only 34 black high-school students in Texas enrolled in courses in hygiene and home nursing, 1,805 in manual training, and 2,535 in agriculture. In contrast, 4,702 students were enrolled in Latin, 4,920 in literature courses (2,186 in English and 2,734 in American), and 10,278 in either English grammar (2,449) or composition (7,829). White educators professed to be baffled by this disparity:

> There is no logical reason why the largest enrolment group of negro pupils should be in formal subjects that will be of very little use to them. . . . It will be a better day for the negro schools when Latin and three years of high school mathematics are considered of less importance than home economics for negro girls. (D. Taylor 108–15)

Black communities, however, saw the value in liberal arts education (especially for "girls," for whom teaching was one of the few professional careers open). The graduates of black high schools and colleges, both male and female, in turn formed the bulk of black teachers in the state. Based on a count of the early catalogues of Samuel Huston, Tillotson, and Wiley Colleges, which list graduates and their jobs, I estimate that through World War II, approximately half the graduates of Texas's black colleges taught at some point in their careers. This figure corresponds to W. E. B. Du Bois and Augustus Granville Dill's 1910 national survey of black college graduates, which found 53.8% working as teachers (66).

Despite common aims, the differences among Texas' black colleges complicate attempts at generalization, demonstrating the importance of institutional microhistories and local contexts in evaluating curricula. Schools varied widely in degree of religious emphasis, student freedom, political tenor, faculty makeup, administrative independence and stability, financial security, academic rigor, explicitness of race-conscious ideology, and class tensions. For example, the American Missionary Association–sponsored Tillotson, founded in 1877, did not obtain its first black president until 1924, and the faculty remained predominantly white until the mid-1930s (Heintze 91). Tillotson's catalogues in the years 1900 through 1935 barely refer to race; if not for the pictures of black students, Tillotson could be any small, religious school. Meanwhile, the nearby Samuel Huston College, a black-run Methodist college, preached an inspiring message of race pride. While all these schools promoted Christian ethics, in general, the more independent the college was from its chartering body and the greater the black control, the more explicit the integration of this mission with the message of racial uplift and activism. Due to the small size of these schools, an individual administrator or faculty member could also have significant effects on institutional mood and direction. Under the administration of President Mary Elizabeth Branch, Tillotson, which had been previously struggling, flourished, as did San Antonio's St. Philip's College under Artemisia Bowden. In contrast, Wiley College, after a period of long stability under President Matthew Dogan, underwent significant upheavals under Egbert C. McLeod, leading to a nationally reported student strike and, eventually, Tolson's departure in 1947.

In addition to their differences, black colleges were often in competition or conflict with one another, especially across interfaith lines. Clarence Norris, a Bishop College faculty member who later became dean of St. Philip's, noted that competition between the Baptist Bishop and the Methodist Wiley, both in Marshall, was so fierce that when, in 1933, he taught as a dual appointee at the two schools to substitute for a Wiley professor on leave, he felt "caught in the middle" between their presidents and under pressure to declare his loyalty: "During their entire existence both colleges were very antagonistic to each other" (Norris 49). Such interfaith rivalries were not limited to schools. Wiley graduate Robert E. Brown, who grew up in Hempstead, Texas, near Houston, recalled his mother's disapproval of his "running with" the daughter of one of their neighbors. "One [reason] was the fact that Annie Mae was about three years older than I, but the strongest reason was that she was a member of the Baptist church" (13–14).

Religion and Rhetoric at Wiley

Wiley was founded in Marshall, Texas, in 1873 by the Freedmen's Aid Society of the Methodist Episcopal Church (MEC), chartered by the state in 1882, and offered its first bachelor's degree in 1888.[6] Like other black denominational colleges, Wiley sought to provide a classical liberal arts education within a religious environment:

> The chief purpose of Wiley . . . is to furnish a place for young Negro men and women of the Southwest to obtain a liberal and Christian education that will fit them for leadership. Wiley differs from the average secular institution in that its training is distinctively Christian. It believes that knowledge is power, capable of destruction as well as construction; and that it is imperative that the power which is given to the youth be properly directed and constrained. It believes that with mind culture should go along heart culture and there is no feature of the University of which those in authority are prouder than this distinguishing characteristic. (*Catalogue 1921* 12)

Wiley's Methodist affiliation served it well. Of the white-dominated religious bodies operating black colleges in the South, the Methodists were arguably the most progressive on the issue of race. From the outset, the church's Freedmen's Aid Society established colleges with the goal of granting them black control. Declared the society's 1868 *Report*: "Teachers for the freedmen must eventually be furnished by their own race. We must aid them in establishing good schools for the training of teachers and preachers, and then as soon as possible deliver these institutions over to them for a permanent support" (16). The Methodists were also committed to liberal arts education for African Americans as a right of citizenship. In 1904, the bishops' address at the opening of the general conference declared:

> [T]he essential conditions of public welfare in a country like this require that men of every nationality, color, and language shall be free according to his personal merit to rise in the ranks and above the ranks. While, therefore, there is ample reason to rejoice in the great recent advance in manual training for both colored and white youth, there is also absolute need for higher and the highest intellectual opportunities to be open to both. ("Episcopal Address" 144)

By 1915, 71% of faculty members at black Methodist colleges were black, as were ten of twenty-three presidents (Heintze 89). In Texas, the MEC's two schools both had early black control. Samuel Huston opened in 1900 with an all-black faculty, staff, and administration. Wiley appointed its first black president, the Reverend Isaiah B. Scott, in 1893 and had an all-black faculty by 1918 (Heintze 91).

Throughout its early history, Wiley offered a curriculum rich in language instruction. In 1892, twenty-four credits in ancient languages and twelve in modern languages—43.9% of the curriculum—were required for graduation. By 1920, English had taken a central role, with twenty-four credits required, though twelve credits in Latin and twelve in modern languages were still required (Heintze 61). Table 1.2 shows the development of language requirements at the college.

Table 1.2. Changes in language requirements as credit hours required for a B.A. at Wiley College, 1892–1950

Course	1892	1920	1930	1950
Languages				
Ancient languages	24	12	0	0
Modern languages	12	12	12	12
English	6	24	18	21

Source: Data from Heintze 61

Oratory, as at other private black colleges, played an important role both in the classroom and in campus life. At the time of Tolson's arrival in 1923, Wiley had three literary and debate societies, one for the college proper, one for its high school, and one for its normal school. All of these clubs were coed. The normal school's Francis Harper Literary Society, whose members were "principally young women, [was] one of the livest in the school." A belletristic-minded Reader's Club, open to all students, met weekly, "for the purpose of cultivating a taste for good and useful books, and to develop general literary culture" (*Catalogue 1921* 22). In the early 1920s, the school also had a debating club, which met weekly for intracampus discussions and debates, and a department of expression, which offered classes in essentials of public speaking, argumentation and debate, and interpretation of dramatic literature; for several years, debating was required of all students. In addition to classes in public speaking, public speaking was integrated into freshman English instruction; students studied both "written and oral expression" and were required "to make several formal addresses before the class" (*Catalogue 1920* 37) in addition to writing daily themes.

Wiley's limited archival record makes it difficult to obtain a detailed picture of texts used in writing classes, as well as how they were used. Worth noting, however, is that in 1920, Wiley's English faculty, Jason Grant, who held an M.A. from the University of Chicago, and Lenora Williams, who held an M.A. from Fisk University in Nashville, used Fred Newton Scott and Joseph Villiers Denney's *Paragraph-Writing* in freshman rhetoric. Scott and Denney's rhetoric book appears to have been used in a number of black Methodist colleges, also appearing in the catalogues of Samuel Huston and Lincoln University in Pennsylvania, where Melvin Tolson studied as an undergraduate. Though Scott and Denney's textbooks cover much of the same ground as traditional textbooks, they do stand out for their emphasis on rhetorical context and audience, a reminder that current-traditional practice was not monolithic in the early-twentieth-century composition classroom. "The forces which urge young persons to express themselves with tongue or pen," Scott and Denney wrote in 1900's *Elementary English Composition*, "are partly individual, partly social,—partly impulses from within, partly solicitations from without" (iii). By the 1911 *New Composition-Rhetoric*, they were able to declare, "Composition is regarded as a social act, and the student is therefore constantly led to think of himself as writing or speaking for a specified audience. Thus not mere expression but communication as well is made the business of composition" (iii). *New Composition-Rhetoric* includes an extensive section on argumentation as well as explicit instructions for setting up a public debate. *Paragraph-Writing*, despite having a title that suggests endless stacks of daily themes—and, indeed, Grant and Williams required one-page themes each class day and three-page themes weekly (Wiley College, *Catalogue 1920* 37)—makes a good claim for studying the paragraph as the building block of written discourse, multiple-paragraph essays being too large, requiring paragraph conventions to be mastered first, but also sentences being too small, as sentence construction depends on the relationship between sentences. Given the often-reductive nature of college textbooks that were available at the time, Scott and Denney's book appears as a refreshing choice and perhaps one fitting with the civic mission of black colleges.

A Black College in the Segregated South

Until World War II, at private black denominational colleges, religious rules and restrictions on campus life were the norm. In the eyes of administrators, students faced dangers not only from sin but from segregation; keeping students on campus and out of town kept them not only morally safe but physically so. From their inception, Texas's private black colleges generally required some form of service to the school (such as working an hour or two a week in the cafeteria or on the grounds), regular chapel attendance, and courses in religion. "Familiar acquaintance with the Bible and its teachings hurt no one, but lifts all," reported the Baptist Guadalupe College catalogue in 1892 (qtd. in Heintze 157). The old course in moral philosophy, discontinued elsewhere, remained a staple of the curriculum. At some schools, dating and dancing were forbidden. Until the end of World War II, when returning veterans began attending school and protesting conditions, few of the private black colleges in Texas even allowed student governments. Writing in the 1930s, President Dogan's biographer praised him for his early "progressive" support at Wiley of then-controversial campus introductions, such as college sports, student government, and Greek organizations (Gibbs 48–54).

In 1906, Wiley required that students attend three separate services each Sunday (Heintze 157), and through the 1920s, students were required to give one hour per week in service to the university. Wiley did not drop required chapel attendance until after World War II. Despite the school's strict religious trappings, however, students were freer in practice than in principle. In 1892, a near-riot and student strike occurred when the college announced plans to increase the tuition of the women's industrial course.[7] President Dogan, during his tenure, frequently took pity on students who had committed some expulsion-worthy infraction and would not send them home. And despite prohibitions against dancing and dating, students could be found doing both and even holding hands in public or meeting in the gardens after dark (Farmer 120).

The frontier atmosphere of East Texas also belied the college's self-representation of strict control of its students. Robert E. Brown, who attended Wiley in the 1890s,[8] recalled the majority of men on campus owning guns. On one occasion, faced with a bully, he determined to settle his problem with a duel. Fortunately, he merely pistol-whipped rather than shoot his antagonist, and they eventually became close friends (45–50). A few years later, during a brief stint as an instructor at Philander Smith College in Little Rock, Arkansas, Brown once bluffed an openly armed student out of the classroom by pretending to reach for his own weapon. "I know you are wondering how many guns I had on me when I tackled the bully. Well, I didn't have a single one on me nor in my room, but he didn't know what I had, but he knew one thing and that was I was from T E X A S; and as a rule, that meant (in those days), I had a gun if I had a shirt on" (108). Even in Austin, the state capital, the administrators of Samuel Huston thought it dangerous for students to travel home during Christmas: "Drunken men are shooting and staggering about, and we are uneasy about those who go home until they return to us" (*Catalogue 1914* 24).

A generation after Brown's experience, it appears that little had changed in Texas. Upon Tolson's arrival at Wiley, a fellow professor invited him to his apartment to give him "the lowdown."

> In the center of the room was a huge table piled high with books. His friend had a forty-five on the table and was applying vaseline to some bullets. He carried a cane loaded with lead and also a razor. This was far from Tolson's concept of a professor's accoutrements, but his colleague stated his case clearly: "There are bad Negroes here and 'badder' white folks." Experience would prove the truth of his friend's statement. (Flasch, "A Critical Biography" 11–12)

Tolson's students recall the campus as a relatively peaceful place. It was outside school where the real dangers lay. Although the population of Harrison County (of which Marshall was the county seat) was over 60% black in the late nineteenth and early twentieth centuries, the power structure was white. Marshall, despite the mediating effect of two black universities, was still a highly segregated, small Southern town. George Dawson, who was born near Marshall, witnessed a lynching in the center of town around 1908 (Dawson 3–13), and violence against blacks was common in the state throughout Tolson's entire tenure at Wiley. Civil rights activist James Farmer, Tolson's student (and the son of Wiley professor James Leonard Farmer), depicted these conditions in Marshall in his autobiography:

> Blacks, on the average, exceeded whites in educational level in Marshall [which had two black senior colleges and one white junior college]. . . . But education was not a factor in segregation. Houses of educated as well as uneducated blacks were on unpaved streets, unless they happened to be on the thoroughfares. Educated and uneducated alike were denied the privilege of trying on clothes in most downtown stores and eating in places where food was served. Education merely made it harder for the brain to adapt to the demeaning things the system told it to do. (121)

Hamilton Boswell, who came to Wiley from Los Angeles, was even blunter: Marshall, he says, was a "very segregated, mean and nasty" town.

In some ways, Wiley's isolation was to its advantage. Gail K. Beil, in her study of James Leonard Farmer's effect on the civil rights movement, suggests that one of the unintended benefits of segregation was that local white communities didn't know—and little cared—what was being taught at black colleges. About Wiley, she notes,

> There is no evidence that any member of the white community was reading Tolson's columns, Farmer's . . . appeals for racial justice, or [Oliver

Cromwell] Cox's denouncement of capitalism as a tool for keeping minorities in their place as a cheap labor force. So far as developing black
leaders determined and brave enough to lead the modern civil rights
movement was concerned, it was probably for the better. (67)

Whites in Texas were certainly not unaware of Tolson. He organized sharecroppers, led boycott threats, and spoke at schools and churches, both black
and white. But the daily goings-on at Wiley were rarely covered in Marshall's
newspaper, and the school's faculty had an academic freedom that was
sometimes denied white scholars at state-supported institutions.

Negotiating with the White Community

Much of the open academic atmosphere at Wiley was due to the long and
in many ways progressive tenure of President Matthew Dogan, from 1896
to 1942. While Wiley's official message of racial pride was more subdued
than its sister Methodist school in Austin, Samuel Huston—which might
have reflected its rural location—the school did tolerate some activism on
campus. In 1937, despite his personal misgivings, Dogan allowed student
James Farmer to form a campus chapter of the National Association for
the Advancement of Colored People (Beil 49–51). Dogan was able to attract outspoken, activist scholars, such as James Leonard Farmer, historian
Andrew Polk Watson, and sociologist Oliver Cromwell Cox. Even Tolson,
despite being pegged as the campus radical and frequently at odds with
the administration, never felt his academic freedom violated. His main
problem was the pressure to obtain an advanced degree; although he began
coursework for a master's degree at Columbia University in 1931, teaching
duties kept him from completing his thesis, "The Harlem Group of Negro
Writers," until 1940.

Dogan's administration demonstrates the fragile position of black college administrators—and black colleges—in the early twentieth century.
Despite the authority that black administrators had on their own campuses,
their position in the larger white community was tenuous at best, as they
continually struggled to negotiate for the survival of their schools. In his
memoirs, James Farmer poignantly describes the difficulties Dogan and H.
B. Pemberton,[9] principal of Marshall's black Central High School, faced.

[They had] influence with the white world and power in the black. . . .
Yet, they had to respect the etiquette of the caste system: they were called
not "Mister," but "Doctor" and "Professor," and there was some grin-
ning and bowing and scraping and foot shuffling. They treated whites
like sacred cows in their presence; but behind their backs, they talked

about them and laughed at them. It was a classic case of role playing. Many students considered them "Uncle Toms," but that did not define them; they were not owned by the whites, just rented. They were fully conscious of the role they were playing. They served their wards as well as their masters. Pemberton got money from the white school board for the segregated black high school, and Dogan raised a $600,000 endowment for Wiley. (121)

One of Dogan's greatest triumphs was securing funding for a Carnegie Library, even though he had no matching funds to put up as normally required. This was such an unprecedented event that the foundation sent Booker T. Washington's private secretary, Emmett Scott (who had studied at Wiley), on a secret mission to ensure that Dogan would not divulge the terms of the agreement (Beil 37–38).

Dogan also played an important behind-the-scenes role in reducing friction between the campus and the community and in ensuring that whites policed their own. Recalls Hamilton Boswell:

[Life in Marshall] was dangerous, but the white businesspeople realized that those two black colleges supported a tremendous amount of business. If those two colleges quit trading on the streets of Marshall, Texas, then Marshall, Texas, had to turn down their lights. That's just how powerful that economic advantage was, and Tolson knew it, Dogan knew it, and the white businesspeople knew it. [If Wiley students were mistreated,] Dr. Dogan knew he could call up the Chamber of Commerce; "You know we're having a little too much trouble out here, and maybe we'll go over to Longview to do our shopping." The subtleties of that man—They called him an Uncle Tom and maybe he was in a way, but he did it for a reason, and out of that day's society he got more out of Marshall than anyone with any other approach could have gotten. . . . It was an age and a time, but they knew they had an economic advantage, and they could use it and the white businesspeople knew it. . . . The KKK was held in abeyance by the white businesspeople.

Dogan's own politics were relatively conservative, at least as compared to those of Tolson or James Leonard Farmer. Dogan also knew that it would not serve the school's mission to be known as a breeding ground for radicals. Black schools gained much support by positioning black education as part of the patriotic process of training all Americans for citizenship. In a 1910 essay written for the volume *Methodism and the Negro*, Dogan assured white churchmembers that Wiley was producing "level-headed" students of "a conservative turn of mind" willing to work toward the "development of our common country" (87). But he also believed that liberal arts training would produce sober, reflective, moral individuals as an antidote to the crass materialism of the times.

> The average American's idea of education is faulty in that it is too practical. This is in keeping with the spirit of the times. America is now in its material age, when financial gain is the motive power and every system of philosophy must adjust itself to this measuring rod. . . . The development of the finer qualities of mind and soul are reckoned as of secondary importance. . . . With us here in America just at this time it is matter, not mind; it is wealth, not culture; it is cents, not sense. (83–84)

Dogan therefore supported his faculty's intentions, even if he did not always agree with their methods.

Unfortunately, the same factors that allowed Dogan's successful administration—the college's small size, religious hierarchy, and tight administrative control—also allowed the somewhat troubled administration that followed of Egbert C. McLeod from 1942 to 1948. McLeod's heavy-handed dealing with faculty and students led to two nationally reported student strikes in 1947 and 1948 (Heintze 119–20, 164–65) and was to some degree responsible for Tolson's decision to leave Wiley for Langston University in Oklahoma in 1947, where his former student Hobart Jarrett was chair of the English department.

Tolson's Integrated Pedagogy

As was common with English teachers at small black colleges, Tolson taught a wide number of subjects, including composition, literature, debate, and drama. Tolson's rhetorical instruction was grounded in two distinct traditions: the classical liberal arts tradition, with its emphasis on Latin and Greek, Socratic dialogue, and instruction in grammar, logic, and rhetoric; and African American religious oratory, with its easy accord between style and substance, use of jeremiad, and emphasis on racial pride, community uplift, and political activism. Both of these mixed with a homespun, muckraking, democratic populism. Tolson came of age in the progressive era, and all his life he maintained a faith in the possibility of radical political reform. But the key to his approach was an unabashed integration of traditions and embracing of contradictions. *And* was his favorite conjunction. He called his *Washington Tribune* newspaper column "Caviar and Cabbage." In the classroom, he combined the rigorous, disciplinary instruction in logic, prescriptive grammar, and usage of current-traditional rhetoric with a social-epistemic understanding of—and an explicit faith in—the power of language to effect radical and progressive social change. He was unburdened by worries that teaching dominant language norms would deracialize or disrupt the agency of his students. He saw his classroom practice as empowering, liberatory, radical, and mainstream.

Tolson was born in 1898 in or around Moberly, Missouri (Farnsworth 7, 303). A precocious child—"Like my father, I was a bookworm" ("Poet's Odyssey" 193)—he had, from an early age, an interest in poetry, history, art, and African American culture, fueled not only by his reading but by an "old Bantu scholar with tribal holes in his ears and an Oxford accent" who would visit the house. "Mother cooked chicken pie so that he would regale her children with tales of black heroes and poets and artists" ("Odyssey of a Manuscript" 5–6). By the age of twelve, he counted both Shakespeare and the Haitian revolutionary leader Toussaint L'Ouverture as inspirations.

Tolson's formal education was thoroughly in the black liberal arts tradition, steeped in classics, religion, language, and oratory. At Kansas City's Lincoln High School, Tolson took four years of English and Latin; such coursework was not uncommon, as black high schools commonly molded their curricula to meet college entrance requirements. Like many black liberal arts colleges during this time, Lincoln University in Pennsylvania, where Tolson studied next, required four years of English and Latin or Greek for entrance. As Lincoln strove to "communicate . . . a liberal and Christian education to worthy young men who may become leaders of the colored people" (*Catalogue 1922–23* 12), four years of Bible study were also required. Tolson's freshman course in rhetoric and English composition featured essays and orations in addition to daily themes and employed texts by Scott and Denney and John Franklin Genung. Forty years later, he "still cherish[ed] the old rhetoric of Professor Genung" and maintained, "Rhetoric is the eternal enemy of the cliché." Tolson's other English courses included Milton (which featured "special attention to meter, diction and wealth of allusion"), English literature, English poets, Shakespeare, American essayists, American poets, Tennyson, Emerson's essays, and Lincoln's writings (which featured "a study of Lincoln's Public Addresses and State Papers, with a view both to their style and content"). Indeed, it seems that the only English class Lincoln offered that Tolson did not take was philology (Lincoln University, *Catalogue 1922–23* 45–46; Tolson's transcript). Although Tolson highly valued his rhetorical education, he would eventually come to regret the limitations of his literary one. He liked to tell the story of discovering Carl Sandburg's "Chicago" during his senior year. "Deeply moved by its power," he ran excitedly to his favorite professor, who told him, "Mr.

Tolson, you leave that thing alone" (Flasch, "Melvin Beaunoris Tolson" 13), delaying his introduction to the moderns for a number of years. Years later, Tolson would tell the story of his entry into the wider world of contemporary American and African American arts and letters while studying at Columbia University for his master's degree: "In 1932 I was a Negro poet writing Anglo-Saxon sonnets as a graduate student in an Eastern university. I moved in a world of twilight haunted by the ghost of a dead classicism." After writing a sonnet on Harlem, he showed it to his best friend, a German-American fiction writer, who told him it was "damned good," but derivative. "You're like the professors. You think the only good poet is a *dead* one. Why don't you read Sandburg, Masters, Frost, Robinson? Harlem is too big, too lusty, for a sonnet. Say, we've never had a Negro epic in America. Damn it, you ought to stop piddling!" (Tolson, "Odyssey of a Manuscript" 8–9). But Tolson was never truly disengaged from the world around him. At Lincoln, he was a champion debater at a school that prominently featured the sport. During his time there, the school offered no fewer than six annual prizes in oratory and debate. In addition to leading the debate team, Tolson also won the junior orator contest, held on commencement day, and the Obdyke prize for best individual debater (*Catalogue 1922–23* 38–39). Around campus, he was widely known for his ability to talk.

Thanks in part to his college training, Tolson had a complex understanding of rhetoric's epistemic functions. He was keenly aware of the difference between the private and publicly constructed face. He celebrated the *hypokrinesthai* in Greek theater—"the speaker's stage voice instead of his real voice" (letter to *Partisan Review*). Time and time again, he insisted that art, scholarship, and even "being human" were all "unnatural." "To be natural on the stage is to [be] unnatural. A scrub woman cannot play a scrub woman; it takes an actress to play a scrub woman. . . . A naturalistic work is unnatural" (Melvin Beaunoris Tolson papers). "A work of art is an illusion of life" ("Poet's Odyssey" 187). Indeed, creating an illusion of naturalness was to him the essence of being human. He therefore disavowed totalizing philosophies of race and human nature. He believed in nurture, not nature; he was, he insisted, not a "hereditist" but an "environmentalist": "How can a Negro be anything else?" ("Poet's Odyssey" 190). He believed, following Oliver Cromwell Cox, that race was a social construct and one deeply entwined with class divisions. Truth to him was epistemic, "a matter to be arrived at by collective argument" (Farnsworth 54).

Tolson's father was a Methodist minister who had taught himself Latin, Greek, and Hebrew and who often discussed philosophy with him (Flasch, *Melvin B. Tolson* 20). Tolson frequently invoked this background when launching into his own secular sermons. "I am the son of a preacher, who was the son of a preacher, who was the son of a preacher," he often said (*Caviar* 26). It was partially due to his father's influence that he obtained his position at Wiley College following his graduation from Lincoln in 1923.

According to some, Tolson was privately agnostic (Boswell). However, he was active in church—indeed, the only person at Wiley who could be guaranteed to fill the chapel when he spoke (H. Wells)—and an outspoken proponent of the social gospel. For Tolson, Christianity and progressive social activism were inseparable. "Only radicals can be Christians," he declared (*Caviar* 46). Jesus, he often said, was a socialist. This was a common trope at the time—forwarded by such influences as the critic V. F. Calverton, an early champion of Tolson's poetry, and theologian James Leonard Farmer, Tolson's colleague at Wiley—but Tolson worked it like no other, speaking from the lower frequencies.

> You talk about Karl Marx, the Communist! Why, don't you know Jesus was preaching about leveling society 1,800 years before the Jewish Red was born? . . . Jesus had white Christians and black Christians meeting together. . . . Then Jesus wanted the rich Christians to take what they had and give it to the poor. . . . Then Jesus ran around with bums: He didn't know how to pick the right company. Jesus went into the colleges and universities and started the students thinking. Then Jesus walked into Wall Street and started breaking up the rackets. . . . If Jesus returned, we'd lynch Him before a cat could sneeze. (*Caviar* 43–46)

As a teacher, Tolson's style was consciously oratorical, influenced both by his formal debate training and religious upbringing. His son Melvin Jr. still vividly recalls his classroom style: "Dad was a debater and orator, the son and nephew of preachers. He developed himself at Lincoln as a debater, and that's the way he conducted his classes. 'Question, question, question, question.' You had to defend your position. It was enlightening, but it could also be rather embarrassing if you were trying to mask your ignorance with bravado. That was his Socratic method of teaching." For Tolson, the classroom was both a performance space and pulpit. To a student who failed to define a simple vocabulary item, he might declare:

> Jones, Jones! I'm so *glad* you came to this university! I'm so glad you're in *my* class! What if you'd gone to some other college and revealed all that compounded ignorance! Girls, take a good look at this poor boy from the backwoods. Don't you marry him or the one just like him sitting next to you. You wait till you get your degree! . . . Now, Jones,

explain to the class how it's possible for a student to live eighteen years,
spend twelve of them in an educational institution, and arrive at college
so completely uninformed about the English language. (qtd. in Flasch,
Melvin B. Tolson 37)

As befits a Methodist, Tolson believed in methods. A stickler for precision,
Tolson had, in the words of his first biographer, Joy Flasch, a "lifelong fas-
cination with grammar. . . . His dictionary was his constant companion
and the primary textbook for every class he taught" (*Melvin B. Tolson* 33).
He insisted that students bring their "Bible"—the dictionary—to class and
often declared that "the only difference between a bank president and a
janitor is vocabulary" (Melvin Beaunoris Tolson Papers; Flasch, *Melvin B.
Tolson* 37). He was, he said, first attracted to T. S. Eliot by his syntax, especially his "inverted participle phrase, because I was grounded in grammar,
and I knew Eliot was 'doing something'" (qtd. in Flasch, *Melvin B. Tolson*
33). When espousing an unpopular opinion, he would often jokingly refer
to himself as being "always in the objective case." Unsatisfied with commercial textbook offerings, he wrote a pamphlet on the "Forty Uses of the
Noun" and over the years developed what amounted to his own textbook
for teaching grammar; "You didn't generally find textbooks that would have
forty uses of the noun, or even twenty," notes Melvin Jr.

Tolson's use of language—he is universally remembered as a brilliant
speaker—and his insistence on precision in its use inspired awe and fear
in his students. "You didn't dare turn in an essay with a spelling mistake,"
says Henrietta Bell Wells, who listed him as the school's "crabbiest teacher"
in her 1931 yearbook but still counts herself as "a disciple of Mr. Tolson. . . .
He would walk in the door. 'Bell! What is a verb!' And you'd better know.
He was hard on his students. They were scared, but when they got out, they
knew English." Tolson was well aware of the effect he had: "'Prof, you scare
us.' Answer: 'You know why you have as many people in heaven as you do?
They were scared of hell!'" (Melvin Beaunoris Tolson papers). Not even his
family was spared his prodding. In 1939, Melvin Jr. graduated high school
and prepared to enroll at Wiley:

> My father suggested that I audit his grammar and composition course,
> with the prospect of taking it in the fall. I assured my father that I had a
> grammar and composition background and that I didn't really need to
> do that. It turned out that the course he had invited me to audit was the
> only one still open. The first day, my father asked me the definition of a
> non-restrictive adjective clause. I had to finally admit I didn't know the
> term. He turned to the class and said, "You see, ladies and gentleman,

this is the young man whose grammar background was so thorough that he didn't need to audit my course."

For Tolson, prescription was never an end it itself, of course, but rather always in the service of a higher good. "I'd rather be a good reasoner and a bad grammarian than the reverse," he said ("Poet Thieves"). Though proud of instilling in his students a love for the precise use of language, he hoped that they would put it to good use and not merely employ it for snobbery's sake or as a class marker. At one point he joked that, despite his best efforts to radicalize his students, "[t]he college turned out . . . Colored ladies and gentlemen who did not split infinitives" (qtd. in Farnsworth 105).

Although Tolson privileged the prescriptive syntax of Standard American English (SAE), he also privileged the rhetorical features of African American Vernacular English (AAVE or BEV—Black English Vernacular). As Valerie M. Balester notes, because much of the early work done on African American language practices was by linguists, the differences between SAE and AAVE are often thought of in terms of "grammar, syntax, and phonology" (33). But, as scholars, such as Balester, Geneva Smitherman ("Blacker," *Talkin*), Roger D. Abrahams, and Keith Gilyard and Elaine Richardson, have shown, it is in the discourse features where the richest divergences (and perhaps correspondences) can be found. In "The Blacker the Berry," Smitherman codifies ten common features of African American discourse: rhythmic, dramatic, evocative language; reference to color-race-ethnicity; use of proverbs, aphorisms, and Biblical verses; sermonic tone reminiscent of black church rhetoric; direct address-conversational tone; cultural references; ethnolinguistic idioms; verbal inventiveness; stressing of cultural values and community consciousness; and field dependency (86–87). In his teaching—and in his public writing, which I treat in this volume as an extension of his classroom—Tolson employed the full range of these strategies: he loved signification and sermonizing; he wrote and spoke from a highly personal, community-situated, "black" subject position; he made extensive use of wordplay, analogy, Biblical, literary, and black cultural references; and he also encouraged his students to employ similar strategies.

In giving lessons, Tolson was a firm believer in the old rhetorical exercise of *imitatio*. He taught himself poetry and playwriting through self-study. His practice was to "imitate the masters, learning the rules for the various forms through using them" (Flasch, *Melvin B. Tolson* 28). As he became enamored of modernism, he sought to make use of its formal techniques while applying the subject matter of race and class consciousness. A poet must use the techniques of the time, he often insisted. However, the similarities ended there. "[W]hen you look at my ideas and Eliot's, we're as far apart as hell and heaven" (letter to Benjamin and Kate Bell). To students, he stressed, "Imitation must be in technique only. We have a rich heritage of folk lore and history. We are a part of America. We are a part of the world. Our native symbols must be lifted into the universal" (qtd. in Flasch, *Melvin B. Tolson* 70).

To push his students, Tolson would often appeal to racial pride. "Your grandpa had the choice of being a preacher, a teacher, an undertaker, or a bum" went a common appeal. "From the looks of these papers, I'd say that you're settling for the last choice, even though the professions are wide open to you today. You know where white folks put information they want to hide from you? Books and magazines and newspapers—that's where!" (qtd. in Flasch, *Melvin B. Tolson* 38). "Question everything," he insisted. "You are competing with students from Harvard and Yale" (qtd. in Flasch, "Melvin Beaunoris Tolson" 19). Such prodding was consciously performative. "He never spoke against other groups," says Wells. "He seemed to believe in loving everybody, but he realized that as a race to receive our due and compete, we had to work hard."

Power and Authority in the Classroom

Tolson's radicalism and rigor made him a legendary figure on campus. At both Wiley and Langston University in Oklahoma, where he later taught, it was widely acknowledged that a "student's education wasn't complete until he had taken a course from [Tolson], even though he may be running the risk of flunking" (Hare). How did he get away with it? First, Tolson's position as a black instructor at an all-black college gave him a powerful ethos. As an African American with rural, religious, and Southern roots, Tolson shared a cultural background with his students and represented a model for them to aspire to. Furthermore, his students, raised in a tradition where sermonic and jeremiadic church oratory was common and attending a school in which the enactment of in loco parentis had full parental support, would not have seen his classroom admonishments as out of the ordinary. Tolson also visibly practiced what he preached. He sent out his poetry to be published (and invited his students to critique it), wrote newspaper columns and articles for the black press, and actively worked for civil rights and social justice at the risk of his own safety, organizing sharecroppers, both black and white, and giving incendiary speeches against lynching, racism, and class inequities. Simply put, his ethos gave him authority, which he successfully exploited to encourage his students to achieve. Said one, "I have decided to strive for excellence because Dr. Tolson made me see that mediocrity is not good enough" (Flasch, "The Man" 4). Wells echoes this sentiment: "He wanted you to strive to be the very best. There was no middle ground."

Such naked exercise of power might strike us as dangerous: do the ends justify the means? In this case, I think so. Recently, Patricia Roberts-Miller called attention to the pedagogical value of Hannah Arendt's distinction in "What Is Authority?" between authority and coercion. Arendt sees authority as a function of a ruling body's legitimacy, against which its power can "be checked" (97): "Authority implies an obedience in which men retain their freedom" (106). Coercion, on the other hand, is simple force. Applied to the classroom, argues Roberts-Miller, authority is what is students grant teachers whose power they recognize as legitimate. "[S]tudents choose to do what the teacher says because they think s/he knows what s/he is doing, rather than because they fear his/her punishments" (140). Coercion is what teachers must rely on when their ethos or authority is not enough. "Authoritarian teachers," she writes, "have no authority" (140). In this light, Tolson's teaching might be regarded not as authoritarian but, to use Roberts-Miller's term, as *authority-based*.

As a small, black, religious school in a segregated town, Wiley was very much self-contained. Tolson used this to his advantage, frequently catching up to students as they walked through the campus in order to discuss the news, invite them to his house to share poetry, or quietly pull them aside and encourage them to study harder. In his autobiography, *Lay Bare the Heart*, James Farmer recalled one such incident that illuminates Tolson's ability to simultaneously chastise and praise his students—and challenge them to do better. One day during Farmer's freshman year, while he was walking across campus, Tolson yelled out, "Farmer, what are you reading these days?" When he told him *War and Peace*, Tolson replied, "I'm glad to know that at least you are drinking the broth of knowledge; why don't you eat the meat?" Soon after that, he asked Farmer to stay after class. In the space of five minutes, he threatened to fail him, gave him extra reading assignments, and invited him to join the debate team:

> Farmer . . . you're doing good work. In fact, you're doing A work, but if you don't do better, I'm going to flunk you. . . . You're blessed with a good mind, an analytical mind, but you don't dig. You're lazy. You're not using half your mind, and like most youths with a gift for self-expression, you try to conceal your ignorance with filibustering.
>
> Well, I'm not going to let you get away with it. Above and beyond the class assignments, you're going to read and study and dig. Finish *War and Peace* and then go on to his other works. Then I want you to tackle

Darwin, Freud, and Marx. Don't just taste them; chew them and digest them. Then we'll get together and argue about them. I'll take a devil's advocate position, and you defend your views. That's the way you sharpen your tools—in the clash of opposing views.

Speaking of opposing views, my varsity debaters . . . come over to the house every Tuesday and Thursday evening. . . . You come over, too. Some of them, at least one, will try to make hamburger out of you—a young upstart, and Dr. Farmer's son—so fight back, my boy, fight back.

All right, Farmer, I'll see you tonight. (118)

Moments such as these stayed with Tolson's students, and a number of them credit him with giving direction to their lives. Farmer attributed to Tolson his political awakening. One evening, in an all-night bull session, Farmer and his friends railed against segregation. "We buried it and wrote its epitaph and danced on its grave." Feeling pleased with himself, he went to the movies. When Tolson found out, he told him, "You hate segregation; but you've paid your father's hard-earned money for the privilege of being segregated" (120). He then tossed him a copy of "Civil Disobedience."

Hamilton Boswell was another student who experienced the Tolson treatment. Boswell came from a respected, well-to-do family—his grandfather had been one of the earliest black physicians in California, and his father was a Methodist minister—but he had been "going nowhere fast" before arriving at Wiley. His first week in school, Tolson caught him unprepared in class:

He wanted to know if I had read the lesson for the day. I hadn't, so I got up and filibustered around for a while. Mr. Tolson said, "Wait a minute, Mr. Boswell, you come from Los Angeles, don't you?"

"Yes."

"They have some of the best schools in the United States, isn't that right?"

"That's right."

I thought he was just admiring of me, so I kept on filibustering. Finally he said, "Mr. Boswell, just sit down a minute." Then he went to the other side of the room and asked a young man if he had read the lesson. He said he had. Then he said, "Mr. Jones, where are you from?"

"Tupelo, Mississippi."

"And what school did you go to?"

"Well I went only went to school about five months out of the year. School was always out when the cotton crop was to be picked."

There I was with all my fancy tailormade clothes, coming from Los Angeles, and I was very embarrassed. So I walked out of the class. About a week later I was walking across campus, and all of a sudden Mr. Tolson came around the corner. He said, "Mr. Boswell, you are a very smart man, but you are lazy." And from that moment on, I began to listen to Tolson. He turned me back around. (Boswell)

Tolson applied such treatment again and again. "You couldn't shock him," says Wells, "but he would often shock you."

Tolson, who modeled himself after Socrates and Diogenes, did enjoy shocking people. But he also knew that "nothing educates us like a shock" ("Richard Wright" 22). Education, he felt, like scholarship and art, should serve a moral purpose." "Use the Word. It is a two-edged sword for democracy and justice" (*Caviar* 233). I suspect also that given that African American rhetoric tends to be comfortable with agonistic discourse and values linguistic virtuosity, Tolson's students would have been savvy enough to understand his pedagogical performances *as performance* and thus would not likely to have been unduly offended. As Joy Flasch related, "It was an honor to be singled out by Tolson as the horrible example of the day . . . for the student knew he was a favorite" (*Melvin B. Tolson* 37). And while Tolson raised the bar through his daunting depth and breadth of knowledge and his enviable ability to think quickly on his feet, he also tempered his ethos by poking fun at himself. He was not only notoriously absentminded and disorganized—he frequently misplaced his briefcase or, more alarmingly, his still-lit cigar—but cultivated these quirks to his advantage. He simply left his house without his shoes too many times for it to be *always* accidental. And such incidents gave him the perfect opportunity to perform: "Well, Boswell, think of that poor cow that died so you could wear shoes" (Boswell).

Not everyone, of course, was impressed with his teaching methods, at least not at first. His indifferent dress, occasional absentmindedness, resistance to convention, love of shock, and insistence that his students meet the high standards he had set for them undoubtedly turned some students off. "He's the queerest weirdo teacher you'll ever meet," said one (qtd. in Sloss 13). But for the most part, his students were won over. Minerva A. Sloss, who graduated from Wiley in 1942, eulogized him a decade after his death in an article in *Oklahoma Today*. In what must have been a familiar arc for a student in Tolson's classroom, at first she was terrified. Before the first day of class, she had "heard so much about how difficult and strange this poetic genius was" she could hardly sleep. On the first day of class, she couldn't help staring at his feet, having heard the rumor—true, of course—that he had once shown up to class barefoot. "Yes, I'm wearing my shoes," he snapped, as if he could read her mind, "just to please 'your world' and its invading-individual-privacy societal rules" (13). On his "moody" days, she found him frightening to behold:

> [H]e would express deep-seated disgust for anyone who was incompetent, unknowledgeable, and unconcerned about bettering his lot. . . . He was impatient, shockingly embarrassing, cruel, to any lack of understanding or display of "I don't care" attitudes. . . . He daily stressed *reading* and *listening to the media* to be aware of what was happening all around us "in your world." (13–14)

But her terror soon gave way to respect as his deep concern for his students became clear, and he awed the class with his erudition and eloquence.

> Although he constantly pounced on the "wrongs" and "cruelties" of the world, most of us began to know him not as a rebel American, but one who truly loved America, yet also loved his ancestral African heritage. He believed we should be ever aware of the inequalities in our nation, that this knowledge, however, should not make us bitter: but should make us realize the necessity of being ever prepared mentally, physically, and academically to cope with these inequalities. . . . I believe my acceptance of myself as a black woman with capabilities to go as far as my educational preparations, aspirations and physical endurance would permit . . . became more realistic as a result of my experiences in his class. . . . I learned much more than mere facts: I learned about life, about myself, my fellowman, my own people. I learned to be concerned about others, that each human being, black or white, is unique and plays a part in the development of our great humanity. (14)

But Sloss is a rare documented critique. Indeed, in researching and writing about Melvin Tolson, it has been difficult to avoid descending into hagiography. He is almost universally remembered as an inspirational teacher and exceptional man (Bickham; Biggers; Farmer; Flasch, "Melvin Beaunoris Tolson," *Melvin B. Tolson*; H. Wells; Boswell; Jarrett, letter). "You're scary and unscathed, really heroic to me, a great man (word I always try to shun)," Karl Shapiro wrote to him after a visit. The writer William Melvin Kelley echoed this sentiment soon after meeting Tolson: "You are a great man. And that word MAN is a very heavy word." Having examined his papers at the Library of Congress and spoken to former students and colleagues, I can attest to the truth of Joy Flasch's statement, "He inspired devotion bordering on adulation in many who knew him well" (*Melvin B. Tolson* preface). Even

Robert M. Farnsworth's finely balanced and carefully researched biography does little worse than suggest that Tolson's love for argumentation may have intimidated his children, who nonetheless respected him and loved him dearly. His eldest son, Melvin Jr., himself a professor of languages, who retired to devote more time to studying the African Diaspora, unabashedly calls him a genius.

Tolson's influence on his students was lifelong. They took their lessons outside the classroom, many becoming activists, teachers, writers, and dramatists, as well as remaining lifelong friends. James Farmer, perhaps his most well-known student, became a celebrated and crucially important civil rights activist. He organized the campus chapter of the NAACP in 1937, at a time when many whites thought the organization insurrectionary, and many blacks, including the college president, thought it too dangerous to join. He later cofounded the Congress of Racial Equality, led the Freedom Riders at the dawn of the civil rights era, and, as assistant secretary of Health, Education, and Welfare under President Richard M. Nixon, was one of the earliest proponents and architects of affirmative action.

Others include Benjamin Bell, who helped organize sharecroppers with Tolson in the 1930s; Thomas Cole, the first black student to receive a PhD from the University of Texas and later president of Wiley College; and Heman Sweatt, whose pioneering lawsuit, headed by Thurgood Marshall, against the University of Texas School of Law in 1946, led to its desegregation by the U.S. Supreme Court.[10] Sweatt cited Tolson with providing him with the courage to initiate his lawsuit and being the second most important influence in his life, after his father; Tolson, in return, gleefully acknowledged contributing to Sweatt's "contamination" (Gillette 163).

Those who entered academia include Hobart Jarrett, chair of the English department at Langston University and later a professor at City University of New York, Brooklyn; Johnnie Marie Van Zandt McCleary, chair of the English department at Texas Southern University; debater Bertram Lewis, who taught at City College of San Francisco and Southern University and A&M College, Baton Rouge; and Robert E. Hayes, president of Wiley College. Hamilton Boswell, now a retired Methodist minister and former chaplain of the California State House, entered the ministry soon after graduating from Wiley, becoming in Tolson's estimation "the most radical young clergyman in the race" ("Man Against" 32), a charge that stuck with him all his life and one in which he still takes delight. "Jesus was a radical," he says, echoing his mentor. "They didn't lynch him for shooting anybody, they didn't lynch him for stealing anything—it was his ideas they lynched him for." Bertram Lewis also showed his teacher's influence. Studying for his PhD in New York in

1950, nearly twenty years after he graduated from Wiley, he described Tolson's suggestions for his dissertation as "one of the oases in the intellectual desert. Of great help. If you have more water to sprinkle, rain down, brother, rain down. Remember, there is a water shortage here in Hicksville-on-the-Hudson; and that goes for water on the brain also" (Lewis).

Tolson's students, in return, encouraged him. He often shared his works in progress with students at his house, running back to the typewriter to make corrections as they offered critiques. His students were flattered to be asked their opinion. And, as befitting their training, they gave it. "As a Negro poet you are tops," Henry Heights wrote to Tolson in 1944 after receiving a copy of his critically acclaimed *Rendezvous with America*. "But you are too big to be a Negro poet. Take up the cause of humanity and become a world poet."

Adventures in Interracial Debates

Although Tolson was an inspirational English teacher, his most intimate relationships with his students were probably as a debate coach. Here, he blurred the line between classroom, extracurricular, and recreational activity as he encouraged his students to apply their rhetorical training in a public sphere. At Wiley, as at other black colleges, debate was not merely a campus diversion. Rather, oratorical competition served, practically and symbolically, as a means of both individual and community achievement. Speakers and audiences alike saw themselves as stakeholders in a public—and publicly performed—enterprise of racial uplift.

In the first decades of the twentieth century, debate became a popular collegiate activity. The Harvard-Yale debates of 1892, though not the first intercollegiate debates, garnered national attention and helped spread the practice (Potter 23–26). The annual yearbook of college debating, *Intercollegiate Debates*, began publication in 1909, and the forensic honor society Pi Kappa Delta was founded in 1913. The 1929–32 *Readers' Guide* lists twenty-nine articles under "Debates and Debating," nearly all on school debate, from "Woodrow Wilson as a Debate Coach" in the *Quarterly Journal of Speech* to "How to Talk Your Way around the World: Bates College Debating Team" in the *Literary Digest*. In 1930, the Sixth National Intercollegiate Oratorical Contest on the Constitution awarded $5,000 in prizes, including $1,500 to the winner, an enormous amount in the Great Depression.

Debating between black colleges can probably be traced back to 1906, when Talladega College met Morehouse College (then known as Atlanta Baptist College) in Atlanta. The schools, which thereafter met annually, were joined by Knoxville College in 1911 and Fisk in 1920, and the practice rapidly spread, fueled, in part, by a strong tradition of intramural debate in black colleges by campus literary societies (Parker, "Status of Debate" 146–47; E. Jones 293–95; Brawley 126). By 1939, debate and drama were the most popular nonathletic extracurricular activities in black colleges (Parker, "Status of Debate" 147), and orators were prominent figures on campus, often garnering "sizeable followings of loyal and devoted fans" (Little 137). In addition to intercampus and league matches, teams from two colleges would often team up for exhibition tours throughout the South. Wiley toured with a number of schools, including Tuskegee, Fisk, and Talladega (Tolson Jr.; H. Wells), and Melvin Jr. recalls full halls—and ofttimes paying audiences—from Dallas to Atlanta. "It was so much a part of the culture," he says, "no one thought to record it."

Arriving at Wiley in 1923, Tolson, fresh from his own experience as a collegiate debater, was eager to organize a team. His first year, Wiley debated nearby Bishop in the school's first intercollegiate debate. No records of this debate have survived, but it is likely Tolson coached this team. Early in his second year, he formally established the school's Forensic Society (Farnsworth 32), and the team soon hosted Bishop College in a major event on campus, the program featuring an invocation by the dean and a recital by the school orchestra. Tolson and his team must have anticipated the event keenly; in addition to the Methodist Wiley's traditional rivalry with the Baptist Bishop, Bishop was coached by E. E. Ware, a graduate of Bates College, which was famous for its debate team. To "the deep regret of all concerned," however, the debate was a nondecision one (Melvin Beaunoris Tolson papers).

In the spring of 1930 in Chicago, Tolson's team made history by participating in what has been reported as the first interracial debate in the United States,[11] meeting law students from the University of Michigan. The nondecision debate, held at a packed downtown theater, was set up with the help of a member of the Wiley community with University of Michigan connections. Chicago was chosen as a relatively safe, neutral site. The Chicago debate was also notable for featuring Wiley's first female debater, Henrietta Bell (now Henrietta Bell Wells). In the 1930s, it was common for women to participate in forensics, though usually in oratory rather than debate, and in separate competitions.[12] Wells was the first woman to compete on one of Tolson's teams and almost certainly one of the few women anywhere to participate in mixed team debate. Wells, a high school valedictorian, had been trained in drama—"that's where I learned how to speak"—but had never debated. Soon after her arrival at Wiley, Tolson recruited her for the team. In addition to being a good student, says Wells, she "didn't look at the boys. Plus the matron wouldn't have allowed me to travel if I had been that kind of a girl." Tolson treated Wells with the same rough kindness as he did the men on his team, calling her "Bell," never "Miss Bell" or "Henrietta." "He treated me like I was another boy," she says. Unfortunately, Wells was unable to remain on the debate team for financial reasons. As an Episcopalian, she did not qualify for school aid—Dogan told her, "Daughter, if you were a Methodist you wouldn't have to work at all"—and she finally had to quit the team for fear of losing her several jobs, which her friends had been holding for her while she traveled. Fortunately, "Mr. Tolson was also the dramatic coach, and most of the plays were held on campus. He said, 'Well, Bell, you can get in dramatics.'"

In 1931, the Wiley team reached a perhaps even more dramatic milestone, the first interracial collegiate debate in the South. On March 27, 1931, on the safe ground of Avery Chapel African Methodist Episcopal Church in Oklahoma City, Wiley met a team from the Methodist-affiliated Oklahoma City University (OCU).[13] "The decision was in favor of the Negro team," the student newspaper dutifully reported ("Debaters Leave"). The decision must have been especially sweet for the competitive Tolson, for OCU was then a regional powerhouse, with a number of state championships and strong national showings. As recently as 1928, their two-man debate team had placed fourth in the Pi Kappa Delta national championships, and in 1929, an OCU student had won the Women's Christian Temperance Union's National Oratorical Championship. At the time of the debate, the school was set to host the Pi Kappa Delta national convention in 1932, having won out over UCLA ("Debaters Win").

How was such an event received in the segregated South? While an intercollegiate debate was groundbreaking, racially mixed events were not unusual at OCU. Through its Methodist affiliation, the school maintained ties with black educational and cultural institutions. The student newspaper, the *Campus*, and the community newsmonthly, the *Torch*, note a number of interracial events, including a performance at OCU by a black gospel group and a visit by the school's own gospel group to the black Langston University. These events are reported with such journalistic detachment, however, that it is hard to tell whether the writers were truly blasé about such happenings, begrudging of them, or writing tersely to avoid offending the sensibilities of the surrounding community. As a point of reference, in 1947, the nearby University of Oklahoma cancelled its annual Religious Emphasis Week when the governing board of the student union refused to allow the attendance of a black chaplain who had been invited to speak (Fisher 107–8, 190).

A front-page article in the *Torch* in 1930 described the OCU team as "typical of Oklahoma, young, with the aggressiveness of the West, yet the graciousness of the South" ("Debaters Win"). The same might be said of Tolson's team. Writing about interracial debates in the NAACP's *Crisis*, a forum in which he would have had little reason to pull punches, Hobart Jarrett recalled that while the Wiley team was on occasion nearly lynched "for practicing social equality," its white opponents were never anything less than gracious. "These interracial debates have been pleasurable, instructive, friendly, and broadening. Our opponents have been gentlemen always" ("Adventures" 240).

During Tolson's tenure as debate coach, the team traveled an estimated sixty thousand to seventy-five thousand miles. In the 1930 season alone, in addition to traveling to Chicago, the team met Arkansas State University, Virginia Union University, and Wilberforce University in Ohio, then met Fisk at home, and began touring with them in exhibition matches in Texas (H. Wells). By 1935, the team had been to Wisconsin, Kansas, New Mexico, and California. That a team from a small black college could travel so widely—much less compete successfully—during the height of the Depression is a remarkable achievement. The federal interstate system had not yet been built, and roads were rough and travel slow. Wiley was struggling financially and had few funds to spare; the team met expenses by borrowing the president's car, staying with friends and families in the Wiley and Methodist communities, and collecting ticket receipts from exhibition matches and competitions.

For African Americans, even those of means, travel in the South was not only difficult but, due to segregation, dangerous. Travelers were regularly denied food, gas, and lodging, and stories of being forced to drive a hundred miles or more just to obtain a sandwich were common. Accordingly, the Wiley team survived breakdowns, car accidents, shootings, and angry mobs:

> Beebee Arkansas! It is three A.M. The White River has gone mad and leaped its banks. A mob, with flaming torches, is scattered along the road, looking for a Negro tramp. A deputy sheriff has been killed. . . . Off in the swamps the hounds are baying. The Wiley debaters are on the road and the road leads through the tremendous circle of mobsters. But there is a mulatto in the car. Coach Tolson tells him to take the steering wheel. The darker debaters get down in the car. The night is friendly, protecting. The mulatto salutes nonchalantly the grimfaced members of the mob, allaying their suspicions. And the debaters reach Memphis and read about the mob in the morning newspapers. . . . (Jarrett, "Adventures" 240)

Throughout the 1930s, Wiley debated dozens of white teams, including the University of New Mexico, University of Kansas, and University of Oxford, England, reportedly without losing a match ("Debaters to Meet"; Scherman 42; L. Hughes; Gibbs 51–52; "Wiley College and Kansas"). Tolson and his students took great delight in defeating white colleges. Said Jarrett, "For centuries, the Caucasian has believed that his superiority lies in his brain power. Debates involve a direct clash of intellects. There was a time when white colleges thought that debating against a Negro institution was mental dissipation, but that view has passed forever" ("Adventures" 240).

On April 2, 1935, the team won its most celebrated victory, defeating the national champions, the University of Southern California (USC), before a paying audience that filled the school's Bovard Auditorium.[14] ("Debaters to Meet"; Jarrett, "Adventures" 240; Scherman 42; Tolson Jr.; Flasch, *Melvin B. Tolson* 25–26; Farnsworth 50). The teams debated that year's national topic, "Resolved: That the nations shall agree to prevent the international shipment of arms and munitions." Before the debate, Tolson toured USC's speech department, which according to legend was almost as big as the Wiley campus. When asked by his team about their upcoming opponents, he casually told them, "They're not so much. We'll visit them after we win the debate, just to show them we're good sports" (qtd. in Randall 57). The victory brought the team wide attention: Mae West insisted on meeting Tolson, and the editors of *The Forensic*, the journal of Pi Kappa Delta, the national debate society, invited Tolson to write an article, although as a black college, Wiley was forbidden membership, and its victory had no official sanction. But it was a sweet victory nonetheless. At a time when the intellectual capacities of African Americans were the subject of public debate, Wiley's long string of decisions over white teams presented a sounding rebuttal to racist ideologies and propaganda. And at a time when black civil rights were still largely suppressed, Wiley's competitions against white teams suggested the hope of interracial harmony and the promise of coming better days. In a 1945 interview in which he foresaw "a real people's movement coming alive" in the South, Tolson noted debate as one of its indicators: "I have seen the organization of inter-racial unions. I have seen the Negro win the vote in the Democratic primary. I have seen white boys and Negro boys debate in places where the Negro was never to say more than 'yessir' to the white man" (qtd. in Lowe).

Tolson was an inspirational model for his teams, which were noted for their "use of logic, wit, strategy, exquisite diction, authoritative facts, and eloquence" (Davis). Besides being a brilliant—and endless—talker, Tolson was a formidable debater, with a great ability to think on his feet. Legend had it that "one Texan who led a mob against him later gave a piano to his Little Theatre" (Lowe). At a party in New York, a professor who had unsuccessfully tried to bait him all evening finally conceded defeat. "Tolson, you just can't be insulted, can you?" "No my friend," Tolson replied. "You see a less intelligent man than I can't insult me, and a more intelligent one won't" (Flasch, *Melvin B. Tolson* 29).

To train his team, Tolson, who loved few things better than a good argument, drilled his students endlessly, often meeting with them three or four nights a week until one or two in the morning, until they were thoroughly versed in their subject and could argue either side equally well. When he exhausted his own prodigious store of information, he would drag in other Wiley professors or visiting lecturers and have his students clash with them on their field of expertise. As Hobart Jarrett, one of the stars of the 1934–35 team that beat USC put it, "We worked like hell":

> Tolson's system demanded perfection. He did such things as putting six men on stage and having them speak three different speeches simultaneously. At any given moment he would yell "stop." We then were signaled to begin where we left off. Suffice it to say that the selected varsity men knew not only the issues pro and con but could argue them in their sleep, almost. And I frankly do not remember EVER having heard an opponent advance an argument for which we had not worked out an answer. This is how the rebuttals mowed down the opposing team." (letter)

Tolson placed great value on audience and in taking advantage of the kairos of the moment. He encouraged his students to find the least-interested person in the audience and try to win him or her over, a technique that Jarrett used in his classroom throughout his career. "Speak to the student who is obviously not really interested, get him or her with you and you've got it made" (letter). One of Tolson's tricks was to have students memorize the names of local landmarks or prominent community members and work them into their speeches. This got the audience's attention, though not always the desired one. Henrietta Bell Wells recalls that at the famous Chicago debate, Tolson, who thought the opening of her speech was not catchy enough, told her to open with, "It has always been my desire to walk down the street with a Chicago Romeo." The next day, she says, the newspapers praised all the debaters, black and white, but noted, "Miss Bell strayed from her point to give vent to her ambition to meet a Chicago Romeo" (H. Wells).

At the core of Tolson's training program was the "Latin logical fallacies." Tolson sought always to find the "crack" in the other team's logic and, by doing so, "go after the ugly truth" (*Caviar* 240). One should always attack the idea, he stressed, not the man. In one of his earliest published writings, a defense of Langston Hughes's "Goodbye Christ," he admonished Reverend J. R. Henderson for his use of the ad hominem attack ("Langston Hughes"). Of course, Tolson himself was no stranger to signifying, and in fact he delighted in elaborately worded put-downs and intellectual one-upmanship if he thought it justified. Of fellow columnist and Howard University professor Kelly Miller he said, "He can say nothing with more dignity than any other man before the American public." Not even W. E. B. Du Bois escaped his barbs: "Our captain has left the No Mans Land of racial strife and retired to Atlanta on a lucrative salary, and from his ivory tower he issues each week his sugar-coated nothings" ("Wanted" 10–11). For Tolson, a student of Aristotle, ethos was everything, and he paid attention to detail in ways that might be unfathomable today. He insisted his male debaters wear tuxedos and his female debaters dress suits. He even asked Wells to cut her hair so as to appear more businesslike. Tolson's visual ethos must have had some effect. Henrietta Bell Wells has kept photos of the teams Wiley debated in 1930, and even by the impeccable fashion standards of the day, the Wiley team looks sharp in comparison. "The fellows from Fisk," she says dismissively, "they just had on suits."

Unfortunately, World War II disrupted college debate, as it did many extracurricular activities, and in 1939, the school was unable to find an opposing team to tour with. The advent of the Cold War also had a chilling effect, as it was no longer advisable to debate certain topics, such as the relative merits of socialism (Tolson Jr.). The spread of mass media, such as radio and television, also contributed to debate's decline as a spectator event. Benjamin Bell, however, who debated at Wiley from 1936 to 1939, suggests another reason for the decline: "Schools were afraid of debating us. . . . Every time they did, they got their pants kicked. How do you think they felt, getting spanked by a little Jim Crow school from the badlands of Texas?" (qtd. in Scherman 40).

Embracing Contradictions

Tolson had a powerful faith in the power of education to uplift—both spiritually and economically—and in the promise of American democracy as espoused by Jefferson and celebrated by Whitman. He was also an unabashed optimist, which he considered a function of his belief in the possibility of change; if human nature was fixed, he said, there was no cause for hope. This is not to suggest, however, that in teaching his students to aspire to "good" English and better citizenship, that his was an uncritical assimilationism. Said Tolson:

> When a white man uses the term *democracy* in the presence of a Negro, it has the effect of adding zero to googol. The compound of *demos* and *kratos* is a semantic echo escaping from the walled-out world in which the lack of pigmentation makes men like gods! . . . When Franklin D. Roosevelt points to the mistreatment of Jews in Germany, Adolph Hitler refers him to the lynching of Negroes in the South. The pot insults itself when it calls the skillet black. ("Man Against" 30)

Tolson did not shy from confrontation in racially mixed company. In a memorial speech soon after his death, Joy Flasch said that he "thoroughly enjoyed shocking his white acquaintances who sometimes had difficulty comprehending a Negro intellectual" ("Melvin Beaunoris Tolson" 9). If a well-meaning white told a "black mammy" story, he would blithely counter with tales of his beloved "white mammy." Ada Lois Sipuel Fisher, whom Tolson assisted in her attempt to desegregate the University of Oklahoma,[15] recalled that though he rarely told racial jokes, when he did, "the African American always won against 'Massah,' 'Mr. Charlie,' or 'The Man,' the weapons of choice being innuendo, slyness, trickery, and cunning" (Fisher 106). The poet Thomas Whitbread depicted one such moment in his elegy to Tolson, "In Praise of M. B. Tolson": "I remember Tolson, summer of '65, / Throwing a half-eaten McDonald's hamburger, in its paper, out the window / Of a moving car / And later describing that hamburger as white America" (45).

Tolson was also a fierce advocate for social justice, practicing what he preached inside the classroom and out. Before predominantly white audiences, he spoke against the "brutal fascism of the South," "the local gestapo" that controlled life "below the Smith and Wesson Line" ("Man Against" 31). He praised Richard Wright's "acid-syllabled words" in *Native Son*, in which at last "Negroes stand up, strike back, find in death the courage of life" ("Richard Wright" 19, 24). In 1946, Tolson gave two speeches in Austin that caught the notice of the press, the first in March at the Community Congregational Church, where he argued that freedom of speech was a meaningless concept without a "decent wage" (H. Campbell 4), and the second in October at the University of Texas, where memories of President Rainey's firing for his support of academic freedom were still strong. There, Tolson "blasted three groups: the government; the upper classes; and the weak-kneed intellectuals" (Rollins 1).[16] In response to Tolson's habit of agitation, Wiley President Matthew Dogan once told him, "Tolson, I won't be a bit surprised to hear some morning that you've been strung up to a tree" (Flasch, "Melvin Beaunoris Tolson" 15). This was a grim joke. On more than one occasion, Tolson barely escaped violence after a particularly incendiary speech, as when, in 1938, he was invited to speak at a black high school commencement in Rustin, Louisiana, where the principal was a Wiley alum. The day before the ceremony, four blacks had been lynched nearby; tensions were high enough so that Tolson's wife, Ruth, forbade him to take Melvin Jr., and student Benjamin Bell, who accompanied Tolson, literally packed his pistols. Tolson boldly told the assembled crowd, which included the sheriff, the president of the school board, and other white dignitaries, "Where were you good folks when these men were lynched?" Afterwards, black residents advised him to leave town by a back road (Farnsworth 103).

Tolson made few distinctions between his politics and his pedagogy. Tolson, as Herbert Aptheker said of W. E. B. Du Bois, "saw education (to be truly education) as partisan and—given the realities of the social order—fundamentally subversive" (xiii). Yet how partisan or subversive could he be given his conservative attitudes toward language and his liberal faith in American democracy and human nature?

A number of scholars have warned of the potentially deracializing effects of rhetorical instruction that seeks to inculcate majority values or linguistic standards. Sharon Crowley in particular has charged freshman English with erasing students' home voices and disciplining their subjectivities (*Composition*). Geneva Smitherman has called attention to the presence of integral African American rhetorical figures in black student writing and warned against instruction that ignores these practices ("Blacker," *Talkin*). In light of these concerns, race-aware scholarship and pedagogy are critical. As Jacqueline Jones Royster and Jean C. Williams assert, "Neutrality often erases the presence of students of color with the resultant assumption that, in not being marked as present, they in fact were not there" (568). Of course, lack of neutrality offers no guarantees. At early-twentieth-century Howard University, writes Scott Zaluda,

> "[G]ood English" meant practicing writing conventions sanctioned by Anglo-American society. . . . and doing so in correct and proper form and style; *good*, moral English also meant publicly criticizing African American apartheid with regard to academic, social, political, and economic communities. (237) However . . . to produce at Howard generally meant to reproduce prevailing social relations as those are constructed by academic disciplines. (241)

Zaluda is careful to describe his study as merely "one institutional context" within a twelve-year span, yet his description of the instructional dilemma at Howard can be safely applied to Wiley and other black colleges of the early twentieth century: "[F]aculty and student writing across the curriculum entered into a unique paradox where prevailing ideas and the social forces that reinforce them simultaneously had to be reproduced and contested" (233). Indeed, this paradox is one of central political dilemmas of the freshman English classroom today. Many members of the post-1960s generation of rhetoric and writing scholars share a deep distrust of institutional authority even as they embody it, and many of our curricular innovations—expressivism, decentered classrooms, students' right to their own language—have been a response to this dilemma.

Such concerns with academic "whitewashing" are not new. In *The Mis-Education of the Negro*, first published in 1933, historian Carter G. Woodson decried an educational system that "justified slavery, peonage, segregation, and lynching" (xii) and that taught blacks "to admire the Hebrew, the Greek, the Latin and the Teuton and to despise the African" (1). "If the white man wants to hold on to it, let him do so; but the Negro, so far as he is able, should develop and carry out a program of his own" (xii). Woodson was especially critical of those who he felt had bought into white bourgeois values or who had internalized the self-loathing they had been taught by their oppressors, whether black or white.

> The "uneducated" Negro businessman . . . is actually at work doing the very thing which the "mis-educated" Negro has been taught to believe cannot be done. . . . If the "highly educated" Negro would forget most of the untried theories taught him in school, if he could see through the propaganda which has been instilled into his mind under the pretext of education, if he would fall in love with his own people and begin to sacrifice for their uplift . . . he could solve some of the problems now confronting the race. (44)

Certainly, class factions divided black communities. Michael Fultz, in his analysis of black newspapers in Chicago between 1900 and 1930, argues that their treatment of education was skewed to middle-class concerns, stressing the need for support of colleges and college students while paying less attention to issues such as universal primary and secondary education. And black college campuses, like their white counterparts, had the potential to perpetuate and exacerbate such class divisions and other tensions. Even at Wiley, it was reputed that the school limited the enrollment of darker-complexioned students, and sororities and fraternities, which dominated campus life, were resented for their "phoniness and pretense" and exclusion of poor students (Beil 36–37; Farmer 122–27).

Tolson was no stranger to these conflicts. All his life he was an enemy of what he considered bourgeois values. He exhorted his students to think beyond their own socioeconomic advancement and consider their community. He continually sided with the young against the old, the powerless against the powerful, the "little dogs" against the "big dogs," be they black or white, and he welcomed social change. "Conservatives," he declared, "have stood for prostitution, blood-letting, polygamy, illiteracy, ignorance, witch-burning, voodooism, piracy, plagues, child labor, social diseases, and cannibalism" (*Caviar* 38). "The status quo is a boat with a hole in the bottom. . . . If a man isn't a liberal or a radical, he is a joke or a foggy among intelligent folk" ("She Can't" 6). In his public writing, he mocked complacent middle-class blacks and "Negro misleaders" for casting their lot with "the Big White Folk" and selling out their people. "If you want to be . . . a Great Big Negro," he wrote in *The Oracle*, the journal of the black fraternity Omega Psi Phi, "be a snob and marry a high yellow woman" ("Recipes" 16). In his poetry, he tried to meld high-modernist techniques with an African American consciousness to create a voice that would speak across both race and class boundaries. And yet, toward the end of his life, with the rise of the Black Consciousness and Black Arts movements, he and his work were attacked for being too white.

One manifestation of black consciousness was the articulation of a separatist black aesthetic, unpolluted by white, European influences, that combined with a wider cultural turn against establishment values and a deep concern for authenticity. This movement saw the most legitimate black voice as bound in the language of the street, of "everyday people." A generation prior, Zora Neale Hurston had been castigated by her peers for writing in dialect. Now Tolson got into trouble for being too high toned. This critique was not universal, of course, As late as 1965, *Muhammad Speaks*, the organ of the Nation of Islam, celebrated him for writing "in Negro" in *Harlem Gallery* ("One Harlem Poet" 17). And Gwendolyn Brooks understood what he was doing:

> [*Harlem Gallery*'s] roots are in the Twenties, but they extend to the present, and very strong here are the spirit and symbols of the African heritage the poet acknowledges and reverences. He is as skillful a language fancier as the ablest "Academician." But his language startles more, agitates more—because it is informed by the meanings of an inheritance both hellish and glorious. . . . I believe that it will receive the careful, painstaking attention it needs and deserves when contemporary howl and preoccupation are diminished. (51–52)

But many critics looked at Tolson's complex syntactic structures and esoteric allusions and saw a black man trying to imitate Ezra Pound or T. S. Eliot. In 1973, Ronald Lee Cansler neatly summed up the problem of Tolson's literary reception:

> A major part of the problem in getting Tolson read and accepted as a great twentieth-century poet is that he is both a modern and a black poet. . . . [W]hite readers and critics could not simply put Tolson in their curio shelves because, as Joy Flasch says . . . "The theme of almost all his poetry is his people." On the other hand, however, many black readers and critics gripped by the powerful separatist urge condemned Tolson's work as part of the white world. (115)

In perhaps the most blistering published commentary, poet Sarah Webster Fabio, a leader in the Black Arts Movement, attacked Tolson—and Karl Shapiro's assertion that Tolson wrote "in Negro" (Shapiro, introduction 12)—by saying he most assuredly did *not* speak Negro but a pale imitation of white speech. She was especially infuriated by Tolson's assertion in *Harlem Gallery* that "[t]he Negro is a dish in the white man's kitchen— / a potpourri." "[A]ny notion of Negritude which extols the virtue of being a rotten pot with flowers and petals for scent is lacking a full understanding of this concept," she sneered (54–55).

The charged political atmosphere of the mid-1960s probably made such readings inevitable. Yet the passage she derides, like much of Tolson's poetry, is a celebration of the richness of the African American experience and an explicit warning against definitions that would limit that experience. It is also playful and funny, which might not have been fully appreciated given the earnestness of the times.

> The Negro is a dish in the white man's kitchen—
> a potpourri,
> an ola-podrida,
> a mixie-maxie,
> a hotchpotch of lineal ingredients;
> with UN guests at his table,
> the host finds himself a Hamlet on the spot,
> for, in spite of his catholic pose,
> the Negro dish is a dish nobody knows:
> to some . . . tasty,
> like an exotic condiment—
> to others . . . unsavory
> and inelegant.

White Boy,
the Negro dish is a mix
like . . . and *un*like
pimento brisque, chop suey,
eggs à la Goldenrod, and eggaroni;
tongue-and-corn casserole, mulligan stew,
baked fillets of halibut, and cheese fondue;
macaroni milanaise, egg-milk shake,
mullagatawny soup, and sour-milk cake.

Just as the Chinese lack
an ideogram for "to be,"
our lexicon has no definition
for an ethnic amalgam like Black Boy and me.

(352–53)

When he wanted to, of course, Tolson's public writing could be as gritty and down-home as anybody's. He was pleased when an early critic discovered blues rhythms in his poetry. But he also believed that modern poetry was here to stay and that the use of modern forms by contemporary black writers represented a maturing of the craft. "The day of the simple Negro poet is gone forever. It is too late now for even a Negro Robert Frost" ("Foreground" 35), Tolson wrote in 1962, and he loved Robert Frost.

Poetry and Pedagogy

Though it is beyond the scope of this chapter to take up a detailed study of Tolson's poetry, his poetics can shed some light on his classroom practice. To Tolson, there was nothing definably "white" in his poetry, nor would there have been in the elegant oratory of Martin Luther King Jr. or in the precise diction or learnedness of James Leonard Farmer (Tolson Jr.). Tolson did not worry whether the master's tools could tear down the master's house; he did not believe the tools belonged to the master in the first place—or, for that matter, the house.

Certainly, black Americans of Tolson's generation would have made racial and class distinctions based on dialect. But correct English was not necessarily synonymous with white English: "There is no Jim Crow line in English," Tolson said (Melvin Beaunoris Tolson papers). Arguably, such a view may have reflected an internalization of the dominant culture's dialect. Yet black Americans long had access to and ownership of this dialect, not merely through proximity to white literate culture but through the Bible (the mastertext of nineteenth-century cultural literacy for both blacks and whites), the black press, slave narratives, broadsheets, public speeches, black churches, literary societies, and a powerful activist oratorical tradition dating back to the antebellum era. Even illiterate blacks would have been familiar with the cadences of the King James. Indeed, what some whites thought of as Black English, many blacks in Tolson's era would have seen as the language of uneducated whites. In his autobiography, *Man of Colour*, John Alexander Somerville, the first licensed black dentist in California, describes his matriculation at the University of Southern California. After a tense beginning, he eventually became close friends with many of his fellow students:

> There was one student, however, who never spoke to me for the whole three years. He was from Louisville, Kentucky. He spoke with a pro-nounced drawl. . . . They gave us all pet names. Mine was "Summertime." They called the Kentuckian "Nigger." I have heard that name applied to individuals many times, but that was the only time I ever heard it applied so appropriately. (43)

Tolson had no trouble code-switching. Though he most commonly used Standard English syntax in public forums, he modified his diction ap-propriate to his audience. His tastes and moods were catholic; in the same column or speech, he might refer to Shakespeare and "Sambo," Coleridge and "cracker." If anything, his use of a wide range of registers was an iden-tifiably African American rhetorical strategy. Though pleased to have his poetry accepted by the white literary establishment—considering it a sign not only of black achievement but of white maturity—he also insisted that caring "what the white man thinks" was one of the greatest problems the black community faced. In response to Robert Hayden's comment about himself that he was "a poet who happens to be a Negro," Tolson famously responded that he did not *happen* to be anything. "I'm a black poet, an African-American poet, a Negro poet. I'm no accident—and I don't give a tinker's damn what you think" (qtd. in Llorens 62–63). On the other hand, he saw racialism as a dead end: "Negritude is a stage in the march of man" (Melvin Beaunoris Tolson papers).

Several writers have suggested that for Tolson, class trumped race, a conclusion his son Melvin Jr. considers fair. "Race and class were inevitably linked in his mind. It was 'People of the world, unite.' He had no idea that blacks would be freed without the other." I would like to complicate that position somewhat in regard to Tolson's published writings. Certainly, for Tolson, as for many black activists of his era, the problem of race was folded into the one of class. Events such as the Great Depression, the Soviet "experiment," and the Italian invasion of Ethiopia led many to see racial discrimination as a function of capitalist exploitation. I think the difference for Tolson, when treating race, was one of audience. When discussing poetry, he frequently cited poet John Ciardi's distinction between "vertical" and "horizontal" audiences. A horizontal audience was the contemporary one, the vertical all an author's readers through time. A writer might have a wide horizontal readership, but what counted, in the long run, was the vertical one. Over time, more readers would be affected by Shakespeare than a popular but ultimately forgettable doggerelist of the day.

For seven years, 1937 through 1944, Tolson wrote a column for the *Washington Tribune*, a black newspaper, contributing as many as fifty pieces a year. Written under the demands of a full teaching and coaching load, public-speaking engagements, and labor activism, these columns were not meant for posterity but to speak to important contemporary issues. Using accessible, colloquial language, Tolson wrote extensively on racial injustice but also on intrablack issues, such as class snobbery and religious hypocrisy. He was ceaseless in his invective against "big Negroes" and "great big Negroes" and "mouth-Christians," for whom bourgeois values took precedence over social justice and racial solidarity. No one could mistake him in this forum for "speaking white." Indeed, to his predominantly black audiences, he did not need to confront the question of racial identity; it was something they shared and the departure point for his politics. His poetry was also designed to speak to African Americans but not exclusively so and not to the same ends as his journalism. On the newspaper page, on the stage, and in front of the classroom, Tolson was expected to perform as if he had the answers. In his poetry, however, especially his later poetry, he had room to ask questions. Here, his voice is more speculative than argumentative as he explores the complexities and contradictions of identity.

Tolson knew his poetry was difficult. "My poetry is of the proletariat, by the proletariat, and for the bourgeoisie," he joked (Melvin Beaunoris Tolson papers), and he knew his esoteric allusions and complex syntactic structures made some of his readers uncomfortable. But he also had faith that his work could be appreciated by the mass of readers, both black and white. He refused to patronize his readers by writing down to them, or to patronize himself by limiting his forms of expression. Nor, as his work matured, did he want to be limited to what the poet Yusef Komunyakaa has termed "service literature." His work surely reflected a desire to "define just what the essence of being black in America is about" (qtd. in Gotera 222), but it did not stop there. In Ronald Cansler's measured words, Tolson "chose to be a Negro, but he also chose to work in the poetic form and tradition most effective for him" (115). Tolson's poetry reflected his pride in both his American and African American heritage, their intersections and departures. Says Komunyakaa, "[H]e brings together the street as well as the highly literary into a single poetic context in ways where the two don't even seem to exhibit a division—it's all one and the same" (qtd. in Gotera 222).

Not everyone agrees, of course. Michael Bérubé treats Tolson's masterwork, *Harlem Gallery*, as if it were a black *Waste Land*, arguing that its two central figures, Hideho Heights and the Curator, who respectively argue for populism and high art, oral and written discourse, cannot find common ground, and that the poem is ultimately divided against itself. If only, he writes, "Tolson sought not to discredit oral narrative as a possible language for the Afro-American artist, but sought instead to author-ize *both* the Curator *and* Hideo Heights, as twin emblems of the richness, diversity, and potential subversive utility of Afro-American art" ("Avant-Gardes" 210–11). Yet that is precisely what Tolson *is* doing here—and elsewhere in his life. Everywhere, Tolson sought to integrate traditions and experiences. He titled his newspaper column "Caviar and Cabbage." He addressed his poems to "white boy" and "black boy" both. He mixed dialects with ease and pleasure in both public and private settings. In turning Tolson's complex aesthetic consciousness into a "cultural schizophrenia" ("Avant-Gardes" 194), Bérubé misses much of his humor and some of his shades of irony. As the artist John Biggers put it, Tolson was simply "humorous as hell," possessing both a profound sense of irony and a generous capacity for self-mockery. Only a man quite sure of his identity could quip that he hoped to teach his students "how to ape, instead of monkey" (Flasch, *Melvin B. Tolson* 40). Nor did Tolson share the modernist despair. On the contrary, he said, "the pessimism of the white man throws into new relief the new Demiurge in Negro life and Africa" (qtd. in Nielsen 245).

Aldon L. Nielsen argues that what critics have identified as modernist and, by implication, "white" in Tolson's poetry—the esoteric allusions, the circumlocution, the rhythmic techniques, the elevated language, the linguistic virtuosity—all have traceable roots in African and African American linguistic expression.

> Tolson's later style, far from being a mask adopted simply to gain entry to the master's house, is a means by which Anglo-American claims to the ground of modernism are set aside. (241) [H]e came to see modernist poetics as having been already arrived at by African aesthetics, thus rendering the African-American tradition primary rather than merely imitative. (246)

In light of this, Tolson's claim—"I have hidden my identity as a Negro poet in words. Thus I am more militantly a Negro" (Melvin Beaunoris Tolson papers)[17]—appears not as a paradox but as a guide to his work:

> You know, poets like to do a great amount of double talking. We think very often that the modernists gave us that concept of poetry, which is untrue. Because I can go back into the Negro work songs, the spirituals and jazz, and show you that double talk of poetry. And I can even go to Africa . . . and show you that double talk of poetry, especially in metaphors and symbols. So I'm doing some double talk here. (qtd. in Nielsen 247)

Nielsen is right to suggest that Tolson's poetry expresses a powerful African American aesthetic, though, I would add, one rooted in a distinctly *American* experience. Indeed, for Tolson, the two were inherently conflated: "A Negro [is] more American than any other American" (Melvin Beaunoris Tolson papers). And it is this sense of himself as an American, which he expressed in every public forum he participated in, that makes him an enormously complicated and valuable subject of study. Tolson turned his double consciousness into a powerful rhetorical tool, demonstrating the possibility of interrogating identity without losing one's identity, or being narrowly defined by it.

Learning from Tolson's Practice

Melvin Tolson's practices at Wiley College add to the growing body of evidence of activist, embodied rhetorical instruction in an era that has often been described as monolithically current-traditional and divorced from the world outside the academy. For Tolson, grammar, modernism, and literary criticism were ways to engage the world, not retreat from it. His work also suggests that pedagogical practices cannot be understood apart from pedagogical intentions and student desires. Although Tolson was an iconoclastic teacher, his teaching style was very much in keeping with the ethos of the black liberal arts college.

The curricula at Wiley and other private black colleges also encourage a reassessment of conclusions within rhetoric and composition about the decline of oratory. In late-nineteenth- and early-twentieth-century black colleges, oratorical training remained an essential part of both the curriculum and campus culture, even in freshman composition courses. Furthermore, the classical liberal arts tradition remained a prominent feature of instruction well into the 1930s, with required classes in Latin, Greek, and theology and a broadly based, language-centered, humanistic curriculum at odds with the more "pragmatic" models then emergent, especially the industrial-training model favored by many whites for black schools.

To the work of historiography, my research suggests the need for more cross-disciplinary communication. Although the persistence of the classical rhetorical tradition in black colleges is well noted in African American and general curricular histories, we have been slower to make note of this in rhetoric and composition. We should also look beyond the freshman English classroom for evidence of rhetorical practices. At black liberal arts colleges and other small schools, disciplinary splintering and professionalization in the early twentieth century were less pronounced than at larger schools, and thus rhetorical instruction was able to remain more integrated throughout the curriculum. Yet this integration would not have persisted without conscious desire. For Melvin Tolson and his students, his debate teams, drama clubs, and late-night discussions at his home were a natural extension of the classroom.

My research also speaks, perhaps most problematically, to the problem of how to respond as instructors in diverse, integrated classrooms in an era in which the very value of diversity and integration is being questioned. The last decade has seen movements toward sex- and race-segregated primary and secondary schools and vociferous arguments over whether boys or girls are more shortchanged in the classroom. Minority parents have resisted liberal efforts for bussing and bilingual education and are often among the most firm advocates of rigorous instruction in grammar and Standard English, despite protests from within the academy. Progressive instructors tend to resist classifying students by race and class, and yet such classification may assist colleges in outreach to and retention of underrepresented students. Certainly, the religious and racial separatism of Wiley and other black colleges contributed to black community strength and allowed the incubation of future political leaders. As a black instructor at a small, residential black college, Tolson had access to a range of rhetorical tropes and pedagogical strategies that cannot easily be duplicated—yet that are no less critical to understand.

Tolson taught in the heyday of the black liberal arts college in America. Today there is no question that many historically black colleges and universities (HBCUs) are struggling to survive. Despite the widening of educational opportunities for African American students since desegregation, HBCUs still play an important role in black education. Although their absolute enrollment figures have declined, historically black institutions still graduate black students at a significantly higher rate than predominantly white ones. In 1997, the nation's 106 HBCUs enrolled only 14.4% of black undergraduates, yet produced 27.3% of black baccalaureates. HBCUs also continue their traditional role of providing higher education for African American women, who in 1997 made up 61.1% of black HBCU students (Wilds 19, 29, 80, 86). Perhaps most importantly, HBCUs still play an important cultural role for African American students. "At Howard," says President H. Patrick Swygert, "you can be as smart as you want to be and as black as you want to be, and both your blackness and your intelligence are assumed" (qtd. in Schemo).

Black colleges also tend to share several important institutional features that contribute to student success, most notably a strong service ethic, close student-teacher relationships, and a highly personal, at times authoritarian teaching style (Roebuck and Murty). Of the three, I suspect that most contemporary English professors would be least comfortable with the latter. Tolson, who "demanded excellence, was quick to praise when students worked, and ready to lambaste when they did not" (Flasch, *Melvin B. Tolson* 38), insisted upon a rigor far beyond what we commonly demand of students today. Tough love gets little mention in the journals. One never sees a Conference on College Composition and Communication panel on students' right to *our* own language (though many of us covertly insist upon it in the safety of our classrooms). And few would be up to replicating Tolson's exacting instruction in grammar, either by temperament or training. Given his highly context-bound pedagogy, what then can we learn from his practices?

I take away from Tolson two important lessons. His ability to teach students dominant discourse norms and liberal culture and make them rightly feel it was part of their own cultural heritage, indeed, their birthright—that's a worthwhile achievement, and one that doesn't just cleave along race lines. In a recent *Oxford American* essay on teaching Emily Dickinson, William Bowers, an English instructor at Santa Fe Community College in Gainesville, Florida, writes poignantly of the difficulty of helping students, whatever their backgrounds, to make meaningful connections between their lives and the works he teaches. Says one student in what is probably not an uncommon refrain in many classrooms, "Seems like all we read in here is freaks" (46). Whatever obstacles Tolson's students had to overcome, anomie was not one of them; they were well aware what was at stake in their attending college. By engaging in public debates of the day and by encouraging his students to do so, Tolson helped demonstrate that writing and speaking matter.

Examining Tolson has also made me more comfortable with the tensions inherent in the desire to be both nurturing and rigorous in the classroom.

As teachers, we rarely hold to the absolutes we sometimes advocate for in our scholarship, and rarely do our students. Although individuals may have a particular epistemological style that is dominant at a given moment, that style contains a "mix of approaches"; indeed, cognitive research suggests that "people can simultaneously hold elements of different epistemologies" (Charney, Newman, and Palmquist 301). Depending on the topic and their investment in it, students may stake out positions ranging from absolutist to relativist to evaluativist. Likewise, as teachers we range from objectivist to expressivist to constructivist, oftentimes in the same class period. Through Tolson, I have become more sensitive not only to these variations in my own teaching style but to differences in discourse practices between my students and me.

For those of us committed to more powerful pedagogies, the successes of Tolson and his students at Wiley—and students and instructors at other black colleges in the first half of the twentieth century—suggest what can be done with limited resources. At the same time, they force us to confront the issue of our own limitations as instructors when faced with our students' widely varying backgrounds, goals, and needs. Is it possible for a white professor to participate in the traditional role of the black HBCU professor as an interpreter of the cultural experience (Roebuck and Murty 118) for her black students? And certainly such problems of identity difference are not limited to race and gender. Even when our students look like us, it is rare that they behave or think like us. We might be urban, liberal, Catholic; they might be rural, conservative, Protestant. We trained, perhaps, at a research institution in a major city; we teach at a small-town college. We value engagement over silence; they value politeness over conflict. Can these tensions be resolved? Is there hope for progressive, integrated education that is responsive to the needs of all students? I believe so. But as the example of Melvin Tolson suggests, rather than try to resolve the contradictions in our teaching, the answer may be to embrace them.

2

Balancing Tensions at a Public Women's University

The amount of knowledge the average student in the Freshman Class has of English grammar when she enters C.I.A. is pitiable. Fully thirty per cent of the students who come here from well reputed high schools cannot write a clear, forceful English sentence.—Susan Cobb, class of 1915

Our language is not permanent; it has been changing and developing ever since the beginning of a language, and it will go on changing; therefore, I say it behooves us to be progressive enough to use the latest and best on the market. . . . Everyone should strive to speak so that it would be easy to enter into a conversation in which neither of the persons would understand the other.—Marie Erhardt, class of 1914

In his 1907 commencement address at Texas Woman's University (TWU), Paul Whitfield Horn, Houston school superintendent, scolded the "ambitious woman" who "deliberately sets out to make a brilliant career for herself," arguing that instead women should be humble "paving stones" on the streets of humanity.

The bricks that form the paving must be content to lie close upon the earth. They can never form part of a lofty temple. They can never be things of beauty. They will never attract much attention, for even the men that pass over them will frequently give them only the scantest notice. All they can do is to lie still upon the silent earth—and keep human feet from stepping in the mire. (*Catalogue 1907* 77)

Horn's speech is surely indicative of the widespread resistance to women's rights in America and particularly the South at the turn of the twentieth century. Yet that he felt compelled to speak at length on the subject—his speech is over five thousand words of lofty Victorian prose—suggests that "ambitious" women were not merely confined to "New England, or to some other section" (79) as he claimed but were popping up dangerously close to home. Indeed, TWU itself was founded and sustained largely through the efforts of brilliant and ambitious Texas women who were decidedly not content to be paving stones—and who hoped their daughters would have the option of brilliant careers, if they so chose.

Founded in 1901 as a vocational public women's college through the activism of Texas women's club members, TWU eventually became the nation's largest residential college for women. The school promoted students' professional development through a curriculum that blended literary and vocational training, and it encouraged participation in public life through its close association with Texas women's organizations. By 1947, nearly ten thousand women had received bachelor's degrees, going on to be wives, mothers, homemakers, teachers, writers, health professionals, home economists, chemists, librarians, social workers, physicians, college professors, and public citizens. The history of this important site of women's education is little known, however. Indeed, the role of TWU and other women's colleges established after the Civil War as alternatives to antebellum liberal arts colleges and seminaries has received little attention from scholars in rhetoric and composition and English studies. We therefore lack a full accounting of the diversity of women's educational experiences in the era, particularly in the South, where changing expectations of women's public and professional roles created new institutional contexts for emerging national trends.

Our picture of women's rhetorical education in the late nineteenth and early twentieth centuries has also been unbalanced by our literary heritage. As Katherine H. Adams notes in her recent history of college writing courses and American women writers, *A Group of Their Own*, European figures, such as Virginia Woolf and Simone de Beauvoir, loom large in our collective consciousness as symbols of women's experiences and expression. Yet their experiences of isolation and circumscribed agency were not necessarily representative of that of their contemporaries in America: "The difference for American writers was college education" (xiv). In 1900, 36.8% of American college students were women; by 1920, women accounted for 47.3% of college students (Newcomer 46), a figure that would not again be equaled until 1976.[1] By 1929, women—often college trained—made up 25% of journalists and 40% of literary authors (K. Adams xvi). Despite a growing body of scholarship on women's rhetorical activities in the late nineteenth and early twentieth centuries, we often still think of the era, especially in the South, in terms of Woolf's fictional Judith Shakespeare, the silenced author, rather than, say, very real, vocal, and effectual public figures such as Ida Tarbell or Ruth Hale.[2]

While scholars, such as Anne Ruggles Gere, Shirley Wilson Logan, Susan Miller (*Assuming*), and Wendy B. Sharer, have recently produced a rich, complex, and contextualized understanding of women's writing and rhetorical practices outside of institutional environments, our understanding of women's college experiences is less well developed and to a large degree still reliant on a narrow range of elite, Eastern, private women's colleges. Helen Lefkowitz Horowitz's *Alma Mater,* for example, concentrates on the Seven Sister Colleges—Mount Holyoke, Vassar, Wellesley, Smith, Radcliffe, Bryn Mawr, and Barnard. Leslie Miller-Bernal's *Separate by Degree: Women Students' Experiences in Single-Sex and Coeducational Colleges* examines only private colleges; her and Susan L. Poulson's recent edited collection, *Going Coed*, meanwhile, treats women's experiences at former men's colleges. Lynn Gordon's *Gender and Higher Education in the Progressive Era* treats a broad cross segment of schools but represents the South with two private colleges, Sophie Newcomb and Agnes Scott. Amy Thompson McCandless's *The Past in the Present: Women's Higher Education in the Twentieth-Century American South* treats the region exhaustively but, like any broad, general history, cannot fully account for important institutional differences.

Much of the scholarship that does focus on college women's writing in the late nineteenth and early twentieth centuries has found it to be highly circumscribed due to lingering antebellum and Victorian ideologies that limited both the public roles and rhetorical training of women. Even in elite women's schools, administrators and faculty sometimes dismissed women's writing and discouraged women's public speaking and political participation (Conway; Gordon). The turn-of-the-twentieth-century Wellesley described by JoAnn Campbell is almost indistinguishable from antebellum Mount Holyoke. That institution, committed to separate gender spheres and a culture of domesticated angels, "failed to create a climate for expression" for its students, "not just one-way personal expression but deeply social, dialogical expression" (J. Campbell, "A Real Vexation" 768). A generation later, despite the numerous systemic changes that had taken place in women's education elsewhere, especially in normal colleges and state universities, a Wellesley woman was still expected to be "a lady first and a college girl afterwards" (Ruth Bradford, qtd. in J. Campbell, "Freshman" 117). At Radcliffe, women were subjected to an even more reductive and disciplinary version of the current-traditional rhetoric then in vogue at Harvard (J. Campbell, "Controlling Voices"; Simmons). Even in Wisconsin's Platteville Normal School, an otherwise progressive, coeducational teacher-training college, women's writing shows "little evidence of women's presence in the community" (Fitzgerald, "Platteville" 295–96).

Against such barriers, we are told, women students often found little room to maneuver. While their campus lives were characterized by "optimism and self-confidence," their writing, at least the stories they wrote for campus literary journals, belied their "subterranean fears":

> Sadness about women's limited options and occasionally self-mockery about their aspirations pervade this student fiction. Most of the stories display no literary merit but evidence college women's strong conscious-ness and accurate perceptions of the cultural and social barriers they faced on and off campus. (Gordon 9–10)

Scholars have suggested that women writers in the era were faced with dual-istic, gendered choices in their writing, which complicated the struggle for developing satisfying, effective forms of expression in any genre but espe-cially in college writing assignments. Joanne Wagner, for example, describes the tension that existed between plain (or practical) and self-expressive, belletristic styles of rhetoric in women's colleges. Even when women sought to institute more flexible rhetorics, they were stymied by the predominance of current-traditional ideology, which perpetuated gender, race, and class divisions by insisting on dominant discourse models. Jane Greer, writing on Marian Wharton's instruction at People's College in Kansas, finds a complex weaving of "alliance and antagonism, of free choice and restricted options, of accomplishment and failure"; while Wharton promoted a radical pedagogy, her "unacknowledged acceptance of existing hierarchies among competing linguistic systems disrupt[ed] her pedagogical project" (249).

Though TWU was not immune to the tensions of the era regarding women's rights and roles, its institutional goals and the education its students received set it apart from many of the schools that have been the subject of rhetorical histories. It is a public, not private, institution; his-torically, it educated students of modest, not comfortable, means. Unlike many women's colleges, TWU neither functioned as a normal school nor was it exclusively a liberal arts college. Indeed, it was founded as a practical alternative to "ornamental" antebellum liberal arts schools for women. Its curriculum was more in line with coeducational land-grant institutions; however, its students never suffered from the second-class status they might have experienced at coeducational or even coordinate[3] institutions.

Women ran all of the campus student publications, including the literary magazine, yearbook, and newspaper, and they competed on equal terms with men at other Texas colleges, both public and private, for state prizes in journalism. They participated in public-speaking activities that for many years would have been forbidden to them at the state's flagship institution, the University of Texas at Austin, and they campaigned for and held office in TWU's numerous literary, social, and political societies, gaining practice in organization, networking, and leadership. Economically, they received training in practical skills; the school promoted industrial education at a time when women were prohibited from attending the state's A&M school and when UT refused to introduce courses in home economics. The school also promoted women's culture and maintained a strong symbiotic relationship with the Texas Federation of Women's Clubs, which supported the school politically and financially. TWU's impact was also wide-reaching. The school provided not only educational opportunities for thousands of Texas women, many of whom would go on to teach in the state's public primary- and secondary-school system, it provided a focal point for women's political activism in the state—and continues to do so. The history of TWU thus presents an opportunity to more completely examine the complex, intersecting forces that affected women's education in the late nineteenth and early twentieth centuries.

TWU's curriculum was of course by no means unique. Between 1884 and 1908, eight public colleges for women were established in the South, reflecting a growing public desire to educate women for a rapidly changing social and economic order; nearly all of these began as vocational institutions and eventually came to offer a hybrid of vocational, literary, and teacher-training courses. The first quarter of the twentieth century also saw an explosion in the number of four-year Catholic colleges for women, from three in 1900 to seventy-three in 1932 (Bowler 90). While these schools promoted a gendered vision of service, they also mixed liberal arts and vocational training and "promoted careers as a source of mobility for their clientele," many of whom came from working-class backgrounds (Chamberlain 113). The rhetorical education of women at both these types of institutions deserves further study.

This chapter introduces the history and educational philosophy of TWU, set against the context of tensions in women's education in the era and the region. I examine the role of both literary and vocational training in the curriculum, the contributions of women's social networks to the life of the school, and the means by which classroom English practice reflected the school's goals. To fully gauge the impact of classroom practice, of course, it is necessary to go outside the classroom and beyond the textbooks that have commonly formed the basis for historical inquiry. Thus, I also examine the role of student-run literary societies and publications—particularly the *Daedalian* literary magazine—in students' rhetorical education. Though attempting to be as comprehensive as archival source material permits, I have also allowed the available material to shape my inquiry. While unfortunately little evidence remains of specific classroom practices in the form of syllabi, class notes, and student assignments, there is a wealth of evidence of the university's educational ideology through official publications, autobiographical material of faculty and administrators, and faculty scholarship, and of student rhetorical practices through student publications, such as the newspaper, literary journal, and yearbook. I have relied heavily on these source materials to reconstruct as best as possible the educational atmosphere of the university and especially student responses to instruction.

The goals and curriculum of TWU corresponded to the educational needs of white Texas women in the early twentieth century. Whereas for other marginalized groups, such as African Americans, a classical liberal arts education was seen as the epitome of educational attainment, for white women in Texas, gender-centered vocational education represented an important avenue of socioeconomic and political advancement. Though home economics has been criticized for reinforcing gender roles, for the supporters of TWU it was seen as progressive and even feminist; the school's vocational focus meant that the campus could never serve as a cloister, and the ever-present support of activist clubwomen gave students powerful role models for participating in the public sphere. In the English classroom, current-traditional, belletristic, and social-epistemic practices all mixed in the service of women's education, and students engaged in a wide variety of rhetorical practices, including participation in literary and debating societies, speech and drama clubs, journal writing, journalism, letter writing, and political activism. Unlike many of their peers at elite, private women's colleges in the East, students at TWU were consistently encouraged to write and speak in public forums, to take part in political discourse, and to think of themselves as rhetors.

Creating a Women's College

Women's higher education in the late-nineteenth- and early-twentieth-century American South was marked by two dominant tensions. The first was the debate over women's role in society, defined at one end by Victorian notions of gender identity, which limited women to domestic spheres, and at the other by progressive-era politics, which scholars have noted were still often based in fixed notions of gender but did expand women's roles into the public sphere and professional life. Even advocates for women's education could be quite split in their goals. Speaking before the Southern Association of Colleges for Women (SACW) annual convention in 1931, Howard Taylor, dean of Oklahoma College for Women, asserted that "the home [is] the center from which the student should make her orientation to life" (23). Speaking before the same body in 1934, George Peabody College President Bruce R. Payne argued that "these new citizens" deserved every educational, professional, and economic opportunity available to men. "Not the whims of men but the needs of our human society must dictate what woman shall study. The woman's college must not block by limited curricula the great social functioning of women, and the state must not be permitted to deny women to use for human betterment and social well-being that wider knowledge once acquired by them" (61). Overlaid on this split was the debate over the purpose of higher education itself as it became a mass phenomenon; the tensions black colleges experienced between liberal arts and vocational education extended to women's colleges as well. Amy McCandless, in examining the split between what she calls "traditionalist" and "utilitarian" institutions, finds that gender-based arguments about women's nature "both extended and circumscribed the professional horizons of educated Southern women" and "could and would be used to close as well as to open the doors of opportunity" (38).

Tensions between competing visions of women's education and public roles were apparent at TWU from the start. Like the two world wars which would follow, the Civil War altered employment patterns, especially in the South. Not only did women enter the workforce, the massive loss of life and disruption of the antebellum economy kept women in the workforce after the war. The rise of the women's rights movement during the progressive era further provided ideological justification for women entering professional life, and the advent of the women's club movement supplied the political infrastructure within Texas for achieving such goals. At the same time, deep-seated Southern and Victorian domestic traditions caused great uneasiness about what the extent of women's new social role would be. By the turn of the twentieth century, even opponents of women's education often grudgingly conceded women's mental parity; it did not necessarily follow, however, that women should be educated to take on roles previously reserved for men. To policy makers, a well-educated wife and mother was a social asset. An employed working-class wife and mother was a tacitly accepted reality. An employed middle-class wife and mother was an oddity. And a professional single woman was a threat. In establishing TWU, the

Texas state legislature acknowledged the former categories while trying to rein in the latter.

Established by an act of the legislature in 1901 after a long campaign by Texas women's club members, TWU opened its doors in Denton, a small town north of Dallas, on September 23, 1903. Originally called the Girls Industrial College,[4] it enrolled in its first year 186 young women in a college-preparatory program that would lead to a two-year vocational diploma. The 1903 catalogue spelled out TWU's goals. It was open to "all white girls[5] of good moral character . . . who have a knowledge of the common school subjects, who wish to acquire a higher education which includes a thorough practical training for life" (10). "In this institution," declared Regent Clarence Ousley, "the young ladies will be taught to be useful as well as ornamental. . . . One of the great stumbling blocks in our country is caste, and industrial education is intended to break down the barrier existing between the lady in the parlor and the maid-of-all-work" (qtd. in "Launching of College" 1). Students studied English, Latin, history, and political economy, as well as household accounts, dairying, china painting, and care of the sick. To be sure, certain Victorian ideals permeated the curriculum. An essay by Mrs. W. D. Gibbs, formerly of the domestic science department at Ohio State University, included in the school's 1904 *Fall Announcement*, demonstrates the tensions between competing views of women's education. Outlining the ideals of the "new idea" of women's education, Gibbs acknowledges that "the history of primitive woman is of an existence menial in the extreme" but cautions that the current "tendency away from home life" has also gone too far. Domestic science, she argues, is a move toward "equilibrium":

> The woman graduate [of the traditional liberal arts college] finds herself possessed of general culture . . . but with no special preparation for the position in which she most often places herself. . . . [If] Domestic Economy can train young women to more healthful, more economic, broader and more appreciative living, it certainly has its place, and a high place, among the sciences of this day. (TWU, *Fall Announcement 1904* 25–26)

TWU's first president, Cree T. Work (1903–1910), believed that "the duties of women will continue to be, as they have been in the past, largely of a domestic nature" (*Catalogue 1907* 85). At the same time, he believed professional options should be open to women, if they so desired. "Who gave the male sex the monopoly of all industry outside the home?" he asked (qtd. in Thompson 5). A supporter of practical vocational training for women, Work popularized the school's motto, "We learn to do by doing,"[6] and advocated for the school's role in serving a previously neglected population of students. Work also resisted early efforts to merge the school with the University of Texas, especially as the school did not generally support vocational training of the kind that he believed would have appealed to women students (Work, *Biographical Sketch*).

Not surprisingly, given the initially lukewarm legislative support for the institution, Work's goals were sometimes at odds with the legislature. His wife, Mary Brown Work, in a biographical sketch of her husband, recalled that before the school opened, several legislators and even a few regents "were determined to develop the school as a self-help, semi-reform school, and actually encouraged some girls to attend who were in need of reformation." But Cree Work traveled the state lecturing on his goals for the school "and a fine class of students applied for admission." Mary Work, herself a former vice-principal in the Dubois, Indiana, school system, also advocated for the new school, speaking to women's clubs and civic improvement organizations and lobbying for legislative support (McArthur). She considered herself "privileged . . . to hold up [her husband's] arms through his struggles for a more progressive education in American schools" (*Biographical Sketch*) but was also a powerful public force herself.

Student Demographics

The early TWU student body represented the rural and small-town makeup of the state. In 1910, 75.9% of Texans lived in communities of twenty-five hundred or less (United States Bureau of the Census, *Fifteenth Census* 941). Of the 192 students enrolled in the 1904–5 school year at TWU, 177 (92.2%) were from a small town or rural area, and 83 (43.2%) were the daughters of farmers or stockmen (*Catalogue 1905* 52). Table 2.1 shows student demographics for the school year 1904–5.

It is difficult to state with certainty how the families of TWU students compared financially to others in the state, but most TWU students were likely of modest means. Anecdotal descriptions from school officials suggest that many students came from small, rural communities where "cultural" advantages were few. Certainly, the predominantly middle-class small-town and city clubwomen who supported the school had in mind the farmer's daughter, cash-poor but character-rich, as an important part of the school's constituency. "The college . . . is not a fashionable school; it is not a stylish school; it makes no pretension to have been established for the aristocracy of the state," wrote Regent Eleanor Brackenridge (10), who supported a number of students through public and private scholarships, gifts, and loans (Menger 112).

Table 2.1. Student demographics for the school year 1904–5 at Texas
Woman's University

Demographic	Number of students*	%
Regional background		
City	15	7.8
Town or small city	96	50.0
Rural	81	42.2
Educational background		
High school diploma	37	19.3
Teacher or normal-school certificate	14	7.3
Entered on examination	141	73.4
Family background (daughter of)		
Farmer	73	38.0
Merchant	22	11.5
Physician	10	5.2
Skilled tradesman	10	5.2
Stockman	10	5.2
Other occupation	30	15.6
Deceased parent(s)	37	19.3

Source: Data from Texas Woman's University, *Catalogue* (1905) 52–53.
*Total student enrollment = 192

The school heavily promoted its attempts to keep costs low to cautious
parents. "The test of a student's standing . . . is not the amount of money
she has, nor the amount she spends. The spirit of the student body is for
simplicity and economy" (*Catalogue 1908* 83). Students could do their
wash free in the college's laundry classroom, and the school offered a
limited number of part-time work opportunities. In 1907, the estimated
average total yearly costs, based on the expenses of twenty-five representative students, were $220.95 for fees (the college charged no tuition in its
early years), room and board, textbooks, clothing, and incidentals, such
as entertainment, transportation, and laundry expenses (*Catalogue 1908*
83). This was less than half the price of a private, Eastern women's college,
such as Vassar, where tuition and residence costs alone were $500 in 1905
and $800 in 1920 (Daniels), with extras "depend[ing] on . . . upbringing,"
or Smith, where officials estimated total yearly costs, including "books,
clothing, traveling expenses and incidentals" at $750 in 1916 ("Is the Higher
Education" 10). However, even TWU's modest fees would have likely proved
a burden to many families; in 1908 the average American worker's income

was only $564 (Derks 92) and a white schoolteacher in Texas averaged just $394.23 (*Texas Almanac 1912* 130). What is certain is that the overwhelming majority of TWU students were first-generation college students and that for many, TWU represented their only opportunity for higher education. Even for families of more comfortable means, TWU offered their daughters economic mobility. At the time of the school's founding, Texas A&M, the state industrial school for men, did not admit women, and the University of Texas, the state flagship school, did not offer courses in household economics or other subjects of interest to many women.

Development of the Curriculum

Over time, TWU's focus shifted toward a liberal arts curriculum, though the school's vocational roots remained strong. During the school's first year, all students were enrolled in preparatory classes and three-fourths of them in industrial or technical tracks. Said Dean Edmund Valentine White, "[T]he newly created college was a college without college students, and the curriculum was loaded down with non-traditional subject matter. It was a new idea in Texas education" (*Historical Record* 12). By 1908, its first students had gone through both the preparatory and two-year college course, and that year it added a third year of college work. Upon Work's death in 1910, the presidency was assumed by William B. Bizzell, who worked to raise the profile of the school, tightening admissions requirements, hiring faculty with advanced degrees, and lobbying the legislature for increased funding. During his brief administration (1910–14), the school began granting teacher's certificates and had a fourth year of college work approved by the legislature. The introduction of teacher certification would provide the university with a major point of focus, as students in all disciplines sought teacher training. By 1927, 84.9% of students enrolled in the College of Arts and Sciences were taking courses in philosophy and education, and as late as 1937, 66.3% of students were (Vaughn 20). From 1906 to 1938, 8,348 students received teaching certificates. Complete records of student employment do not exist, but of those students registered with the placement office between 1926 and 1938, 58.4% were placed. The actual percentages were likely much higher, "as many positions [were] obtained without the assistance of the Placement Bureau" (Vaughn 35–49).

In 1914–15, two administrators who would have lasting effects on the direction of the institution came to the college. President Francis Marion Bralley, a long-serving administrator in the Texas school system and later director of the Department of Extension at UT, was a strong advocate for the school. "As long as I have anything to do with it, the College of Industrial

Arts will never be the tail of the educational kite of any other educational organization in Texas," he frequently declared. Under his administration, the school revamped its curriculum, strengthening the "literary" course in particular and moving toward becoming a comprehensive liberal arts institution (E. White, *Historical Record* 14–15). The school granted its first three bachelor's degrees and was recognized by the State Department of Education as a college "of the first class" in 1915; had its work approved by the University of Texas in 1918; and was accepted into the Southern Association of Colleges and Secondary Schools in 1923 (E. White, *Historical Record* 15–16). Many of the curricular changes under Bralley's administration (1914–24) were directed by Dean Edmund White, a former administrator with the state Department of Education and UT. White, who served for over thirty years, was actively involved in the academic life of the institution, writing and editing the catalogue, college histories, and bulletins and organizing accreditation drives. White was by no means an educational or political progressive and by his own admission had no qualifications as a man to advise female students on any aspect of their lives beyond purely academic affairs. But he was impressed and to some degree transformed by what he saw as the courage and determination of his students, and he proudly wrote of their achievements in both school literature and his autobiography.

By the time of President Louis H. Hubbard's appointment in 1926, the school had been granting baccalaureate degrees for a decade. Hubbard personally believed "that the average woman would prefer, even when she is preparing herself for a career, to marry a man able to support her, and to give her time entirely to her home and to her children" ("What Young Women Think" 35). Yet he gave full support to career-minded women. He took a broad view of TWU's mission, expanding vocational education while increasing support for the liberal arts.

> [T]he college had been planned chiefly to furnish vocational training to rural and small-town girls, many of whom had had no opportunity to acquire even a high school education. . . . I knew that such young women had been deprived . . . of an opportunity to develop their intellectual capacities, and that they were starving for the cultural advantages which would likely have been available to them had they had the advantages of urban living and more adequate financing. So I dreamed of a college which would envelop its students with these intellectual and cultural advantages and would lead them on to a higher measure of spiritual strength. . . . My ideal for every student who enrolled in our college was for her to become a completely integrated personality. (*Recollections* 173–74)

A former high school English teacher and self-described "progressive" composition instructor, Hubbard emphasized English education at TWU. "[I]f pupils are given the impression that their use of English is important only in English classes," he wrote in his autobiography, "they have two strikes against them in their efforts to improve" (*Recollections* 96). His own pedagogical techniques were complex, combining grammatical rigor and progressive intentions. He encouraged civic participation and voting and urged his students "to read newspapers and magazines and to keep abreast of the times" (*Recollections* 80). He required his students to memorize poems and, to help them learn poetic structures, had them write out their own verses.

> In my grading of these papers I was strict. I hammered away at sentence structure, faulty grammar, and spelling. I required each student to keep a notebook of his misspelled words and later to bring the list to me and demonstrate that he had learned to spell the words correctly.... But I kept firmly in mind that I must not stifle originality or cramp the student's willingness to express himself freely. (*Recollections* 94)

Hubbard wanted to develop TWU into a liberal arts school "of the first-class," but he also kept in mind the school's vocational roots. In his dissertation, "The Place of Vocational Training as an Objective of the Woman's College" (completed at UT in 1929), Hubbard strove to find a workable balance between professional and cultural training, legitimizing the former without condemning the latter. He noted that while the Harvard-influenced Vassar "clung through the intervening years to her cultural, non-vocational masculine objectives" (169), friends of the women's movement sought to broaden women's education for the needs of a new era: "None of these thinkers has been unfriendly to the cultural point of view. . . . But at the same time they have sincerely believed that the subject matter of vocational courses could be so organized as to develop both culture and vocational preparation. They have believed, with John Dewey, that vocational courses, rightly organized, have cultural values" (171).

Hubbard was by many accounts a master administrator, increasing funding for the school even through the Depression, improving the physical plant and overseeing the construction of many new buildings, expanding the school's cultural programs and participation in community affairs, and taking an active role in faculty recruitment, even visiting prospective hires to save them the expense of a visit. He was active in the Southern Association of Colleges for Women, serving as president in 1932, and he remained a lifelong advocate for women's separatist education, believing that it not only provided women with education appropriate to their needs and interests but allowed women leadership opportunities hogged by men on coeducational campuses. By the time of his retirement in 1950, TWU was a large, comprehensive university.

Women's Social Networks and TWU

In 1903, at the opening ceremonies of the college, Regent Clarence Ousley paid tribute to the political skill of the women of Texas: "The honor of the founding of this institution belongs to the ladies of Texas for they were the power behind the throne that caused us men to act. We are simply agents in their hands" (qtd. in "Launching of College" 1). Despite the paternalistic overtones of Ousley's statement, by the time of the founding of the school, Texas women were not merely powers behind the throne but active political players in their own right. That what began as a hesitant experiment by the state of Texas would soon become an important center of women's education is a testimony to the activism of Texas clubwomen. Indeed, the history of TWU cannot be understood apart from the women's clubs that help found and sustain it. Clubwomen not only helped assure the school's survival but by providing models for activism helped promote student engagement in public life. Their combining of conservative and progressive politics also is a reminder of the importance of taking into account local historical contexts in evaluating institutional histories.

Although there had been little tradition of organized women's activism in the antebellum South, women in the 1880s in Texas had begun taking part in what Megan Seaholm has termed the "national contagion" of the women's club movement ("Earnest Women" 2). In the wake of social up-heavals following the Civil War, American women began forming social and civic organizations for a number of purposes: the Young Women's Christian Association in 1866; the American Equal Rights Association in 1866 (which split into the National Woman Suffrage Association and the American Woman Suffrage Association in 1869); the Association for the Advancement of Women in 1873; the Women's Christian Temperance Union in 1874; the National Council of Women in 1888; and the General Federation of Women's Clubs (GFWC) in 1890. By 1905 the GFWC had a half-million members (Seaholm, "Earnest Women" 2).

Hundreds of women's clubs flourished across Texas in the early years of the twentieth century. By 1903, the Texas Federation of Women's Clubs[7] (TFWC) included 232 clubs with 5,000 members (Gammage 18); at the peak of its membership in 1941, the federation had 1,200 clubs and 60,000 members (Seaholm, "Texas Federation"). Many of these clubs were initially formed for the purposes of self-improvement and literary study, but, inspired by social and political challenges at home and the activism of women's clubs elsewhere, they soon took a more activist turn, becoming a powerful social force for change. Through promoting the study and discussion of current events, literature, and art, these clubs served as de facto colleges for "middle-aged middle-class women," allowing them "to discern that their reality often disagreed with the social myths of their time" (Gammage 17–19). Before suffrage, women's clubs in Texas were a significant political force, organizing successful campaigns to establish elementary education, improve teacher pay, increase the age of consent, establish public health laws, and secure women's property rights.

The founding of TWU was the result of a decade-long struggle by women to establish a public women's college in Texas. In 1889, the Texas State Grange first proposed the founding of a public college for women similar in purpose to Texas A&M, which at that time did not accept women.[8] A bill was introduced into the legislature in 1891 but did not pass (Holt; Thompson). The idea then attracted the attention of a number of women's organizations, including the Texas Women's Christian Temperance Union, the Texas Woman's Press Association, and the Texas Federation of Women's Clubs, which began a campaign for the establishment of a school through newspaper articles, public addresses, letters and petitions to the state legislature, and personal meetings with legislators (Toler 60). Helen M. Stoddard, president of the Texas WCTU, redrafted the bill to include a focus on household economics and persuaded Judge Vincent W. Grubbs to introduce it in 1899. Stoddard's revision, modeled on that establishing Mississippi's State College for Women, specified the curriculum to include: "Scientific and practical cooking including a chemical study of foods; also a knowledge of practical housekeeping; also a knowledge of trained nursing and caring for the sick; also a knowledge of the care and culture of children" (Stoddard 187). The bill failed again but was passed in 1901 by tie-breaking votes by the leaders of both the house and the senate. Once the school was founded, women's groups regularly passed resolutions supporting the school and in nearly every legislative session petitioned the legislature to increase funding and support for the college; likewise, the administration commonly called on the TFWC for support when extra political pressure was needed to obtain funding or curricular improvement (McArthur; Toler; Thompson).

Three influential women were appointed to TWU's initial board of regents: Helen Stoddard; Eleanor Brackenridge, president of the Woman's Club of San Antonio and later a prominent suffrage leader in the state; and Eliza Sophia Johnson (wife of State Senator Cone Johnson), who was active in many clubs and would later serve as president of the TFWC from 1905 to 1907. Each used her political leverage to lobby for the school. In 1907, when the legislature turned down the school's request for $6,000 to build an infirmary on campus while appropriating the same amount for a horse hospital at Texas A&M, Stoddard met with the appropriations committee and threatened to have the story reported in every paper in the state. They quickly reassessed their decision (Bellamy 30). That same year, when the legislature failed to come through on a promise to fund a dormitory, President Work gently reminded readers of the *College Bulletin* of the school's continued need. Brackenridge, meanwhile, under no pressure to appease the legislature, took her campaign to the readers of the *Fort Worth Record and Register*. In a forceful editorial, she wrote:

> The value of this school to the homes of the future, the value of this education in the advancement and status of women, no tongue can tell. . . . A wing in the Insane Asylum is favorably mentioned [in the Democratic platform]. Will the state do more for her hopeless past than for her hopeful future? . . . Women nowhere meet with tax exemptions, and surely women are entitled to tax representation, and we have the right to ask that the womanhood of the state should share the benefits. (10)

The legislature ended up appropriating $60,000 to fund the building of Stoddard Hall (Thompson 16).

Throughout its early history, TWU maintained a close, symbiotic relationship with the TFWC: "They were two arms of the same body," says TWU archivist Ann Barton. The school's bulletins often included speeches by women's club members, club officers throughout the state commonly received the school's bulletins (McArthur 38), and in 1928 the college hosted the federation's annual convention (Toler 65). Club members took a strong, proprietary interest in the progress of the school and could be counted on to support it in times of crisis. TWU students, in turn, joined women's organizations and remained active in them their entire lives. A 1941 survey of 288 graduates from 1904 to 1921 found that 67% percent currently held local office and 15% state office in a club, church group, or professional organization (Cornell 51). The 288 graduates held 172 memberships in "study groups," such as a Federated Woman's Club or the American Association of University Women, and 148 memberships in professional organizations, such as the Texas State Teachers Association or the Texas Home Economics Association (Cornell 26–30). Given that at the time, less than half of these women surveyed were working, these numbers suggest many women kept their professional memberships active even after leaving their careers to become homemakers.

TWU women and Texas clubwomen often worked together for joint causes. In 1906 and 1907, the WCTU and the TFWC successfully lobbied together for a pure food bill, under the direction of Mary Brown Work, head of the TFWC Committee on Home Economics and wife of the TWU president. Though they were unable to secure TWU as the home of the new office, they prevented it from being placed under the supervision of either the state health office or—more importantly—the male-only Texas A&M. Instead, they secured an independent commissioner friendly to women's activism, who trained and deputized clubwomen as volunteer inspectors (McArthur 42–45). The passage of the Smith-Lever Act by Congress in 1914, which provided funding for agricultural science, also set off a gender-based power struggle. In Texas, only 24% of the state's Smith-Lever funds were given over to domestic science. Texas clubwomen sought to guarantee that at least 50% be allotted and that TWU be granted authority to participate in the administration of funds. Women failed in securing their demands in this case, but Clarence Ousley, who directed the state's agricultural extension service and was hostile to any changes in the fund's administration, adroitly acknowledged their motivation: "sex consciousness" (McArthur 49–51).

Progressive Politics and Southern Identity

The South has often been portrayed as isolated from progressive political changes that occurred elsewhere in the country. Yet the sometimes-fierce resistance to progressive ideas and policies suggests the movement's influence in the South. Indeed, many Southern women supported a number of progressive ideals. A 1934 poll of Georgia State College for Women students found that 19.8% of them agreed that the United States should "change gradually toward socialism" and that 83.7% supported "a single standard of morality for men and women" (G. Wells 32–33). Informally polling his own students at TWU, President Hubbard found that they were "practically one hundred percent in favor" of equal pay for equal work. "They believe it is unfair to pay women correspondingly smaller salaries, and that, in the long run, the result is not beneficial to men because where there is a difference in the compensation paid to men and women the salary scale tends to be lowered to the level of that paid to women, as in the case of the compensation of elementary schoolteachers" ("What Young Women Think" 34).

Through their participation in women's clubs, Texas women were well aware of the activities and activism of women in other parts of the country. In Denton, the daily newspaper, the *Denton Record-Chronicle*, regularly reported on local, state, and national club meetings. If men were not paying attention to these clubs, women were. In 1928, Fort Worth hosted a regional meeting of the American Association of University Women (AAUW). The evening before the conference, Lois Mathews Rosenberry, former dean of women at the University of Wisconsin and past president of the Association of Collegiate Alumnae, a forebear to the AAUW,[9] spoke at a banquet given by the Denton chapter of the AAUW at the university, attended by about forty-five members. She "told of the connection of the American Association of University Women with all important progressive movements of cities in which there are chapters, gave the scope of its work, which is not limited to college activities, and mentioned its pre-school age educational efforts as important" ("Two Officials" 6). In her introductory remarks to the speech, Edna Ingels Fritz, TWU home economics professor, stressed the importance of women's clubs to women's sense of well-being, identity, and solidarity.

> Were it not for such organizations as the A.A.U.W.—which enables college women not only to meet together in the interests of education but to have the inspiration of being together and mingling with interesting people, some of us would probably slip into the ruts of local interests and self satisfaction. This is especially true of college women who marry and settle down and become absorbed in their homes. (Fritz Collection)

Yet white Southern women—and especially Texas women—brought to women's causes their own interpretation of women's rights and roles. Texas Woman's University was in no way a hotbed of radicalism. As a public university, it had to accommodate public opinion and legislative whims. Texas women, even when organizing for women's rights and social reform, were reluctant to be associated with what was often seen as Northern extremism and could be ambivalent about suffrage. Advocates for TWU, especially in its earliest years, emphasized the school's benefits to women and society within politically acceptable margins while seeking to extend those margins. Training women for work and the "responsibilities of citizenship," argued Mary Work in 1909, "does not necessarily mean that the school makes suffragettes of its pupils, but the course in social economics is such as to create enthusiasm and willingness on the part of the girls to enter reform work in their home communities upon leaving school" ("Home Economics" 12).

Nancy F. Cott has made a distinction between "female consciousness" and "feminist consciousness." The former is based in an awareness of gender difference and can be either conservative or radical, while the latter radically challenges male hegemony. While Cott was rightly trying to correct the tendency to broadly label women's political activities as feminist, no matter what their nature, her distinction does not quite do justice to the complexities of women's activism in the late nineteenth and early twentieth centuries. Scholars have particularly underestimated the importance of state and regional identity in resistance to progressive and feminist political movements in the South. Texans, then as now, are Texans first, and the taint of what was seen as Northern agitation in progressive causes no doubt turned many women off; neither did Texas women necessarily want to give up Southern notions of womanhood, which they felt some strains of women's activism demanded. Instead, Texas clubwomen mixed conservative and progressive social, religious, and political ideals. The same club leaders who were active in promoting women's rights and TWU also belonged to conservative organizations such as the Daughters of the American Revolution and the United Daughters of the Confederacy. Their activities might be termed as "womanist consciousness" (E. B. Brown) or "maternalist politics" (McArthur 3), but it is important to recognize that they saw their activities as feminist—even if they did not always use the term—and as part of a complex web of female, Southern, white, and Texan identity.

Of course, certain tensions in the women's movement in Texas exposed white women's ambivalence toward racial equality and universal sisterhood. Many white Texas women refused to support suffrage, fearing that it would be seen as supporting the enfranchisement of black women and thereby damage their other platforms. And in the prevailing conservative political climate, Texas women's rights activists who saw themselves as radicals were careful not to publicly construct themselves as such. When suffrage was won, wrote Minnie Fisher Cunningham in a letter to a friend, she was going to wear a red dress to a political meeting and "appear in my true colors as the village vamp" (qtd. in Gammage 46). And of course, supporting TWU gave many women a political focus they might have lacked before. As Judith N. McArthur notes, "In defending and promoting the college, many otherwise conservative clubwomen found themselves for the first time agitating a woman's cause. They were keenly aware 'their' college was the poor stepsister of the large and prosperous Agricultural and Mechanical College, and the competition for influence soon exposed underlying gender conflicts" (38). Yet Texas women had their own vision of how TWU should develop; it was a vision inspired by egalitarianism but rooted in a recognition of gender difference and Texas women's distinct educational needs.

Home Economics and Vocational Training

Liberal arts and vocational training are often discussed as if they were mutually exclusive or existed at opposite ends of an educational spectrum. The story of TWU in its first half century, however, is one in which liberal arts and vocational training exist in powerful symbiosis. Both were supported institutionally, and both were valued by students and played important roles in their education and personal development. At the same time, the legacy of antebellum educational and cultural patterns complicated white Southern women's relationship to their college curricula, especially the liberal arts stream.

The antebellum ideal for a Southern lady limited her education to a narrow range of cultural pursuits without practical application outside the home. College was reserved for the wealthy, and graduates were not expected to work. As Christine Anne Farnham notes, "Even to teach was seen as an embarrassment to the family," because it suggested a woman's husband or father could not support her (32). The façade of "true" Southern womanhood began to crack, however, during the social and economic upheaval following the Civil War. Even during the antebellum era, few women had the privilege of domestic indolence; after the Civil War, it was no longer a sustainable model, even as a fiction. The problem this posed for education was well described in 1947 by Dean Hilda Threlkeld of the University of Louisville:

> The objective [of the traditional Southern woman's college] was clear: to train ladies to grace lovely tall-pillared homes, perfumed by the fragrance of magnolias and operated by a retinue of loyal dusky servants. If, by chance, adverse fate through the death of the husband or the loss of the estate brought the Southern lady into financial distress, she retired to the sheltering home of the nearest male kinsman. Frail vessel of charm and spirituality, she should never be sullied by activities in the market place, nor turn her thoughts to the complexities of the political realm. Such a lady was Melanie in "Gone with the Wind," while Scarlet, the aggressor, the realist, was widely disclaimed as no true Southern woman. (35)

For white Southern women, especially of middle-class and working-class backgrounds, liberal arts and "cultural" education often called to mind these antiquated seminary-style academies and finishing schools, whose "chief purpose," said John A. Anderson, Kansas State Agricultural College president, in 1874, "seem[ed] to be that of furnishing intelligent playthings for men possessing exhaustless wealth" (*Catalogue 1874* 31). Addressing the 1905 TWU graduating class, Mary Wilson critiqued "the fashionable girls' school of the past," whose graduates, "with the equipment of a mediocre musician, a little knowledge of polite literature, a small degree of skill in embroidery, and a vague memory of dates, maps and foreign languages, would hardly win social success today, to say nothing of the school or business office" (*Catalogue 1905* 57). Women's clubs, energized into widespread national political action in the 1880s and 1890s, were also eager to shed the mantle of ornamentation. At the 1904 GFWC national convention, President Sarah Platt Decker declared: "Dante is dead. Drop his Inferno, and proceed to contemplate your own social order" (qtd. in Shepard 35).

Despite antebellum and Victorian notions of female delicacy, the South was largely a rural and poor region, and even white Southern women commonly worked, if not outside, then inside the home; it was expected that TWU graduates, few of whom came from privileged backgrounds, would do the same. Unlike women at Wellesley, theirs was not "an economic world where women's education was as inessential as dusting china ornaments," nor did they settle "soundly in a realm of uncontested femaleness" or return "to a life of social teas and visitations" after graduation (J. Campbell, "Freshman" 121–22). On the contrary, TWU women went to school to improve their socioeconomic standing and to learn practical skills. A 1941 survey of 2,775 TWU graduates from 1915 to 1939 found that 60.1% (1,669) were employed[10] (and 97.1% of these full time) and that 97.8% had worked at some point following their graduation. Of single women, who made up 42.9% of the graduates, 94.1% (1121 of 1191) were working; it was an indicator of changing attitudes toward women's employment that the survey's author, Catherine Bentinck, felt compelled to offer a lengthy explanation for those few single graduates who *weren't* employed: Half were students, some were caring for relatives, traveling, or ill, and "one said that she was financially independent" (38–40). Significantly, even among those graduates who did marry, at least 37.5% (548 of 1461) still worked, and many more women retained active membership in professional organizations long after they had "retired" to the concerns of domestic life. For Bentinck, these figures demonstrated not only that the school had a "serious obligation" to continue preparing women for vocations but that "the chances for a TSCW alumna to become a wage-earner and a participator in the economic life of her community are exceedingly good" (39).

Vocational training today has negative overtones, and home economics, steeped as it is in tropes of domesticity and historical limitations on women's public roles, even more so. But for Texas women in the early twentieth century, the stakes of being "efficient housewives and educated mothers" were high (J. Campbell, "Freshman" 121). As Judith McArthur reminds us,

> The "care and culture of children" . . . had special significance at a time when 18 percent died before age five, two-thirds of them before their first birthday. . . . Every mother was essentially her own pediatrician . . . and the mortality rate of physicians' children was only a few percentage points

below the national average. . . . For [activists such as Isadore] Callaway[11] and [Helen M.] Stoddard . . . household economics was an integral part of their feminist protest against women's subordinate status. (36)

Through the first half of the twentieth century, home economics, or domestic science as it was sometimes called, was treated by its practitioners as a *science*—a thoroughly modern subject dependent on advances and advanced training in chemistry, biology, and technology and with the potential to influence human society outside the home.

In hindsight, of course, it is easy to see the early-twentieth-century mania for science and industry as expressed through the home economics movement as complicit in the destruction of local foodstuffs, food traditions, and folkways, and the home economics movement itself as perpetuating women's subordinate social status. But at the time, its ideals were highly valued. For many rural and Southern Americans, the Depression was not a disruption but a continuation of the status quo. Being able to feed and clothe a family on a limited budget was a valuable skill, and one in which contemporary women often took great pride. As late as 1946, Margaret M. Justin could write in the *Journal of Home Economics*, "College courses bearing on woman's responsibility were, and still are, viewed with approbation by parents, students, and the citizenry at large" (198).

At TWU, home economics was given a prominent place in the curriculum from the start. Speaking before the district convention of the Texas Federation of Women's Clubs in 1905, Mary Louise Tuttle, director of domestic science at TWU, outlined her vision of a home economics program as a means of raising women's dignity, both by giving them access to the best scientific and economic practices of the day and by elevating the social status of work in the home. Referring to professional women, she said, "It is often well but not necessary for woman to step outside of her own field of honor and success" (*Catalogue 1905* 63). In the dairy-work sequence, Tuttle, who held a diploma in domestic science from Columbia University's Teachers College, sought to give students "a scientific practical knowledge of different lines of dairy work." This included "dairy bacteriology; the composition and food value of milk, butter and cheese . . . creamery management . . . butter and cheese making . . . handling of milk for butter making and for market . . . [and] the pasteurization and sterilization of milk" (*Catalogue 1903* 21). Included in Edna Ingels Fritz's 1921–22 Clothing 312 class was an extended discussion of children's clothing "from a hygienic standpoint." Clothing, she said, should address not only durability, comfort, season, and the age and growth rate of the child but also their "psychology—temperament, disposition and activity." This material later turned up on the final exam: "What different conditions must clothing meet to be considered hygienic? Are woolen materials suitable for infants' garments? Do you think that a problem in children's clothing should be included in a high school course in sewing?" (Fritz Collection).

Such courses responded to the needs of women students at TWU and other colleges. In a 1933 survey of women graduates of Southern colleges, Doak Sheridan Campbell (later president of Florida State College for Women) asked 803 married participants which subject they wished they had studied more of in school. The largest group, 35.6%, chose home economics, followed by English with 18.3%, and commercial subjects with 12.7% (D. Campbell 15). When, after a long struggle, home economics courses were finally established at UT in 1912, so many students signed up that the building had to be enlarged and two additional instructors hired (McArthur 39).[12] To these students, the value of such education was clear. A March 1912 editorial in the *Daedalian* declared, "A woman with a knowledge of physics does not have to send for a plumber or an electrician every time one of the many conveniences for the household afforded us as the result of scientific effort, gets 'out of fix'" (18).

To the writer of this editorial and many other women, science and service went hand-in-hand, linking women's traditional home sphere with the wider world. "This is an age of science. The men in the activities in which they are engaged, reckon with science. 'Scientific methods' is the cry of the business man. Should the home lag behind in this scientific movement? No, it should lead. Nothing is too good for the home" (19). If the women of TWU accepted home as their sphere, they also redefined it, expanding on the activities they might have traditionally been expected to perform there. "Another species of the overworked woman is she who is a slave to the appetites of her men folks, and usually these appetites exist only in her imagination. . . . In this age of dyspepsia the woman who knows how to make more than three kinds of cake knows too much, anyway, and ought to be suppressed," wrote Isadore Callaway, a *Dallas Morning News* columnist and home economics proponent (15). Instead of simply copying their mothers' recipes, TWU students studied chemistry and bacteriology to prevent deaths due "to the consumption of milk which has been improperly cared for" (Texas Woman's University, *Daedalian* March 1912 18). This service component was especially important to TWU women. The college named its home demonstration school after Ellen Swallow Richards, the first woman to graduate from MIT and a pioneer in food science and sanitary engineering. Among its activities, it operated a home-demonstration railroad car to bring advances in food safety and medical care to rural communities, offered a series of extension courses, and published numerous bulletins on food sanitation and safety. Perhaps the most significant impact of home economics and vocational education on women's lives is that as a career choice, it offered women economic possibilities unlikely in other professions. TWU graduates who worked as home demonstration agents made on average *twice* that of teachers—$2,486 a year versus $1,266 in 1939. Indeed, teachers made less than the median income for all professions practiced by TWU graduates, leading Catherine Bentinck to observe that while "it is quite apparent that teaching is the most popular vocation . . . it [is] equally obvious that teaching is not the most profitable of all vocations" (93–94).

Teaching, of course, was the primary career choice in the first half of the twentieth century for college-educated women, no matter where they attended school. While graduates of elite women's colleges in the East had a wider opportunity to pursue white-collar careers, in Texas and the South the professions were slower to open up to women, and lagging economic development meant that there were fewer opportunities in these fields even for men. While a few graduates of Vassar or Mount Holyoke might have gone on to careers in home economics, for TWU graduates it was the third most popular career choice (Bentinck 63), suggesting that the school was responding effectively to local women's needs. TWU's vocational emphasis had a profound effect on its students, promoting confidence as well as economic independence. "We were taught that neither was there any position we could not hold nor was there any job we could not do if given the opportunity," recalls Jackie Matthews Greer, '29. "My accounting courses were taught so as to provide 'road maps' not only for the time we were in college but the years ahead. We were prepared to be productive professional people." Applying for a job at Shell as an office supervisor following her graduation, Greer was offered a position "as soon as the college of my education became known," making a salary of $110 with the promise of a $25 raise in ninety days, at a time when the average entry-level salary was $75 (30).

Out in the heartland, such sentiments retained their force for a long time, and the association of domestic skills with self-reliance persisted well after the decline of the home economics movement. In 1979, the legendary costume designer Edith Head presented a retrospective at TWU of her work.[13] The *Denton Record-Chronicle* reported her comments.

> "I believe there's a way of dressing for your way of life. . . . The woman who's able to sew has the advantage of choosing color, fabric, and being able to make things over." She added that, if she were to pass a law,

everyone, "even men," would learn to sew. "People sew because they're shocked at the price of ready-to-wear, and some [clothes] are so badly made." (Clark 1C–2C)

The same edition of the *Denton Record-Chronicle* includes a lengthy article praising home sewing as smart consumerism, quoting faculty from TWU's College of Nutrition, Textiles, and Human Development. Especially in a time of inflation and "threatened recession," the ability to save "at least half the cost of a ready-made garment" was treated as a patriotic skill (Vanwinkle 2C).

I do not want to suggest that TWU students did not feel tensions between what they were learning in college and their likely lives outside of school, especially in the institution's earliest days. The first women at the school received decidedly mixed messages as to where they would practice their newly learned skills. Through the mid-1910s, students often commented on the pressure to choose between homemaking and a vocation. "To be (a cooking teacher) or not to be, That is the question," pondered household arts major Bessie Meyers in her yearbook epigraph in 1911 (Texas Woman's University, *Yearbook 1911* 39). Two years later, Edna Duncan asked a similar question: "After the mastery of the Lit. Course, shall I conclude by being a future wife and mother of Texas?" (Texas Woman's University, *Yearbook 1913* 57). As it turned out, Duncan did forgo a career to be a wife and mother, becoming among the first two members of her class to marry, but she was something of an exception; of the forty-eight members of her graduating class, she was the only student who did not take a Texas State Teacher's Certificate (Texas Woman's University, *Catalogue 1914* 145–46).

Rhetorical Instruction

Reading, writing, and speaking instruction played important roles in Southern women's education throughout the late nineteenth and early twentieth centuries, a testament to the persistence of the antebellum liberal arts tradition. Through the 1920s, English was the most popular major and elective of women in B.A. programs. While rhetoric was not often prescribed as a subject, elocution was widely taught, first as a separate subject and later as part of the English curriculum (McCandless 57–58). TWU reflected this tradition as it developed its own curriculum. At the same time, its emphasis on training women for public and professional roles helped ensure that English training was tied to life outside the classroom. Students at TWU in the first half of the twentieth century could expect to participate in a rich textual environment that incorporated both "practical" and "literary" ends.

Of course, rhetorical instruction did not take place only in the English department. The history of the departments of English, elocution, and reading at TWU shows a complex interaction among a number of forces and points out the limited effectiveness of sweeping statements about trends in rhetorical instruction. It further suggests that pedagogical practices cannot always be separated into discrete epistemological or ideological categories, even within the same institution or classroom. I am especially wary of the tendency to look with aversion upon current-traditional practices or other instruction that supposedly reproduces cultural hierarchies; as my examination of TWU shows, instructors often combined elements of varying pedagogical approaches in their practices.

The bill that established TWU stipulated that, in addition to vocational training, the school also provide a "literary" education. As the 1920 TWU *Catalogue* stated, "They did not want the college to become a second-rate trade school on the one hand, or an old-line, classical university on the other hand" (23). English education thus played a prominent role from the start at TWU, "[d]espite the fact that the practical arts predominated the curriculum in the early days" (E. White, *Historical Record* 43). In the school's first years, it offered four sequences of study: domestic arts, fine and industrial arts, commercial arts, and English-science, with composition and rhetoric and literature required of all students.

> It will be noted that in all of the courses literary work has a prominent place. Industrial training is most valuable, but, taken by itself, it is not sufficient. Both for the purpose of training and that of giving information, literary work is indispensable in a thorough education. In the courses as arranged an effort has been made to furnish the two lines of work—industrial and literary—in proper proportions for the best, all-round, practical training for life's work. (Texas Women's University *Catalogue 1904* 15)

The school's goal, as stated in the 1913–14 board of regents' report, was "to send out well-rounded young women. And it will never send them out until it sends out a girl who can write as well as she can cook, who can interpret great minds as well as she can sew, and who can talk and assimilate the ideals of others as well as she can furnish a house" (Texas Women's University, *Sixth Biennial Report* 11). From 1914 to 1919, English was the only liberal arts major, and through World War II, two years of English were required of all students, whether in vocational or liberal arts tracks. Throughout this period, English was consistently one of the most popular major on campus

(E. White, *Historical Record* 43–44). As with other parts of the curriculum, the work of the English department at TWU was commonly linked with both school and community life. In 1922, the English department published *Programs and Suggestions for Study for Women's Clubs* as part of the college bulletin. In 1939, the department began an annual writers' conference, which is ongoing. In 1949, under the direction of Autrey Nell Wiley, the department began a series of summer workshops for secondary-school and college English instructors on current trends in English (Palmer and Martin).

Rhetoric and Composition in the Early Curriculum

As might be expected, in the first decade of the school, grammar and composition courses dominated the English catalogue, most likely due to its founding as a vocational institution and the predominance of college preparatory students in its first years. Yet instruction in grammar was not meant to screen out working-class students but to give them access to the language of power. The first English instructor, Lucy Fay, held a master's degree from the University of Texas. At first glance, she appears to be a stern traditionalist, emphasizing grammar as the backbone of language and logic: "The aim in the study of Grammar will be to insure a thorough working knowledge of the subject, as a basis for the succeeding courses in Historical Grammar, Composition and Literature" (Texas Women's University, *Catalogue 1903* 13). She assigned themes drawn from student life, which she corrected primarily on the basis of "spelling, punctuation, sentence structure and paragraphing" (Texas Women's University, *Catalogue 1903* 13). By her students' testimony in the 1906 yearbook, Fay had a reputation as a fearsome grammarian: "Deals in wholesale examinations and low grades of compositions" (11). "F stands for Fay, / so beautiful and tall, / If you don't know your English, / She'll sure make you squall" (Texas Women's University, *Yearbook 1906* 102). However, her students respected her rigor and loved her for her obvious concern. One even wrote her a devotional poem, loosely inspired by Poe's "Annabel Lee." While other teachers could be sucked up to with flattery—kissing their children, laughing at their jokes, pretending to listen—there was only one way to "stand in" with Miss Fay: "Be bright and never act timid" (Texas Women's University, *Yearbook 1906* 111).

Another early English instructor was Etta M. Lacy, hired in 1908. Her March 1912 editorial in the *Daedalian*, "English as She Is Spoke at C.I.A. [College of Industrial Arts]," offers a window into the early-twentieth-century emphasis on grammatical correctness. At first glance, she too appears to be the stereotypical current-traditional grammar maven, made "dizzy" by the "violence to pure diction" and "barbaric thrusts" she hears students utter, both in the classroom and out. However, her attention to usage also had practical rhetorical intent:

> A recitation on one of the poets stated that he wrote about "nature and everything." "And everything" is such a big, broad, embracing expression for one to take refuge in, unless there is a hot pursuer in the person of a pedagogue on the trail. "And all" is another hiding place for the mind that does not care to disclose all its wealth of information. (4)

Her attack on her students' "extravagant use of adjectives" is also difficult to fault:

> The things that were described as "perfectly lovely" ranged from a well-browned pancake to Raphael's Madonnas. "Nice" was prefixed to a variety of things from such questionable sanitary edibles as hot tamales to the promised auditorium we are to occupy in June. "Pretty" and "cute" had as wide a range. I even heard that Miss Justina Smith [director of elocution] was the "cutest little old girl." (4)

Lacy was not merely reacting to student slang or favoring masculine models of discourse over feminine ones—no doubt she would have taken men to task for similar practices—but saw such language as masks for sloppy, imprecise thinking, which led to ambiguous writing: "A paper on 'How to Darn a Stocking,' without mentioning needle and thread, told me to run around the hole several times before beginning to darn" (6). Moreover, Lacy maintained a sense of humor about herself and her students that, one suspects, carried over into the classroom. In her essay, at the end of her long day of battling student slang, she can finally take no more. Incoherently babbling "Words, words, words!" she runs from the classroom and bolts herself in her room but to no avail, for waiting for her are a stack of themes, which finally drives her to bed. "[I]t has made me batty, I reckon, or kinda sorter crazy as the day ends up" (5–6).

Expansion of the Curriculum

Despite her emphasis on composition, Lacy oversaw a gradual increase in the teaching of literature at TWU; in 1911, literature courses accounted for more than fifty percent of English offerings for the first time (Palmer and Martin timeline). This change, consistent with trends in other public women's colleges and in English departments nationally, reflected an increasing emphasis on liberal arts within the university and an increasing diversity of interests among the student body. By 1915, soon after the school began offering four full years of college work, the department had grown to five faculty, changing its name from English Language and Literature to simply English, reflecting the new departmental major. Though the English department was led by dedicated teachers throughout the school's early history, its academic professionalization began in 1919 with the appointment of Dr. Lee Monroe Ellison, a University of Chicago graduate, as professor and chair. Ellison served during a period of great expansion for the college, working under administrations that supported liberal arts education and the recruitment of well-trained scholars. A philologically trained Romanticist[14] who favored faculty with similar training, Ellison brought in graduates from recognized programs such as Virginia, Michigan, Columbia, and especially Chicago; at times the department had as many six University of Chicago M.A.s and Ph.D.s employed. However, he also recognized local talent, hiring outstanding TWU graduates as well. Ellison remained department head until his retirement in 1947, upon which the chair was assumed by Autrey Nell Wiley, a TWU graduate and University of Texas Ph.D., who had served as a faculty member since 1922.

By 1920, there were ten English faculty. Despite Ellison's own research emphasis, under his direction, the department subscribed to no one stream of rhetorical instruction but instead offered a comprehensive series of courses that reflected contemporary scholarly and pedagogical influences. The 1920 *Catalogue* emphasized the department's newly formulated goals:

> The courses in English seek to accomplish three practical ends; to train students in the processes of clear thinking and effective expression, both oral and written; to develop in them a sureness of taste which will sharply distinguish the artistic and the wholesome in literature from the meretricious and the unwholesome; and to promote in them an adequate sense of the importance of literature as an interpretation of life. (67)

That year, the department offered three courses in composition, a year-long required freshman composition course, a one-semester review course for students who failed first-semester composition, and an elective in advanced composition.

TWU's writing courses reflected both the school's emphasis on practical training and the English department's emphasis on developing "sureness of taste" in literature. Each semester in the first-year course was dedicated to a different mode of expression: exposition in the fall, argumentation in the winter, and description and narration in the spring, a common-enough division at the time. But instead of daily themes detached from rhetorical context, assignments were either "correlated with the work of the other departments" or took the form of explicitly genre-specific writing. In freshman composition, students wrote "club papers, book reviews, and speeches for special occasions," argumentative exercises "based upon current problems," and narrative assignments such as "letters, character sketches, and original stories" (Texas Women's University, *Catalogue 1920* 67). Mamie Walker, for many years the sponsor of the *Daedalian* literary magazine, "skillfully assigned the composition of poems or short stories in such a manner as to assume appropriate copy for the publication"; to enroll in her class "was automatically to volunteer as a writer for the *Quarterly*" (Huey 20). In advanced composition, students studied "modern prose style in newspapers and magazines, and the techniques of the short story" and wrote, published, and presented "newspaper articles, club papers, demonstration lectures, and short stories." Only the remedial composition class focused on features now associated with current-traditional rhetoric and disciplining student subjectivity: "grammar, sentence-structure, paragraph-structure, and punctuation" (Texas Women's University, *Catalogue 1920* 68–69).

It is somewhat difficult to tell from the available record exactly what was valued in student writing in classroom papers. Unlike the familiar, red-inked daily themes from turn-of-the-twentieth-century Harvard students, the English papers on file in the TWU archives show surprisingly minimal marking. The most extensive collection comes from Autrey Nell Wiley, who was a student from 1918 to 1922. Of the various papers from her English classes, only a handful have written comments beyond a grade, and these are usually brief: "Good!"; "lacks unity"; "Very satisfactory report"; "Some good points. More criticism regarding plot structure and treatment of theme is desirable." Wiley, who received only one *B* in English and composition courses during her time at TWU, was a good enough English student to be hired as an assistant professor upon graduation—at a time when the department was filled with advanced-degree holders from elite institutions—so it is possible the lack of commenting was a function of the quality of her writing. At a time when English instructors commonly marked for errors and deficits in Standard English usage, it is possible that a paper that did not exhibit these features attracted little commenting. The only mechanical feature of her writing her professors repeatedly commented on was "a tendency to over-punctuate," and where these errors were noted, no more than one or two examples in the essay were circled, with an occasional instructive comment such as "Study rules for use of [the semicolon]" or "Don't use too much punctuation" (Wiley Collection). But even comments such as these were rare. If absence can be read as presence, it seems that, in Wiley's case at least, in-class practice placed the responsibility for attending to errors on the student.

Public Speaking and Public Life

Rhetorical instruction, of course, was not limited to the English department. In the school's second year, the Department of Elocution, Physical
Culture, and Vocal Music was formed. This department was reconfigured
as the Department of Reading in 1918, strongly influenced by Charles Wesley
Emerson's innovative Emerson College of Oratory in Boston; in 1920, five
out of six TWU faculty members were Emerson graduates. The department,
which compared favorably in size and scope with the University of Texas's
Department of Public Speaking,[15] integrated reading, writing, and speaking
instruction through an interdisciplinary degree in literary interpretation. At
a time when women were prohibited from participating in debate at UT,[16]
TWU students were encouraged to study public speaking and performance;
reading majors took a structured sequence of courses in English, drama,
debate, public speaking, literary interpretation, and physical training.

The emphasis of the reading department was not on parlor skills but
on public ones, fitting students for "the work of the home, the church, and
the community . . . the many responsibilities of social life and for teaching
the subject of Reading." A year-long sequence in debate, designed to help
students "acquire ease and fluency while speaking from the platform," was
open to all students, no matter what their major, "interested in becoming
successful demonstrators, public speakers, club leaders, teachers, or church,
settlement or extension workers." Public speaking was designed to aid students "in meeting the demands of social and public life." In platform art,
students were required to write and present before the class stories, mono-
logues, and lectures as well as cast and direct either a dramatization of a
work of fiction or an original one-act play. Courses in reading and literary
interpretation had a decidedly belletristic emphasis, emphasizing the "development of the student's capacity to respond to the spiritual life of a poem
or any form of literature" and the "psychological principles which underlie
the development of any art." These courses were enormously popular, so
much so that the department also offered numerous sections—as many
as ten per semester—of a four-year sequence in individual instruction in
reading for students outside the department (Texas Women's University,
Catalogue 1920 130–36).

Literary Clubs and Cultural Life

In addition to flocking to courses in English, reading, speech, and drama,
students enjoyed a wide range of extracurricular cultural activities. In the
early years, literary societies were the most popular clubs on campus, attract-
ing over half of the student body.[17] Indeed, it was common for new students

to be asked whether they were going to be an "M.E.B. or a Chap" (*Daedalian* October 1912 6)—a member of the Mary Eleanor Brackenridge Club or the Chaparral Literary Club. "We believe that no girl who enters C.I.A. is getting the full benefit of the school, the real college spirit, until she decides upon one of the literary societies and becomes a member, identifies herself with the Y.W.C.A., and above all, becomes an *active* member of the Athletic Association," declared the *Daedalian* editors in October 1912 (14).

The clubs maintained a friendly competition, inviting each other's members to their yearly get-acquainted parties, and a democratic spirit, welcoming students of all socioeconomic backgrounds. Of course, part of the popularity of the literary clubs can be attributed to the prohibition on sororities at the college. In their absence, the literary societies functioned as de facto social clubs. However, even if the primary motivation of some students was social—and the clubs did hold dances, teas, and other recreational functions—the main activities of these clubs, like their women's club counterparts outside the academy, were educational and civic in nature. The Mary Eleanor Brackenridge Club, named after the well-known women's club leader and advocate for women's education, was formed "to raise the general standard of knowledge among its members; to establish higher ideals of womanhood, and ultimately to develop a nobler sympathy for humanity." Its members studied "art, music, literature, and especially the widening field of activity open to women" (Texas Women's University, *Yearbook 1915*). The Chaparral Literary Club established the school's yearbook and literary magazine, running the latter until its supervision was taken over by the English department in 1915 (Palmer and Martin 5). Other clubs flourished over the years as well. The Adelphian Club was formed "to develop the individual thorough social, cultural, and creative experiences; and to encourage him to participate in both leading and following roles." The 1919–20 program for the Athenaeum Literary Club, which met semi-monthly, gives an example of a typical range of study topics: "modern violinists," "the art of story telling," "modern poets," "great singers of today," "modern novelists," and the "most prominent magazines of today" (Hook Collection). In addition to joining the established literary clubs, it was common for TWU students to form semi-formal reading circles, sometimes supervised by a professor, sometimes by the students themselves. These circles would meet on a weekly basis, usually outdoors in good weather, and often treated popular literature not studied in class.

Extracurricular activities such as these also provided students opportunities for close interactions with their teachers. In TWU's first half-century, over 90% of faculty members were women. Men, wrote Eleanor Brackenridge, "have been found wanting in the necessary tact and ability" (10). Though conventions at the time prescribed that teachers often maintain strict discipline and clear lines of authority in the classroom, teachers at TWU often maintained quite personal relationships with their students after class hours. Even as subtle a move as rearranging the chairs for a reading circle had a large symbolic effect. During her tenure at TWU, history professor Jessie Humphries led the English History Club, reading to the students "under the trees" stories connected to their studies while they did light handwork. During bad weather, they met in the history room. "[B]y changing the chairs, Miss Humphries [changes] it from the stiff, orderly class-room into a homelike sitting room" (Texas Women's University, *Yearbook 1907* 85). Lucy Fay also led a weekly reading circle, devoted to Thackeray. Said one student, "Seeking out some quiet spot, we have, in these intervals of relaxation, thrown care to the winds and allowed our fancy to follow its own sweet course. These hours have been to us the pleasantest and happiest of all" (Texas Women's University, *Yearbook 1906* 84). In a strikingly informal yearbook photo, about two dozen students sit outdoors casually doing needlework or studying as their teacher reads.

TWU offered numerous formal and informal opportunities for students to present their work in public forums. Students regularly presented their work in public recitals, plays, and debates, and for at least twenty years performed a Shakespearean drama at commencement exercises (Palmer and Martin 12). Shakespeare, it seems, was everywhere; he is referenced constantly and casually through the years in the *Daedalian* magazine and yearbook. In 1911, for example, the junior class described themselves through Shakespearean quotes:

> Alderson, Inez—"Is she not a modest young lady?"
> Ellis, Stella—"I'll break a custom."
> Grace, Hybernia—"My books and my instruments shall be my company."
> Koepke, Ethel—"Man delights not me."
> Robertson, Oberia—"I'll keep mine own in spite of all the world."
> Rogers, Bettie—"I had rather hear a dog bark at a crow, than a man swear he loves me."
> Shropshire, Ruth—"Who chooseth me shall get what many men desire."
> (Texas Women's University, *Yearbook 1911* 55–56)

In its second decade, TWU began to develop a reputation for bringing in writers, scholars, and performing artists. During President Bralley's administration, from 1914 to 1924, visitors included William Butler Yeats,

Robert Frost, Carl Sandburg, Alfred Noyes, John Masefield, and Rabindra-math Tagore. Other visitors over the years included Ruth Draper, Charles Laughton, Martha Graham, Edna St. Vincent Millay, Arnold Toynbee, Arthur Rubenstein, Isaac Stern, Yehudi Menuhin, Robert La Follete, Thomas Mann, Archibald MacLeish, Will Durant, Sinclair Lewis, Frank Lloyd Wright, Eleanor Roosevelt, and Amelia Earhart. Poets and writers were especially favored by the students, who would often write critical essays on their work in the *Daedalian*. Toynbee stayed a week, and Frost, Sandburg, and Millay each made multiple visits. These programs eventually earned Denton a reputation as a cultural center, to the point where it on occasion preempted neighboring Dallas as a concert venue. Louis Hubbard, who made the promotion of the series one of the priorities of his presidential administration, still recalled "with pride" some twenty years later that when the San Francisco Symphony Orchestra was on its way East, the only campus stop it made in the Southwest was at the college (*Recollections* 209). For TWU students, especially those from small rural towns, the opportunity to interact with such notable cultural figures must have seemed amazing. After the baritone Mack Harrell gave a recital in neighboring Greenville, *Dallas Morning News* amusement critic John Rosenfield read a "most knowing and beautifully written" review by a TWU student. "She told me she was a girl from a small Texas town, that all the music she ever heard was part of her four years at T.S.C.W., that she was a Journalism major and hoped she would make a good critic" (qtd. in Hubbard, *Recollections* 207–8).

TWU also offered students numerous opportunities to publish their writing. The earliest yearbooks included a literary section with student poetry, short stories, and essays, in addition to class and club notes. The campus literary magazine, the *Daedalian*, began publication as a monthly in 1906, and the newspaper, the *Lass-O*, as a weekly, in 1915. All these publications were "managed entirely by the students," with only "slight supervision" by faculty (Texas Women's University, *Catalogue 1920* 191). Given the often paternalistic atmosphere of residential colleges in the early twentieth century, especially Southern women's colleges, the free rein allowed TWU students to direct their own publications is quite remarkable; judging by their often irreverent and sometimes downright cheeky editorial tone, they took full advantage of their freedom.

Student Voices

In December 1905, members of the Chaparral Literary Club formally resolved "that they would have a college paper"; by the following spring they had published their first issue of the *Chaparral Monthly* (Texas Women's University, *Yearbook 1907*). Soon renamed the *Daedalian*, the journal published continuously until 1980, when it was merged with the yearbook as an annual publication (Palmer and Martin 21).[18] In the years before the founding of the *Lass-o* newspaper, the *Daedalian* served as a combination newspaper–literary journal. Typical contents included short stories, literary essays, editorials, alumnae notes, campus news, and accounts of club, athletic, and social activities. By 1912, the magazine had developed a fairly stable classification of five departments: literary, editorial, society and clubs, athletic, and exchange, the latter featuring reviews of other college papers from the United States and Canada. By 1914, the literary department had grown into the largest section in the magazine, and, by 1917, as other departments were either dropped or spun off into their own publications, the *Daedalian* had become chiefly a literary and cultural journal. By the 1920s, issues of from eighty to one hundred pages are common, with as many as twenty-five contributors per issue. The *Daedalian*'s pages contain a remarkable record of student rhetorical production at TWU over the years, offering a window into the wide range of source material that inspired the students, the topics that concerned them, and the kinds of writing they valued. Student writers at TWU display both confidence and competence, suggesting a campus culture that was supportive of their rhetorical activities and connected to the world outside the classroom.

In the first years of the *Daedalian*, the editorial teams occasionally exhibit the deferential self-effacement Lynn Gordon sees as marking the student writing of the period. "The girls welcomed [the magazine] with open arms and petted it and fed it on all kinds of things, from overdone jokes to the freshest of current events. Notwithstanding the variety of its diet, it thrived and grew, until . . . it was able to make a great many funny and interesting little noises" (Texas Women's University, *Yearbook 1907* 99). But this attitude soon disappears. By 1911, the editorial voice of the *Daedalian* is self-assured and confident, with a practiced ironic superiority replacing previous self-effacement. An essay that year, "To a College Editor's Waste Basket," demonstrates that self-criticism was not just for women. The writer, mocking her own attempts at writing, speaks of her wastebasket as being a long-suffering best friend, fed a "pasty, starchy, frequently acidic" diet resulting in "a most highly exaggerated form of literary dyspepsia." But it is not only the editor who commits literary crimes. She notes a supposed example from President Bizzell, "T'would be always doleful weather, if't were nothing else but Spring," which goes on "for ten or twelve stanzas" with only minor variations in punctuation.

This pathetic and affecting poem was written by Dr. Bizzell, on violet scented note paper, with pale blue ink, besplotched with many briny tears, and yet—none of these things availed, and when the waste basket had swallowed it boldly, it glowed with soft, effulgent light, conscious of having well performed a duty, and of having become a great benefactor to humanity in general. (Texas Women's University, *Yearbook 1911* 124)

During this time, the editors were being trained to think of themselves as journalists and to conceive of journalism as a rhetorical act, as Maybelle Brooks did in May 1912:

A very effective definition of journalism has been given us by Dr. Edwin E. Slosson: "Journalism is the art of timely and effective presentation in print." Dr. Slosson classes journalism as an art. By a timely and effective presentation in print he means that which is written at an appropriate time for a specific and immediate effect. This differentiates it from the larger body of literature in general, where the element of timeliness is eliminated or subordinated. The journalist is writing for his contemporaries, not for posterity. Of course he may accomplish more than his aim and give to the world material which will be read generations after. . . . The fundamental object of journalism is to incite the thought and correct the judgement to action. Like oratory, it aims to instruct, convince, guide, and control. (*Daedalian* May 1912 9–10)

Frequent editorials in the *Daedalian* forward this professional ethos. In addition to speaking out on political topics of the day, the editors address topics of professional concern, such as calling for higher standards and more journalism education. A 1911 essay by Jessie Bozeman presents a brief history of the development of college papers at institutions such as Harvard, Yale, and Stanford. By her tone, she suggests that the *Daedalian* should be considered among the ranks of those schools' publications (Texas Women's University, *Yearbook 1911* 11–12).

The editors of the *Daedalian* had a broadly conceived sense of audience. On the one hand, the journal was designed for the TWU community, which included students, faculty, family members, alumnae, and clubwomen throughout the state, who were known for keeping an eye on campus affairs. Older students mentored younger students through the sometimes serious, sometimes tongue-in-cheek editorials and advice essays written for freshman and through the regular publication of freshmen writing in the journal. (Instructors commonly assigned essays with publication in the *Daedalian* in mind.) The *Daedalian* was an enculturating tool, advising students on norms of the college, tuning them in to inside jokes, and helping maintain a spirit of solidarity against institutional authority. At the same time, writers and editors took their work seriously and hoped that it would appeal to an audience beyond the school, as evidenced by the journal's exchange department. In the early twentieth century, it was common for schools to exchange copies of their journals and offer criticisms in their pages, commenting not only on the writing but also the look of the magazines, such as the illustrations, cover, quality of paper, and layout. (The attention of the *Daedalian* editors to visual elements of other magazines suggests deep involvement in their own magazine's production process.) Through the exchange department, the *Daedalian* editors were able to both keep up with what other publications were doing and assess their own work in comparison. They were especially enthusiastic in this activity, exchanging with up to eighty schools at a time in forty states, actively seeking the critiques of other schools and offering sharp, irreverent ones of their own: "We note by this magazine that smoking is forbidden on the campus and think it pertinent to inquire, 'Where do you smoke?'" (*Daedalian* February 1910 21).

One of the more lively exchange editors was Margaret Sackville, who served as president of the Texas Intercollegiate Press Association (TIPA) and assistant editor of the *Daedalian* in 1912–13, her senior year. An outspoken suffragist and progressive, with a cutting sense of humor, Sackville was a sophisticated critic of language, placing quotation marks around the prescribed "he" when referring to herself in the third person and taking delight in "editorial wiseisms." In 1913, she edited the yearbook's yearly joke edition of the *Daedalian*, "devoted to the highest interests of yellow journalism" (188):

> We recently read something else which attracted our attention. . . . "An authority is attempting to explain why girls don't marry. After viewing some members of the male sex no explanation is required." We have expressed our opinion of this rather obvious statement, but believe the author really meant, "After viewing the views of some members of the male sex, no explanation is required." This is merely a suggestion as to the trend of views which a claimant to the hand of a Suffragette should cultivate. (190)

As exchange editor, Sackville increased the size of the department, actively sought exchanges, and harangued other schools to do the same. About the numerous publications the school received, she commented, "Not many have come without our sending the first 'Please Exchange,' but then we are not all equally anxious to build up our departments, and receive magazines from far and wide" (*Daedalian* May 1912 21). Given the acerbity of her reviews, it is not surprising that some schools might have been reluctant to send issues. While she could laud journals she liked—she was especially generous with those whose editorials were "progressive in spirit"—she was unforgiving in lambasting those that failed to meet her standards, tossing off pithy, sardonic insults like a Texan Dorothy Parker:

- *The Aster* (Miss Craven's School, Newark, New Jersey): The literary departments in these exchanges from girl's schools certainly do show the feminine touch, and to such an extent as, we are sure, would gratify the hearts of all the many masculine opponents of woman's suffrage.
- *Hemnica* (Red Wing Seminary, Red Wing, Minnesota): We have been reading for some time very favorable comments on "The Hemnica," but we have decided they must have been given by institutions from the same part of the country who could appreciate the exceptional amount of local color depicted therein.
- *Blue and Gold* (Aberdeen, South Dakota): The stories are very good as juvenile productions and we suppose March in South Dakota is too early for the spring romancers to start writing.
- *Black and Red* (Northwestern College, Watertown, Wisconsin): There is always a long dissertation in German which we take for granted is most excellent, but just put off reading.
- *The Comet* (Milwaukee, Wisconsin): "The Comet" is as progressive as the city from which it hails. . . . We are sure the advertising brings in good money and doubtless the advertisers appreciate your placing other reading matter among theirs, but this detracts from the style of your magazine.
- *The Maple Leaf* (Morristown, New Jersey): "The Maple Leaf" receives plenty of criticism which we would otherwise give, so we will refrain. (*Daedalian* May 1912 22–24)

Literary Criticism and Attitudes toward Language

The literary essays in the *Daedalian* are often written with the same critical eye as the exchange reviews. The earliest tend to be in the form of short, belletristic appreciations of canonical texts, such as Margaret Malone's prize-winning Texas Intercollegiate Press Association contest essay, "Poe and Hawthorne as Short Story Writers." Though Malone makes the sort of rhetorical moves that have been dismissed as masculinist and hegemonic—depersonalized third-person voice, appeals to universal aesthetic standards—the self-assuredness and authority with which she makes her claims suggest ownership of her language, not alienation from it. Nor does she fear challenging the authority of the authors she reviews:

> Poe has painted a picture, while Hawthorne has created an ideal, yet neither has given a flesh and blood character. . . . Poe is without rival in working up to an effective climax. . . . [but] many of his scenes are so revolting that one loses sight of the workmanship. Hawthorne's stories have not so well a defined climax, but Hawthorne has a delicacy of feeling and lightness of touch which Poe lacks. (Texas Women's University, *Yearbook 1915*)

Over the next two decades, the scope of student criticism expands. Essays become longer, exhibit more historical awareness of literature as a field, and address a wider range of topics, including contemporary popular literature. The Romanticists remained perennial favorites, of course—"Is Shelly Lacking in Thought?" "Shelly as a Lyricist of Sadness," "Wordsworth, Moss Back?"—but by the early 1920s, the magazine also includes subjects such as Gertrude Stein, Anatole France, Edgar Lee Masters, and African American poetry, with articles such as "Carl Sandburg: The Poet of Brutality and Beauty," "Striking Parallelisms in Modern Art and Modern American Poetry," "Matthew Arnold's Theory of Poetry Applied to His Own Verse," and "Josephine Preston Peabody, Exponent of Poetic Drama." This shift likely reflects the increasing professionalization of the English department after 1919.

Regardless of their subject, students display a wide range of critical responses and attitudes toward language. In a 1914 essay, "The English Problem at C.I.A.," Susan F. Cobb already sounds like the English teacher she was practicing to become.[19]

> The amount of knowledge the average student in the Freshman Class has of English grammar when she enters C.I.A. is pitiable. Fully thirty per cent of the students who come here from well reputed high schools cannot write a clear, forceful English sentence. . . . The College is not the place to learn English grammar. This art of writing and spelling is supposed to be mastered before the student enters college. (Cobb 10)

That same year, *Daedalian* editor and self-described "newspaper man" Marie Erhardt wrote what amounts to a fierce rebuttal. In her yearbook editorial, she mocks prescriptive grammar, defends "the reckless 'newspaper English' of [the] day" as the "clearest, most concise" form of expression, and praises slang for generating a limitless supply of "fresh, new expressions":

Our language is not permanent; it has been changing and developing ever since the beginning of a language, and it will go on changing; therefore, I say it behooves us to be progressive enough to use the latest and best on the market. . . . [I]t is perfectly shocking to any nice young lady to think the latest, good-looking man can speak perfect English and find nothing in stock except second-rate discarded jabber that he has used ever since Taft's administration. Just think of a grown up man saying, "I should worry," when anybody would know that "Ish Ka Bibble" is the proper form. It should be the height of everyone's ambition to make the language they use sound like a musical comedy. Everyone should strive to speak so that it would be easy to enter into a conversation in which neither of the persons would understand the other. (Erhardt 189)

Mary Tanner, in her January 1923 essay, "'Poetic Diction' in Theory and Practice," writes like a disciple of Matthew Arnold, taking Wordsworth to task for promoting the use of common language: "Though it was a belief inspired by a most democratic view of life, we feel that he failed to take into account the fact that true poetry should be a little above the ordinary plane of our thoughts, and should elevate us" (*Daedalian* 18). In contrast, Justine Harris's spring 1922 essay, "Democracy and the New Poetry," celebrates the contemporary "revolt against the decadence and artificiality of the 'nineties,'" surveying the work of modern poets such as James Oppenheim ("the great humanitarian radical"), Louis Untermeyer, Edgar Lee Masters, Edwin Markham, Edwin Arlington Robinson, Robert Frost, and others who would have "no doubt" made the "average Victorian [raise] his hands in holy horror" (*Daedalian* 37). In the same issue, *Daedalian* editor Lucyle Hook's twelve-page "Naturalism in Modern Fiction," another prize-winning TIPA essay, praises the "sometimes raw, bleeding life" (13) in authors such as Tolstoy, Dostoyevsky, Zola, Hardy, and de Maupassant. "The sordidness which permeates the naturalistic novel reflect[s] back the shining stars of truth to those who have eyes to see" (*Daedalian* 24).

Whereas *Daedalian* writers a decade earlier emphasized the timelessness of literature, Mary Tanner's January 1923 editorial, "A Subject for C.I.A. Novelists," calls for more social realist novels of women in business and notes the problems of genre expectations in depicting reality.

Business men, as a whole, seem to take the matter rather as a state of affairs to be accepted without protest. Happily married women murmur complacently about how much working girls miss, and pity them because of their contact with the "cold world." Unhappily married women covet the independence of the "bachelor girl." But the attitude of authors cannot be so easily defined, for it seems that this startlingly individual class of people has as many opinions on the subject as it has persons. (26)

Most novels, she notes, solve the problem of the businesswoman by having her marry off. This state of affairs "needs no comment" (26). On the other hand, two recent novels also miss the mark. Edna Ferber's *Emma McChesney and Co.* defends "the possibility of rearing a child, keeping a home, and retaining feminine sweetness and charm, and at the same time making a marked success in a business firm," though its superwoman heroine is "a bit too near a paragon." A. S. M. Hutchinson's controversial *This Freedom*, meanwhile, meant "to prove the absolute impossibility" of a woman being a successful businesswoman and mother, is "most unreal." Tanner "wish[es] for a story which takes the middle ground . . . upon which the efficient, admirable woman of the twentieth century is firmly standing" (27). She suggests that her fellow college writers take up the failings of the current literature to create works that respond to their lives.

Tanner's editorial is a reminder against monological readings of the effect of literary ideologies on literate practices. Tanner shows not only that she is acutely aware of and capable of criticizing competing streams of thought but that she herself has a complex, multivoiced response. For example, she was not a fan of what she considered "affectedly queer" modern poetry. She disliked free verse and found E. E. Cummings deficient in "punctuation for clearness," despite the opinions of the editors of the *Dial* (*Daedalian* January 1923 29). She considered Wordsworth too democratic. And she was clearly no political radical. But the same woman who feels that poetry should be a genteel medium above the realm of politics believes that fiction and drama are appropriate forums for the subject.

Satirizing Campus Life

Some of the most fascinating examples of student writing are the poetic *imitatios* satirizing campus life that recurrently appeared in both the *Daedalian* and the yearbook. Despite their light tone, these works are often quite sophisticated, demonstrating both close attention to the content and structure of the source material, as well as satirical skill. In the hands of TWU students, Poe's "The Bells" became, quite naturally, a vehicle to vent against the school's own infernal batch ringing the students to class—"In the startled air of morn, / They are painful as a corn" (February 1914 15); Tennyson's "Charge of the Light Brigade" reminded students of a certain English class—"Theirs not to make reply, / Theirs not to reason why, / Theirs but to do and die: / . . . / Boldly they wrote, and well, / Into the jaws of Death,

/ Into the mouth of—well" (*Yearbook 1911* 178); and Chaucer's *Canterbury Tales* inspired a senior class's history of their own journey—"She algate and ever of the Deutsche language prates, / But 'Ich leibe all meachen,' she never translates" (*Yearbook 1906* 34).

An especially popular topic for satire was the campus uniform code. Like many women's colleges, TWU insisted upon a rigid and, as the years passed, increasingly complex dress code that prescribed specific colors, materials, and patterns that students could wear, according to whether they were attending class, dinner, or chapel. Most dreaded was the "blue chambray" of the standard skirt. While other regulations could be subverted or broken—and often were—there was no avoiding the uniform code. Almost from the opening of the school, the students took every opportunity to protest it, sometimes informally, sometimes by petition. In his memoirs, President Hubbard recalled one dramatic protest:

> And one morning the editor of the school paper *The Lasso*, came to my office and demonstrated the truth of her statement that, as then constituted, there were one hundred and thirty-seven uniform combinations provided by the regulations, in skirts, blouses, coats, hats, accessories, stockings and shoes, which, in her opinion, made the uniform a farce. After that girl's visit I immediately appointed a faculty-student committee to work on the problem. (*Recollections* 225)

The committee unanimously voted to abolish the uniform in 1938; Hubbard made the announcement just before Christmas to "applause and tears" (*Recollections* 225). Until that crucial moment, students made their opinions known by criticizing the code in verse, as in Teresa Abney's "The Rubaiyat of NoMore Uniform": "Wake! for the Rules have scattered into flight / All dreams of new styles from our sight" (*Daedalian* October 1911 6). A particularly deft example is Opal Hughes's "Song of Myself."

> A new girl fetching me a bolt of serge, said,
> "What is the uniform?" How could I answer the girl?
> I do not know any more than she.
>
> I guess it is the handicap of the faculty,
> A constant token and reminder of their
> authority—designedly adopted.
>
> Or, I guess, the uniform is a law, the pet
> child of their regulations.

> Or, I guess it must be the flag of their dispositions.
> Out of hopeless blue stuff woven.
>
> Or, it seems to me, the beautiful, uncut folds
> of restraint.
>
> (*Yearbook* 1911 158)

The prevalence and sophistication of these satires suggest the immersion of TWU students in literary culture, despite the school's emphasis on vocational education. The writers of these verses were confident that their classmates would not only relate to the subject being satirized but would be familiar enough with the source material to appreciate the work.

Political Engagement

If "controversial political topics," as Amy McCandless suggests, "rarely penetrated the classrooms of Southern colleges" (77), they did pervade some campuses. As public women's colleges were frequently dependent on legislative whims and community sentiment for their financing, students had a stake in being attuned to public affairs, and at TWU they were encouraged to do so. In 1912, students in TWU's political economy class publicly debated the topic, "Resolved, that Socialism is an expedient governmental policy" (*Daedalian* February 1912 9). In the pages of the *Daedalian*, students debated politics and history—arguing the relative merits of Woodrow Wilson, the Panama-Pacific Expedition, and free speech laws—as well as the political implications of literature. TWU women read and responded to articles in a variety of publications, including the *Atlantic Monthly*, the *Bookman*, and the *Dial*, and were especially sensitive to articles on the "woman question." In response to Gilbert Frankau's questioning of whether the "modern girl," supposedly masculinized by her achievements in the world, is capable of love, Ruth West asserts her right to both political agency and femininity.

> In placing "love" on a higher, if a more practical plane; in removing it from the show-case of sentiment . . . the modern girl, far from showing in this action an utter lack of reticence, has proved herself the possessor of that fine reserve. . . . It does not prove her "too wise," that she takes into frank consideration the difficulties and problems following "her civil-contract in marriage." . . . And in "most supremely knowing exactly what she wants," it is not blind sentimentality. Being cognizant of her good qualities, her poise, her efficiency, her intelligence, her aim is to be "a worthy co-partner of this existence," capable of self-sacrifice in real

service, a true interpretation of which, for her, has not lessened its value. (*Daedalian* November 1922 28)

These essays and editorials, of course, did not always display the most radical sentiment. The author of an editorial on activist and journalist Ruth Hale, for example, is generally supportive of suffrage but clearly thinks this business of keeping one's own name after marriage is going a bit too far. What is important in TWU student writing is not the individual political positions students hold but the clear assertion of political opinions on controversial topics in a public forum. The issues of the day mattered to TWU women—and they were encouraged to write about them.

The interest of TWU students in public affairs was encouraged by the political activism of the women's clubs which supported the school. Throughout its history, TWU maintained a close alliance with the women's clubs that were instrumental in its founding and continued to offer financial and political support. Accordingly, TWU students sometimes satirized the lack of political interest among some women. Elinor Jones's "How the War Aroused Our Club" mocks dilettantism—"We would have knitted some more [socks for the soldiers], of course, but it was nearly summer time" (Spring 1917 28–29); and Dorris Mirick's "The Flapper in Politics" depicts a stylish young woman more concerned with the state of her lipstick than the state of the union—"What's that girl's name that is running for governor?" (Spring 1922 52). Through the pressure of women's groups to increase public funding for the university, TWU women were continually reminded that the existence and prosperity of their school were contingent on political engagement. "The legislature will meet again some of these days," reminded the *Daedalian* editors in October 1911, "so remember your duty to your school" (13).

Of course, the sensitivity of the students to women's issues regrettably did not always extend to other topics. TWU was, after all, designed for "white girls," a racially segregated school in a racially segregated state. Throughout Texas and the South, white women were often ambivalent—and occasionally hostile—toward civil rights for blacks. Many leaders in the women's movement feared that suffrage would be interpreted as a race issue, leading to the enfranchisement of black women, and commonly maintained a position of active silence on the question of race. Furthermore, although Texas had a large African American population, it was concentrated in the eastern part of the state. Denton County in 1920 was only 7.3% black (Urquhart 68). I have not found any articles opposing black civil rights in the *Daedalian*, and beginning in the 1920s, articles begin to appear in appreciation of African

American literature, albeit in a somewhat paternalistic tone. However, racial stereotypes of the day sometimes appear in its pages. Students may have taken their cue in part from university officials, who tended to display either indifference to or ignorance of black sociopolitical struggles. Dean Edmund White's autobiography shows a man deeply committed to the education of women and respectful of the dignity of all his students, even those who didn't obtain degrees, but the work is literally filled with dialect jokes and "mammy" stories. Indeed, he thought himself something of a connoisseur of African American culture (*Lengthening Shadows*). President Louis Hubbard used humor in the classroom as a pedagogical tool; sometimes this took the form of ethnic jokes (*Recollections* 81–86). The complicated relationship between white and black women's struggles for educational opportunities deserves further study.

Pride and Publication

The experience of writing and editing their own publications gave TWU students a powerful sense of pride in and ownership of their work. This pride was likely confirmed by their participation in the Texas Intercollegiate Press Association. The history of TIPA is worth a study in itself. The organization included a wide range of schools, both public and private, coeducational and separatist, and included Baylor, Texas A&M, North Texas State, Texas Christian University, and the University of Texas. It held enough cachet to attract prominent speakers to its yearly conventions, including Lieutenant Governor Will H. Mayes in 1913 (*Yearbook 1913* 124).

At this time, most journalists were men, and women journalists were frequently limited to women's departments or "soft" features, such as literature and theater criticism. Through midcentury, the field had strong working-class, rough-and-tumble associations. On the other hand, America had long had a strong tradition of women journalists, writers, and public speakers TWU women could look to as models. Students kept up with the work of Ruth Hale, a nationally known suffragist, women's rights activist, and journalist, who wrote for the *New York Times* and *Vogue*, although they didn't always agree with her politics. Certainly, the example of pioneering women journalists helped encourage the confidence of TWU women in their own publications. They also identified with "newspaper guys," reprinting a poem from the *Cleveland Plain Dealer* lionizing the reporter's ability to get in anywhere—crime scenes, sold-out shows ("Star nuthin'! He's one of those newspaper guys"), even the gates of Heaven (March 1914 16). Yet they still faced many restraints. In 1915, women in Texas could not obtain a degree from Texas A&M, could not participate in intercollegiate debate at the University of Texas (Regan 33), and, of course, could not vote. But women in TIPA held their own, delivering papers, exchanging advice, and debating male students on topics of professional concern. At the 1914 annual convention, a male student, Robert Skiles, gave a toast comparing coeds "to the modern-day picture show . . . absolutely unnecessary but impossible to live without."[20] TWU student Corrie Walker stood up and responded with her own verse, redefining "co-ed" as female *and* male students working together toward a common aim. At first, she said, she imagined writing a "clever" speech to "repay" Skiles, but then her "heart went—in the opposite direction." Claiming, unlike Skiles, to have a "pitifully small" knowledge of co-eds, "coming from a girls' school as I do," she decides to embark on a comprehensive study of the subject:

> Well, the more I studied about co-eds, friends,
> The more they appealed to me.
> And so completely filled me with envy
> That only one viewpoint I see.

> And that's of their advantage, could anything lovelier be,
> Than boys and girls working together, helping each other along,
> Sharing each other's burdens, making school life mere song?

> So just here fellow press men,
> In response to the one just read,
> Here's to all these boys and girls,
> These enviable co-eds.
> (*Daedalian* May 1914 17)

Mr. Skiles's response is not recorded. But if bemused paternalism regarding women was common, so was professional respect. TWU was a state leader in TIPA's annual writing awards, and women from TWU and other schools often ran successfully for state office within the organization, including that of president: TWU's Margaret Sackville served in 1912–13 and Margaret Collins of North Texas State in 1914–15.

Whether the writing in the *Daedalian* displayed "literary merit" is perhaps too subjective a call, especially in regard to fiction. As with any broad collection of student writing, it exhibits a range of talent and achievement. Some of the writers and editors went on to become professional writers, scholars, and critics; most didn't. Some of the stories and essays, certainly, are derivative, trite, or merely of the moment. But far more often than not, I find the writing of TWU students consistently sophisticated and often ambitious, reflecting a considerable awareness of literary genres and conventions and an admirable command of language. Whatever their merit, no one could say of the student poems in the *Daedalian* that their authors didn't read poetry. Students were clearly working in and through literary and journalistic traditions and often said as much. And by the professional and academic standards of the day, TWU students were producing good work, with TIPA awards contributing to their sense of pride. In 1922, for example, TWU received first prize in the short story and humorous story, second in the essay and poem, and third for newspaper story. "If everyone who is at all capable will write a serious short story, humorous story, poem, serious essay, humorous essay, newspaper story, or one-act drama," encouraged Nadine Morgan, *Daedalian* associate editor, "there is no doubt that C.I.A. will win more honors than any other contesting college and even more than she won last year" (*Daedalian* January 1923 28). These prize-winning pieces were regularly featured in both the *Daedalian* and the yearbook.

The optimism and confidence the students displayed through their writing can be traced to several sources. First is the spirit of the college. TWU was founded as a grand experiment in the advancement of women in Texas after a long-fought public battle by Texas clubwomen. These clubwomen remained fiercely loyal to the school and continued to fight for its improvement after its founding. With the help of these women and dedicated teachers and administrators, TWU developed a reputation as an innovative institution on the leading edge of curricular and technological advancements. It was not only able to compete with the men's A&M college and even the University of Texas, but in some departments, it was markedly superior. On campus, TWU women faced few, if any, social barriers; it was their school entirely. Furthermore, few TWU students, especially in the school's early years, came from privileged socioeconomic backgrounds, and even those who did often felt that they belonged to a new class of Texas women. For these students, the education they received at TWU greatly expanded their life options, even given other political and cultural constraints. The school may not have been entirely the classless "democracy" it represented itself to be, but differences in social class do not appear to have created great tensions. In 1925, President Lindsey Blayney stated with pride that five of the last seven student presidents had worked part-time in the school cafeteria to pay for their education (6). The pride of TWU students in their school and their excitement at the opportunities they expected it to provide were reflected in their writing. It is telling that while school policies were often critiqued in student writing, English classes—unlike at Radcliffe or Wellesley (Simmons; J. Campbell, "Controlling," "Freshman")—almost never were.

Writing Their Own Way

In writing on TWU, I don't want to make the mistake of reestablishing the "seamless narrative usually told about the rhetorical tradition" (Lunsford 6). As Sharon Crowley and Gary Olson suggest, the ability of students to write with confidence and skill within socially approved margins may in itself suggest internal conflicts or a problematic pedagogy.

In *Disorderly Conduct*, Carroll Smith-Rosenberg writes, "[W]omen's assumption of men's symbolic constructs involved women in a fundamental act of alienation.... If the marginal or powerless wish to challenge the dominant discourse, must they not frame their challenge in the language of the dominant mode?" (266). Perhaps. But students at TWU in the early twentieth century did not necessarily see themselves as marginal or powerless, feel alienated by the assumption of "dominant" modes of expression or men's symbolic constructs, or, most importantly, believe themselves to be assuming alien forms of expression. Just as students at black liberal arts colleges saw Standard English, the Bible, political oratory, and the classical liberal arts tradition as part of their *own* cultural heritage as Americans and African Americans, so women at TWU saw public writing as a human skill they had a right to develop and *could* develop, just as they learned other vocational skills. As befits their audience-based instruction in English, journalism, and public-speaking classes, students wrote in voices appropriate for their tasks, making use of a wide range of rhetorical strategies. I find little evidence that TWU students were subordinating their personalities to write in a plain style or that they were conflicted about expressing their personalities through a more belletristic style. If students at TWU did feel these tensions, they did not write about them. Although the absence of an archival record by itself is not necessarily evidence for the lack of a phenomenon, the otherwise substantial record that students left of what they did worry about is suggestive. In their diaries, editorials, essays, and short stories, they wrote about men, families, friends, and faculty. They were explicitly concerned with their identity as women and their place in the world, especially the options open to them in the future. But they did so with confidence in their ability to use language to explore these ideas, and they made use of a wide range of expressive modes. The same student might write a highly personal, "feminine" book review and a piece of literary criticism in a less personal, "masculine" voice. Or she might do both, at once. Indeed, student writing in the *Daedalian* is remarkable for employing a wide range of registers, from Standard English to contemporary slang, from artless to ironic, and a variety of literary models, including Westerns, romance novels, religious sermons, Romantic poetry and drama, modern poetry, and travel narratives.

If recent research on women's history is moving beyond dualisms, such as separate spheres (Kerber), in men's and women's lives, perhaps a similar move can be made towards the examination of men's and women's rhetorics. Just as what we have identified as seemingly incompatible rhetorics—social-epistemic, belletristic, and current-traditional—often existed in concert at the same time in the same location, so, too, did different writing strategies and modes of expression. Students at TWU certainly didn't feel they were being exposed to a single perspective, nor do they exhibit it in their writing. They did not describe their education in terms of binary oppositions or classify their writing in terms of feminine or masculine discourse. Indeed, they did not sharply contrast between men's and women's rhetoric. Nor did they, for the most part, reject models of gender or seek to create an androgynous world. The "gendered notion of service" that persisted in the early twentieth century in Texas was seen by TWU students not as limiting but as providing a space to claim cultural and political power. The greater comfort of Texas women with traditional gender roles may have also produced a less obvious dichotomy between their education and the burgeoning women's rights movement. Like women elsewhere, women in Texas "linked college education and self-fulfillment with feminism and glorious achievements." But for the "New Woman" of Texas, "repudiating the Cult of True Womanhood" (Smith-Rosenberg 245–47) was not part of her project. Rather, Texas women—who relished their independence as Texans as much as men did—used domestic tropes to advance their cause. Household economics not only brought the latest science and industry into the home but brought the concerns of the home—sanitation, food safety, economy, and ecology—into the public sphere. From the growth of women's clubs in the 1880s through suffrage, white Texas women, despite very real limits on their rights, wielded considerable political influence.

In many ways, the lives of women at TWU resembled those of students at private women's colleges in the East. Students maintained warm relationships with faculty and each other. Crushes and lifelong friendships were common, and students remained loyal to their school. But there were fundamental differences. Academically, TWU was more in line with public A&M and normal colleges, which were frequently more responsive to students' needs in rhetorical instruction than traditional liberal arts colleges (Kynell; Fitzgerald, "Rediscovered"). Indeed, Texas women had a complicated relationship to the liberal arts, which they frequently saw as belonging to an outdated and limiting antebellum finishing-school tradition. Even in the school's earliest years, students at TWU were not cloistered or confined to female-only social spheres. Students regularly traveled to town, football games, and fairs and engaged in intercollegiate activities with men and women from other schools in Texas. More importantly, the school's mission meant that students could *not* be cloistered; the school was designed for working-class women seeking professional opportunities. Finally, the close association between the college and women's clubs gave students models for civic engagement.

Students at TWU thus had different educational expectations than those at colleges such as Vassar and Bryn Mawr. As Southerners, and especially Texans, they also had a different relationship to the women's rights movement than their better-off counterparts in the East. They were more conservative politically and less conflicted about their life opportunities as women. Many graduates happily fulfilled expected roles as mothers, housewives, or elementary and secondary schoolteachers. While TWU was not necessarily breeding radicals or suffragists, it was turning out women who firmly insisted on their equality and dignity, and it gave them the ability to be economically independent if they so desired. Furthermore, the education they received prepared them for the rapidly changing society in which they were to live. TWU provided many of its students with social, intellectual, political, and economic opportunities they would not have had otherwise, even for those women who ultimately chose homelife over a career. In classrooms, literary and social clubs, and especially school publications, students actively engaged the cultural and political issues of the day. The confidence, leadership, and economic skills they gained would remain with them their entire lives and would place them at the leading edge of a new generation of educated, professionally trained Texas women. Before World War II, almost 98% of TWU graduates entered the workforce; of those who married, approximately 40% continued to work (Bentinck 39–40; Cornell 25–26)[21] and most remained active in women's organizations. Nearly half (48.1%) of their daughters graduated from high school; of those graduates, 86.5% attended college (Cornell 47–48). The history of TWU, then, is of a school that, whatever its flaws in reproducing cultural hierarchies or ignoring other injustices such as racism, uniquely answered the needs of its students. It also affirms the value of separatist education for marginalized groups. Finally it suggests how seemingly competing pedagogies can be linked and how binary oppositions—current-traditional and social-epistemic, conservative and progressive, feminine and feminist—may be limited in describing the complexities of institutional ideologies, classroom practices, and student lives.

3

Challenging Orthodoxies at a Rural Normal College

The classroom is the place for the pupil to learn how to use his own powers, and if the teacher usurps this, he is the meanest of tyrants—a tyrant over human souls.—William Mayo

Every lesson learned in the school is more or less a lesson in English.—William Mayo

At first glance, William Leonidas Mayo would not likely be a welcome figure at a contemporary convention of the National Council of Teachers of English (NCTE). His classrooms were anything but decentered, and he would have scoffed at the idea that students had a right to their own language—unless that language was Standard English. The maverick founder and president of East Texas Normal College (1889), an independent teacher-training institution in rural Commerce, Texas, ruled his school with unquestioned authority, boxing unruly students about the ears, sending others home for rule infractions, and insisting upon exacting standards for English instruction. Whole weeks at the campus could be spent in debate on the finer points of prescriptive grammar, and woe to the student who used the subjective case where the objective case was required, in class or out. At the same time, Mayo advocated many practices that anticipated contemporary, student-centered, civically engaged pedagogy; he held that students' changing needs should drive curricula, that each student had a sacred dignity that schools must uphold, that practical, universal education was the basis for a democratic society, and that no student should be turned away for lack of academic preparation or funds.

As a normal school educator, Mayo was at once mainstream and iconoclastic. In his pedagogy, he combined elements of rugged individualism, populist politics, progressive educational ideals, Methodist discipline, and a late-Victorian faith in self-improvement. His motto was "Ceaseless industry, fearless investigation, unfettered thought." He tailored his institution to the needs of the local agricultural community, with no formal admissions requirements, minimal tuition, and ten-week terms, which allowed students to come and go as finances and farm work allowed. He had little use for what he considered the "aristocracy" of academia and little patience for the administrative rules of the state Board of Education. As the school catalogue annually declared:

- Board of Regents—None. We use no names of distinguished politicians or other men of high-sounding titles for mere catch-traps.
- Board of Trustees—None. No such dignitaries to hold us in suspense for weeks or months when we wish to make the slightest change or needed improvement.
- Board of Directors—None. We are not check-reined by such a body of men, who know far less about school work than about the business they follow, and who are ever ready to suggest ideas prevailing "when I went to school."
- Board of Visitors—Everybody. Who desires to attend college, or who has a son, a daughter, or a friend anxious to acquire, under the most favorable conditions, a general practical education at a minimum outlay of time and money. (*Catalogue 1905* 2)

Although not initially accredited—indeed, Mayo opposed accreditation—East Texas Normal quickly became an important training center for teachers. By 1907, its summer teacher's program was the state's largest (Goodwin 41); by the time of Mayo's death in 1917, yearly enrollment had reached three thousand, and the school had long had the largest summer enrollment of any Texas institution save the flagship University of Texas[1] (Bledsoe 49–50). Mayo's graduates formed an important part of the professional class of East Texas in the first half of the twentieth century, and he was long remembered after his death for providing educational opportunities to thousands of ambitious rural students who would have otherwise been unable to attend college because of limited funds or inadequate previous schooling.

Mayo is a figure worth studying for several reasons. First, as the founder of a normal school, he represents a neglected part of the legacy in rhetoric and composition studies; normal school educators played an important role in the NCTE in the early twentieth century and actively contributed to discussions in the *English Journal*.[2] Not only did normal schools, or teacher-training colleges, descend from a different intellectual tradition than liberal arts colleges, their advocates explicitly defined themselves in opposition to liberal arts colleges, which were frequently perceived as part of a conservative and even antidemocratic educational establishment. Normal school educators held that schools must be accountable to the communities they served and that pedagogical practices must meet students' interests, needs, and abilities. Throughout the early twentieth century, English instructors at normal schools revolted against what they saw as the limitations of traditional university pedagogical practices, especially overreliance on textbooks and lectures. As scholars such as Kathryn Fitzgerald, Lucille Schultz, and Beth Ann Rothermel have recently shown, the normal school tradition generated marked differences in the English classroom.

Mayo's institution also served a constituency long overlooked in histories of rhetorical education: white, rural students, both male and female, of modest economic means. For these students, normal schools served a similar function as private liberal arts colleges did for African American students, providing them with a means of socioeconomic advancement and community pride. Mayo geared his curriculum toward his students' interests and needs, paying particular attention to how the school fit into the surrounding community. As an independent normal college, East Texas differed not only from private white liberal arts colleges and state universities in Texas and elsewhere but from other normal schools, especially state-sponsored ones in the East. As a Southerner, Mayo rejected traditional Northern teaching practices as represented by liberal arts colleges, and he tempered secular, Pestalozzian, Midwestern normal college practices with his own brand of Southern Methodist rigor for his East Texas constituency. Despite his flaws and insistence on tight control, in thirty years he built East Texas into an important center of teacher education in the state. As such, he demonstrates the importance of looking to local historical and institutional contexts and material and personal influences on institutional practices in developing rhetorical histories.

Finally, Mayo complicates and challenges attempts to locate pedagogical practices within a discrete ideological or epistemological schema and to connect pedagogical practices to political ideologies or ends. For example, Susan

Kates makes an important and necessary distinction between *mainstream* and *activist* pedagogy in order to show the historical diversity of rhetorical instruction in American colleges. To the extent that Mayo ignored the "politics, ethics, and social organization implicit in language acquisition," devalued "alternative modes of communication," and paid little attention "to racism, sexism, and economic exploitation" (Kates 9–10), his instruction can be considered mainstream. Like Fred Newton Scott and many other progressive-era educators, he shared a universalist, assimilationist view of linguistic standards. To the extent, however, that he "[made] civic issues a theme in the rhetoric classroom . . . emphasize[d] the responsibility of community service as part of the writing and speaking curriculum" (Kates xi) and sought to assist marginalized students by challenging what he saw as the elitist hegemony of liberal arts colleges, his instruction was activist. Mayo did not simply expect his students "to assimilate, as best they could, into mainstream academic culture" (Kates 9) but sought to respectfully provide his students with the tools to succeed in that culture, even as he tried to change it. Though he served a white audience in a segregated state, his rhetoric was "embodied" in his local community as surely as that of African American activist educator Hallie Quinn Brown at Wilberforce University in Ohio. Moreover, he made few gender distinctions in his pedagogy: women took the same classes, participated in oratory and debate, and even delivered commencement speeches. In teaching speaking and writing, Mayo aimed at promoting creative production, even as he stressed the formalistic, prescriptive qualities of language pedagogy often associated with current-traditional practice.

In this chapter, I examine the rhetorical training of students at East Texas Normal College, which I set in the context of Mayo's life, turn-of-the-twentieth-century rural Texas, and the greater history of the normal school movement. I trace Mayo's educational influences and identify four key features of his teaching: his attention to local community needs; his emphasis on oral production in the training of future teachers; his insistence on "learning by doing," which foreshadowed contemporary approaches to teaching writing; and his almost obsessive focus on prescriptive grammar. I argue that the experiences of students at East Texas and other normal colleges challenge many of the generalizations made about late-nineteenth- and early-twentieth-century rhetorical practices in American colleges. Mayo's students experienced a rich rhetorical environment in which reading, writing, and speaking were well integrated; participation in public discourse was encouraged; public speaking and oratory were an essential part of the curriculum and campus life; and textbooks had only a peripheral role in instruction. While faculty at East Texas maintained a rigorous, disciplinary approach to instruction in the "fundamentals" of English that in some ways resembles what has come to be called current-traditional practice, they also sought to spark student interest and achievement. Unlike students elsewhere who complained of the dullness of their daily themes, East Texas students appreciated the standards their instructors encouraged, feeling that it prepared them for professional and civic life.

Mayo's complex pedagogy speaks to challenges contemporary rhetoric and composition instructors still face in finding a balance between inculcating culture and critiquing it, between nurturing students and challenging them, between promoting the love of learning with preparing students for careers. Indeed, East Texas had much in common with today's community colleges and regional and commuter universities; the school catered to students with a wide range of academic preparation, many of whom were the first in their family to attend college, worked to pay for their education, and saw college largely as a means to socioeconomic advancement. Any attempt to develop a critical or responsive pedagogy must take such students into account—even if their goals or vision of education appear to conflict with our own.

The Alternative Pedagogy of Normal Schools

Although it is convenient to speak of the normal school "movement," normal schools in America varied greatly in institutional mission, educational practices, and student makeup. In the East, where the influences of Protestant churches and liberal arts colleges were strongest, normal schools tended to emphasize moral uplift and the training of primary schoolteachers. In the West, where educational infrastructures were not yet highly developed, normal schools, both public and independent, developed as alternatives to private liberal arts colleges and as precursors to community colleges and comprehensive regional universities (Harper; Herbst). Western normal schools, which were frequently founded as coeducational, also tended to make fewer gender distinctions than Eastern normal schools or even Western state colleges, though treatment of women varied from school to school. In the populist, frontier environment of the nineteenth- and early-twentieth-century American West, normal schools held great appeal, providing outlets for entrepreneurial, iconoclastic, even messianic educators, such as Mayo, who were antipathetic toward what they regarded as the elitism and outdated practices of liberal arts colleges. At their most conventional, normal schools reified class and gender boundaries and barriers, even as they provided educational and professional opportunities to new constituencies of students. At their most progressive, they promoted gender equality, class mobility, and educational opportunity on a wide scale (Fitzgerald, "Redis-covered"; Harper; Herbst; Ogren).

The founding of the first school in America devoted primarily to teacher education is generally credited to Samuel Read Hall, who in 1823 started a private normal academy in his home in Concord, Vermont. Though Hall would become widely known for his *Lectures on School-Keeping*, it was with the establishment of the first state normal school in Lexington, Massachu-setts, in 1839 that normal schools began to become a mass phenomenon (Herbst; Salvatori; Lucas). The term *normal school* derives from the French *ecole normale*, a model or ideal school for the training of teachers. Charles Brooks, who had studied the French and Prussian educational systems and who along with Horace Mann campaigned for the establishment of normal schools in Massachusetts, is generally credited with popularizing the term in America. Strongly influenced by Rousseauean Romanticism and Enlightenment philosophy, which emphasized nurture over nature, and the burgeoning fields of developmental psychology and sociology, early European normal school educators sought to develop a naturalistic, holistic method of education that would appeal to children's abilities and interests, develop well-adjusted citizens and human beings, and transform society.

Perhaps the most influential was the Swiss educator Johann Heinrich Pestalozzi (1746–1827): "I wish to wrest education from the outworn order of doddering old teaching hacks as well as from the new-fangled order of cheap, artificial teaching tricks, and entrust it to the eternal powers of nature herself" (qtd. in Silber 136). Pestalozzi would likely have gotten along with Peter Elbow: "The first instruction of the child should never be the business of the *head* or of the *reason*; it should always be the business of the senses, of the *heart*, of the *mother*" (294). To teach children writing, he exchanged pen and paper for slates, which allowed "repeated corrections and improve-ment" (Silber 126). Instead of instructing through textbooks, rote memo-rization, and recitations, Pestalozzi stressed spontaneity, self-development, and learning modeled after children's natural cognitive development. He also emphasized the sacredness and dignity of each student, stressing that love was the foundation of all educational enterprise (Kilpatrick, *Educa-tion of Man* viii). At the heart of his system was the concept of *anschauung*, or sense impression, knowledge obtained directly through observation, experimentation, and experience.[3] Instruction, he argued, should move from the concrete to the abstract, beginning with what students already know, rather than starting with dry lectures and abstract concepts foreign to their experience:

What are words when the heart bows itself in dark despair, or rises in highest rapture to the clouds? . . . Either we lead the children through knowledge of names to that of things, or else through knowledge of things to that of names. The second method is mine. I wish always to let sense-impression precede the word, and definite knowledge the judgement. (Pestalozzi 267, 325)

After Pestalozzi, wrote an American normal school advocate, teaching "was to be no longer a matter of assigning pages of printed material to be memorized, and then of holding the open book while the child repeated the lesson" (Harper 17–18). Pestalozzi influenced numerous other nineteenth-century European educators, including Johann Friedrich Herbart, Friedrich Froebel, and Maria Montessori.

Normal Schools and the American Ideal

The theories of Pestalozzi and his followers found fertile ground in America, where education had long been seen as both a moral and economic force. To the Protestant mind, education not only protected one from sin—"It being one chiefe project of that ould deluder, Satan, to keepe men from the knowledge of the Scriptures," began a 1647 Massachusetts public-education law (Shurtleff 203)—it led to social and economic success. In the new republic, the normal school movement early took a strong populist turn. Speaking for the establishment of a normal school in Plymouth, Massachusetts, in 1838, John Quincy Adams challenged his audience.

We see monarchs expending vast sums, establishing normal schools thruout their realms, and sparing no pains to convey knowledge and efficiency to all the children of their poorest subjects. Shall we be outdone by kings? Shall monarchies steal a march on republics in the patronage of that education on which a republic is based? (qtd. in Harper 23–24)

Wherever they were established, American normal schools shared a fundamental set of assumptions that set them apart from private liberal arts colleges and, to a lesser extent, large public research institutions. They emphasized active student participation and hands-on learning by doing. Tuition and other expenses were intentionally kept low. Though schools included and even promoted traditional liberal arts subjects, they stressed practical and professional training within a flexible, changing curriculum. "[N]o method can be 'Normal,'" declared Alfred Holbrook, president of National Normal University in Ohio, "which is not making improvements upon itself continually" (*Reminiscences* 318).

Founded with the ideal of fostering democracy through universal education, normal schools also paid close attention to the needs of the communities they ultimately served—the public and public schools. As Albert Storms observed at the National Education Association's annual convention in 1907:

> It is still true and should be increasingly true that the little red school-house on the hill is the temple of liberty. . . . There is no civic duty of an educated and patriotic citizen that should stand superior to this of assisting to foster the common school. There needs to be a civic conscience about adequate taxation for this purpose and the encouragement of a high order of character and ability to enter the teaching profession, especially in the common schools. . . . Education must not be for the few but the many. (65)

Normals further stressed the importance of engaging student interest and allowing the individual student to advance at his or her own pace. Though at least one anonymous normal school English instructor preferred the "heartless, cold-blooded way of the liberal arts college" (qtd. in Meadows 43), most subscribed to the ethos of developing curricula that addressed their students' needs. These included a focus on the "fundamentals" of English (i.e., prescriptive grammar), consideration of the wide-ranging educational preparation and abilities of students, an interactive approach to learning, and development of coursework that would be of particular use to future teachers.

The emphasis on pedagogy was a key point of contention between normal schools and older, more established liberal arts colleges, whose faculty frequently maintained that disciplinary knowledge of a subject was sufficient to teach it.[4] "How often we learn of an A.M. or a Ph.D. coming among us from some great northern university," wrote Mayo, "taking a place in a southern school, and being sent back in the course of a few months, as a man knowing plenty of Latin, Greek, and Hebrew, but having no power whatever of getting others to know it" (East Texas Normal College, *Catalogue 1896* 65–66). Throughout the last half of the nineteenth century—and into the twentieth—many traditional colleges resisted or only reluctantly incorporated new fields of professional, technical, and scientific training (Pangburn; Kynell). Weighing in for the *Atlantic Monthly* in 1869 on the future of the "new education," Harvard President Charles Eliot allowed that while "polytechnic" schools might serve a useful function in training the "manufacturer, engineer, or teacher," their subjects had no place in a *true* college. "Just as far as the spirit proper to a polytechnic school pervades a college, just so far that college falls below its true ideal. The practical spirit and the literary or scholastic spirits are both good, but they are incompatible. If commingled, they are both spoiled" (Eliot 214–15). Some twenty years later, he still hadn't changed his mind: "The faculty [of Harvard]," he wrote in 1891, "in common with most teachers in England and the United States, feel but slight interest or confidence in what is ordinarily called pedagogy; but they believe that skillful teachers should be able to give some account of their methods for the benefit of those who are beginning to teach" (United States Bureau of Education, *Report of the Commissioner 1890–91* 1076).

If normal school educators felt slighted by established colleges, they also felt superior to them. Said Mayo:

> There is a fundamental difference between a school of instruction and a school of education. The "lecture system" of universities is a system of instruction. The pupil sits at the feet of the instructor and accepts without thought or question, everything that is said. He takes notes on the lecture, then goes to his room and memorizes them. He learns to follow, not to lead; to accept the opinions of others, not to think for himself; to read the results of their investigations, not to make these investigations for himself. Such is not education. It has been designated cramming. It stupefies rather than develops power. The normal college reverses this plan. (East Texas Normal College, *Catalogue 1896* 71)

Defining their mission in contrast to that of liberal arts colleges, normal school instructors commonly described themselves in proletarian terms, taking great pride in rolling up their sleeves and getting down to what they saw as the true business of education. "The university professor may have his chair and from it satisfy a well-established demand," said one state school superintendent in 1882, "but the normal-school professor must live in his saddle in the field and on the march" (qtd. in Harper 116). Though some of these distinctions were undoubtedly self-serving or exaggerated, they were honestly felt. Evert Mordecai Clark, a graduate of National Normal University (and later chair of the Department of English at the University of Texas), took several leaves from teaching at East Texas Normal while studying for his Ph.D. at Yale. Though he appreciated his graduate education, he found it somewhat wanting: "Yale professors," he wrote in 1905, "are learned men and yet—shall I say it?—men among whom real teachers are rare enough. At least that is the way it looks to a Normalite. . . . [T]he instructor does the work and gives you the results, and then it falls upon you to hold it in memory. The normal teacher tells you where the jewel is to be found and bids you 'dig' for it. . . . I say this, not in criticism of Yale, but because I am proud of the practical pedagogics in the East Texas Normal College" (qtd. in Goodwin 119).

Normal schools served as a powerful democratizing force in American education. Indeed, Kathryn Fitzgerald notes, in the late nineteenth and early twentieth centuries, normal schools "democratized and expanded educational and vocational opportunity far beyond any existing institution, in terms of both class and gender" ("Rediscovered" 228). By 1905, enrollment in the nation's 89 private and 179 public normal schools totaled 65,300, over five and a half times the 11,687 students enrolled in teacher-training courses in other universities and colleges, and more than twice the 28,340 students enrolled in teacher-training courses in all other institutions combined, including public and private high schools (United States Bureau of Education, *Report of the Commissioner 1905* xliv).

One of the most important services normal schools performed was offering summer sessions. These were valuable not only to rural and working students seeking to become teachers but working teachers seeking advanced teaching certificates and degrees. In 1925, Joseph Emory Avent, as part of a study of summer sessions in state teachers colleges, surveyed 2,184 students at five large programs. Summer students, he found, tended to come from large, rural families of modest economic means and were poorer than the general population. Almost two-thirds (62.8%) of summer students were the children of farmers, 39% were supporting one or more dependents, and 81.8% were paying their way through teaching or other work (Avent 173, 388). These were exactly the students Mayo had in mind when he founded his college and who eventually flocked to his program.

Mayo's Path to East Texas

Although many states, especially in the Midwest, developed public normal colleges, private normal schools, often founded by maverick educators with a fervent faith in the movement, played an important role. Mayo descended from a line of such educators. His alma mater, Central Normal College in Danville, Indiana, was founded in 1876 by William F. Harper and Warren Darst, alumni of Alfred Holbrook's National Normal University in Lebanon, Ohio, a model for a number of normal colleges. An influential normal school advocate and a prolific author of books on both English grammar and normal school instruction, Holbrook embodied the fault lines of class and changing socioeconomic conditions underlying the tensions between liberal arts colleges and normal schools. Holbrook's father, an entrepreneurial educator and engineer, was an 1814 graduate of Yale but had little regard for either the school or liberal arts colleges in general, which he regarded as stultifying and backwards, especially for their refusal to teach modern science. An advocate of manual education, he insisted his son could learn more—and more quickly—from employment and self-study than he could from college. Like his "iconoclastic" father, Alfred, who taught himself Greek while working in his father's shop, had little awe for the methods of instruction and discipline in traditional colleges.

> The world moves . . . even though the only places through which the turbid stream of the dark ages still flows are the most highly endowed and the most aristocratic of the colleges. It may be charged, as it has often been, that I am hostile to colleges and to college men. Not in the least. As was my father before, I am bitterly opposed to the evil practices, the antiquated usages, the repressive influences of the colleges, as many of them are yet conducted. (*Reminiscences* 79)

Holbrook indeed had no fault with college men. His maternal grandfather, a Methodist minister, was an intimate of many Yale faculty members and administrators, and Holbrook fondly recalled dinners with those "worthy and dignified gentlemen" at his grandfather's house (*Reminiscences* 61). But he was especially troubled by what he saw as the ill-treatment of students in traditional colleges, and he rejected the "assumption . . . of most college men . . . that boys and young men are necessarily sensual, and prefer idleness and self-indulgence to hard work and determined effort and self-denial" (*Reminiscences* 328). Early on in his teaching career, he concluded that if his students were bored or frustrated, it was his own fault, not theirs. He promoted a dynamic, practical, democratic education that responded to changing needs of students and relied on classroom-tested methods rather than tradition: "[M]echanical training . . . may answer for the schools of absolute Governments like Germany, or possibly for the autocratic management of the charity schools of England, but is utterly abortive with the free spirits of Young America" (*Reminiscences* 296–97). He further promoted the use of multiple textbooks in class instead of one, "to break up the inordinate respect for the authority of the text-book, and to incite more extended and thorough research in study" (*Reminiscences* 318). Mayo would later adopt this approach at East Texas: "The more texts investigated by a class, on a subject, the more interesting and profitable is its discussion" (*Catalogue 1896* 52).

Holbrook's grammar instruction relied heavily on classroom drills but with the aim of instructing students in as organic and enjoyable a manner as possible. He "reject[ed] philological discussion" (*English Grammar* iii), considering it more important, for example, that students could identify parts of speech from sentences than give rote definitions of parts of speech. His textbooks were notable for including scripted examples of classroom lessons driven by student participation, which teachers could use as models. His methods included teaching grammatical terms and usage by parsing examples of everyday speech; relying on current usage rather than "attempting to dictate what usage *ought to be*, as most grammarians vainly assume to do" (*English Grammar* iii); and encouraging students to criticize and teach each other. "Without special care, on the part of the teacher, he will deprive the scholars of this privilege by doing too much of it himself" (*Normal* 102). From today's perspective, these are subtle differences, perhaps, but Holbrook believed they "converted the study of Grammar from a burdensome, hateful, useless process of memorizing definitions and rules, into an exciting and enthusiastic work of comprehending and applying principles in the correct use of the varying forms and arrangements of the English language" (*New English Grammar* iii). Mayo, who employed Holbrook's *English Grammar* at East Texas, likely agreed. Holbrook's reputation in normal circles and public schools was such that he was described by former *Texas School Journal* editor J. E. Rogers as a "grand old 'Prince of Grammarians'" (qtd. in East Texas Normal College, *Catalogue 1903* 50).

Holbrook's principles were enthusiastically taken up at Central Normal College. A popular school, at one time estimated to have graduated or taught one-third of all schoolteachers in Indiana (R. A. Brown, forward; Beeler and Chamberlain 117), Central Normal mixed explicitly Pestalozzian pedagogy with Midwestern pragmatism. "[Our] instruction is professional in tone, organic in character, and practical in results," said the 1878 catalogue (16). As students were expected to become teachers, the school emphasized a hands-on approach to learning, with students leading discussions and teaching lessons in many of their classes. Language instruction, which the school identified as grammar, rhetoric, Latin and Greek, composition, elocution, and especially debate (a required subject for all students each term), played a central role.

> We know of no other institution where pupils have so much drill in public speaking. The entire course is so conducted as to enable each individual pupil to express his own thoughts in concise and elegant language. Humdrumming over the rules of Grammar, memoriter[5] recitations of Latin and Greek, hateful essay-writing, stiff and formal delivery, listening or sleeping under the metaphysical lectures of Professors, committing Rhetorics to memory, are not permitted to profane a normal [school] recitation room, or the study room of a normal student. The *use* of lan-

guage is learned by *using* it, the rules of Grammar by their applications, composition by the expression of thought, and elocution by reading and speaking. Thus the student becomes master of *himself* and can *use* his knowledge. (*Catalogue 1878* 11–12)

Central Normal also prided itself on its gentle treatment of students and accessibility to all. Among the "fifteen reasons" it advertised for the school's success, it claimed:

2. The teachers work with an untiring zeal for the progress of each individual pupil.
3. The custom, so prevalent in many institutions, of "cutting" pupils in recitation for awkwardness or difference of opinion is not *tolerated* in this school.
4. Every pupil is made perfectly at home by the kindly, good-humored feeling which pervades the recitations and all the intercourse of the teachers with the students, and the students with each other.
5. No difference how poor a pupil, how backward in his studies or how uncouth in his manners, he finds himself just as much respected as the wealthiest Nabob, the wisest Solomon, or the most polished gentleman.
6. No pains have been spared to bring the expenses within the reach of the poorest. (*Catalogue 1878* 2)

In 1881, the *Indianapolis Daily Sentinel* published a long encomium on the college. Especially taken with the school's democratic system of governance, which was free of "those obnoxious rules and restraints enforced in most Colleges," its equal treatment of men and women, and its respect for its students, the reporter pronounced Central Normal "the most completely republican institution we have found in all our travels." Even accounting for a measure of boosterish overenthusiasm, his description of the school shows how thoroughly Pestalozzian ideals had taken root in Midwestern normal schools:

This so-called "Normal System of Teaching," is a grand innovation on what has heretofore been considered standard usage. Instead of making slaves of the scholars by making masters of their teachers, and leading the young mind up to a supposed infallibility, whose dogmas dare not be questioned, the new system unites the efforts of both on a rational plane. Here is a school in which the scholars are induced to educate each other, while the very competent tutors watch the proceeding, and only interfere after their limited resources are exhausted. Every student is thus made proud of his or her position in the school. Each one has a sacred individuality worth preserving. . . . It is not a stuffing school, in which young minds are being crammed with the pet notions of any text-book writers. ("Danville" 5)

Mayo was profoundly influenced by his experiences at Central Normal College and counted his instructors there as lifelong influences, especially President Franklin Adams, who taught English and pedagogy. He maintained close ties to the school as well as Holbrook's National Normal University and hired graduates from both institutions.[6] Mayo also adapted many of Central Normal's features to his own school, such as holding morning chapel exercises, accepting students at any time of the year, requiring each graduate to deliver an original oration at commencement, and maintaining a flexible curriculum. But perhaps the most important lesson he took away from Central Normal, which proudly advertised itself as "the School for the Poor as well as the Rich" (Parr 30), was the viability of establishing a college that would serve students of modest means. "Out of the depths of his own experience," wrote his brother Marion of his college days, "he knew how to sympathize with the young man or woman who was hungering and thirsting after knowledge, but thwarted and discouraged because of a lack of educational opportunity" (M. Mayo 166).

Mayo was not simply a product of his normal school training, of course. In his pedagogy, he was both a progressive Pestalozzian and a traditional son of the rural South. Born in 1861 in a small hill community in Eastern Kentucky, Mayo lived through a period of rapid change in American education, with his own schooling spanning the gamut of nineteenth-century traditions. Mayo's father was a Methodist minister, and Mayo grew up in a home of "almost puritanical strictness"; play was frowned upon, secular music forbidden, and dancing considered sinful. As Mayo's brother diplomatically put it, "Froebelian theories[7] had not yet penetrated into mountain culture" (M. Mayo 161). Public education, only marginally established in the state prior to the disrupting effects of the Civil War, was often haphazard; in rural districts especially, schools tended to be poorly equipped—Mayo's lacked even a blackboard—and in session no more than three or four months a year. The local teacher might be a hastily recruited young farmer or preacher with no professional training in either pedagogy or academic subjects. Reading and writing were taught by the A-B-C method[8] and the *McGuffey Readers*, and classroom discipline was enforced, literally, with a hickory stick. Upon taking his first teaching job in the common school in

Little Mud, Kentucky, fifteen-year-old Mayo was given a "formidable switch to be used in maintaining discipline," though he found that merely the silent threat of it hanging behind the door did the job (qtd. in M. Mayo 167).

After graduating from the local common school, Mayo attended Prestonsburg Seminary, a traditional liberal arts school, where he studied "history, geography, grammar, rhetoric, algebra, geometry, Latin, and natural philosophy—the popular studies of the nineteenth century academy," followed by the Cedar Bluff Academy in Virginia, where he won a medal for oratory (M. Mayo 161–65). By this time, he had begun teaching in local schools. He next entered Central Normal College, his interest sparked by an advertisement for the school. Though already a well-regarded local teacher, his decision to further his education at Central Normal caused a local stir. Upon seeing the trunkful of books he dragged home from school, a neighbor commented, "I reckon [William] has about all the books there is, ain't he?" (M. Mayo 166).

The pragmatism and pioneering spirit of Mayo's home community stayed with him and served him well. After graduating Central Normal in 1883, Mayo returned to Virginia as principal of Cedar Bluff Academy, where he had studied just a few years earlier. He initially planned to continue his studies at Indiana University. Hoping to finance his education, upon returning home to Kentucky for the summer in 1885, he entered into a logging venture with the county sheriff, Lindsay Clark, who had helped him obtain his first teaching job. The venture failed, however, wiping out his savings, and he decided to "go West" to seek his fortune. After teaching briefly in Denver, he found his way to East Texas, where some relatives had previously settled, and began shopping around for the opportunity to found a normal school. In 1886, he was hired to direct the local school in Pecan Gap. Three years later, he was hired as superintendent of the public school in nearby Cooper, where he convinced the trustees to allow him to open a normal college. Purchasing the local school building, he opened East Texas Normal College on September 2, 1889 (Goodwin 12).

While in Cooper, Mayo was introduced to Etta Booth, his future wife, who was visiting her sister, Mattie Booth Oliver, an instructor at the school. Mayo initially hired Etta Booth, who had studied at Vanderbilt and the Cincinnati Conservatory of Music, to teach music, elocution, Latin, and English. Etta Booth Mayo became a central figure in the early development of the school. In addition to teaching, nursing ill students and community members, campaigning for temperance and suffrage, and raising her own children (of whom five of eight survived to adulthood), she contributed substantially to the school's cultural life. She led several literary and musical societies. Her correspondence with the Women's Christian Temperance Union brought Carry Nation to campus (Linck and Linck 29). For many years, she took summer sabbaticals—often with the children in tow—to Cincinnati, Chicago, and New York to continue her musical studies, and she frequently attended conferences of the Music Teachers National Association (Goodwin 117). Through her contacts in the music world, she brought many nationally known performers to campus who otherwise might never have been seen in East Texas, including pianists William Sherwood, Edward Baxter Perry, Emil Liebling, and Martin Bruhl, tenor Enrico Palmetto, the Schumann Quintet, the Chicago Glee Club, and music and drama clubs from Harvard and Oxford (Linck and Linck 27–28).

Though East Texas Normal flourished in Cooper, the town eventually proved too small and provincial for the Mayos. The family was reported to have been shaken up by either a public lynching or a hanging visible from their residence at the school, and, in 1894, after the school building was destroyed by fire,[9] they moved to the new and growing town of Commerce, which promised financial support to purchase a plot of land and raise a new building.

Education for the Community

As Mayo saw it, one of the main goals of education was to create independent, thinking citizens. "Normal methods," he wrote in the college catalogue, do not make "the student a mere passive recipient for the learning of others, but [put] him to thinking and telling his thoughts for himself" (*Catalogue 1896* 62). He despised what he considered pretentious displays of knowledge—"Education does not consist in the mere accumulation of facts" (*Catalogue 1896* 72)—academic arrogance, and instructional methods that required students to passively sit in class and regurgitate their lecture notes or textbooks. "If [a student] has been permitted to 'parrot' from memory every recitation, as in far too many schools and colleges," Mayo wrote in the 1903 school catalogue, "constant efforts are made to restore supremacy to his thinking powers" (17). Mayo advocated student participation and active "learning by doing," replacing lectures with seminars and practicums. "[I]nstead of lecturing for [the student], put him to lecturing for you. . . . True, the teacher must direct the efforts of the pupil, but the classroom is the place for the pupil to learn how to use his own powers, and if the teacher usurps this, he is the meanest of tyrants—a tyrant over human souls" (*Catalogue 1896* 72).

Mayo called his approach "normalism." Though he never formally articulated his practice, it blended both the strict, disciplinary rigor and moral uplift of his early home life and education—"All play and no work makes Jack a numbskull and a parasite" (qtd. in Goodwin 162)—with the flexible pedagogical innovations of his normal school training, filtered through a distinctly American faith in rugged individualism, eclectic learning, and capitalistic enterprise. Said alumnus Claude Crawford, a widely published University of Southern California professor of education:

> Instead of putting the curriculum on the top of a flagpole and forcing his pupils to climb or go ignorant, he brought it down to earth where the ordinary boys and girls actually were. He had no false pride that sought to put the academic fences up too high to keep out the humbler and less brilliant students who wouldn't be a credit to the college. He taught calculus and spelling, trigonometry and penmanship, logic and typing, French and first aid, with no thought that a useless subject was more honorable than a useful one. In his efforts to give the elements of an education to the illiterates who came out of the woods and fields at the age of twenty, he did not sacrifice the needs of those who hoped to be scholars, authors, and scientists. (qtd. in Bledsoe 243)

Mayo did not envision the educated citizen as being above or removed from the rest of society. He did not make strong distinctions between vocational and liberal arts training, nor did he try to isolate the two from each other, as did Harvard president Charles Eliot. He did not try to "inoculate" his students from mass or popular culture, as did Harvard rhetoric professors Edward T. Channing or Adams Sherman Hill. He did not fear the "new biology" heralded by Darwinism, as did many religious Southern educators, nor suffer any modernist hand-wringing at the tremors of the new industrial age. Henry Adams, had he been a student at East Texas, would have been instructed to quit whining about dynamos and take a course in basic chemistry—or better yet, find an engine and take it apart to see how it worked. "Perhaps he didn't call it the project method, but he had the psychology of it just the same," said Crawford. "He would have been a good Gestaltist. . . . He believed in the whole method. He didn't care for the process of assembling the abstract fragments of learning. He wanted the concrete from the start" (qtd. in Bledsoe 243).

From the beginning, Mayo sought to make East Texas integral to the local community. He established ten-week terms, five a year, which accommodated the work schedules of rural students. He deferred room and board payments for the fall until after the harvest. He invited community members to college events and, in his school catalogue, annually thanked the residents of Commerce for their support and encouraged them to take part in the life of the school. "[V]isit us more often, and find out more about what we are doing. The growth and prosperity of the school is materially connected with the growth and prosperity of the town" (*Catalogue 1896* 75).

Mayo kept classes in session throughout the year and allowed students to enter or leave at any time without penalty. "If you can only spend a few weeks in school, come to the East Texas Normal College," he urged (*Catalogue 1903* 16). Even one term, he believed, would allow students to "improve as to earn money the more easily and come again" (*Catalogue 1896* 67). The short, nearly year-round terms epitomized Mayo's educational philosophy. First, they served a useful object lesson: "Teach the pupil to throw away three months per year in idle vacations and you teach him to throw away a third of his life. This no one has a right to do" (*Catalogue 1896* 61). Second, they advertised the efficiency of his school. He believed as much or more could be accomplished in ten weeks at his school, four hours a day, five days a week, than at campuses where, in his opinion, classes took weeks to gear up and months to wind down each semester. Finally, they served his students' needs. Mayo believed that overly long semesters and relaxed intervals between classes cheated students of both their time and money. His students appeared to agree. "Especially is this true of those of limited means," testified graduate W. H. Snow, "because there you are not compelled to drag along for months and months over a dry text-book until you are utterly disgusted with the subject, but you are allowed and encouraged to push your work and complete the subject as fast as your ability permits" (qtd. in East Texas Normal College, *Catalogue 1903* 48).

For those students who had to work to support themselves, the ability to come and go as they were able to attend enabled them to obtain an education at their own pace. A typical student experience was that of high school science teacher and guidance counselor Walter Nash. "With a little schooling during the winter months and some farming the rest of the time, I finally obtained my second grade certificate" (qtd. in Bledsoe sec. 2, 30). Many other students worked as teachers during the winter and attended school in the summer and early fall. Because Texas at the time certified teachers primarily by exam, it was not necessary to obtain a degree to begin teaching, especially at the primary level. "You would get a certificate to go out and start, with the thought of that you would come back in the summers to work," said Opal Williams. Opal Rice, for example, "went one winter, got out and taught, and went back every summer until she got her degree" (Williams qtd. in McCown 9). Although many students remained teachers—even though teaching paid poorly it was still "big money to them" at the time (McCown 20)—many also used teaching as a stepping stone to further educational work and careers in law, the ministry, business, and government.

Mayo took seriously his declaration in the school catalogue that "[a]ny person, of whatever age, wealth, or previous advantages" (*Catalogue 1903* 44) who desired to attend East Texas be able to do so. For those who had not had the "advantages of high school training" or felt their public-school training inadequate, he included a preparatory year covering the common school subjects: arithmetic, algebra, geometry, geography, Texas and U.S. history, civics, physiology, rhetoric, grammar and composition, and literature, as well as a miscellaneous program that included penmanship, spelling, parliamentary law, and debate. "Every person," he wrote, "whatever his vocation in life, ought to possess this amount of knowledge, in order that he may perform intelligently his part as an active American citizen" (*Catalogue 1903* 16). Mayo kept costs exceptionally low; in 1905, ten month's room, board, and tuition were only $110. He allowed a number of students to study with the promise—sealed with a handshake—that they would pay him back once they began working. He accepted payment in whatever form students or their families could manage—crops, livestock, building materials, or labor—and commonly extended credit until after the fall harvest. No one who wanted to attend was turned away for financial reasons. "If you had money, okay. If you didn't they'd take you in anyway," recalled one student in what was a common refrain (Jackson 6). Students were frequently employed on campus doing odd jobs, teaching, and, in at least one case, "taking care of Professor Mayo's unruly children" (qtd. in Massey 65). For cash-poor Texas farm families, such measures were invaluable. In Jackson Massey's 1928 survey of twenty Mayo-era alumni, only seven reported receiving financial support from their parents; the rest paid their way with work or loans from the school (64–66). Sam Rayburn, later speaker of the U.S. House of Representatives, swept out the dorms. "If it hadn't been for Mayo's college, his credit system, and his inspiration, I don't know where I'd be today," he wrote in 1960 (25).

Mayo's responsiveness to local conditions contributed greatly to the success of his school. Among civic-minded, rural Southern and Midwestern towns at the turn of the twentieth century, a local college was considered an important cultural and economic resource, as vital to their prestige and future growth as paved streets, a stone courthouse or library, or a railroad. Communities often supported schools through local bonds or grants of land or money and competed with each other for schools. For example, when Central Normal College moved from Lagoda, Indiana, where it was originally established, to Danville in 1878, local merchants were so incensed they refused to sell the wagon drivers food, and one landlord locked his door, forcing students to lower their trunks from their windows (Parr 10). After the fire at Cooper, Mayo's own move to Commerce was prompted in part by the town's financial incentives.

Just as communities competed for successful colleges, colleges competed for community support; those that ultimately survived established interdependent relationships with the communities they served. Without that support, it is unlikely that Mayo, who received no state tax dollars and who because of his policy of "never turn[ing] anyone aside" was often late in paying bills (Galyon 3), would have been able to keep the college going, especially in the competitive, frontier environment of East Texas. At one point, Henry T. Bridges, the president of struggling Henry College in nearby Campbell, about eight miles south of Commerce, began to blame Mayo for his school's ills. As Jackson Massey, who treated both schools in his history of education in Hunt County, described it: "The custom in those days was to give boys and girls credit on their board and tuition to solicit students for their school, and it seemed that the students that went to Mayo's school were better solicitors than those who went to Bridges' school, thereby causing the attendance of Henry College to fall off considerably" (57–58). In both the press and in his school catalogue, Bridges attacked Mayo as a predatory carpetbagger:

> Do not allow yourself to be caught by the glare and glitter of unwarranted assertions of so-called colleges. . . . Their only reality is on paper and in the fevered brain of some fanatic who has had a few months at a typical Western Blow Up, some great National Normal or Normal University and has come South to make his fortune and puff up the youth with the same kind of chaff. This year he is here with the greatest school on earth . . . next year, alas! he is gone, and the only thing left of his pomp and glory is the requiem of the winds, singing of lost time, money thrown away, and disappointed hopes. Young man, beware! (*Catalogue 1896* 8–9)

Mayo tried to answer the charges with a measured response, but Bridges took these as "insults to his southern dignity" (Massey 58). On the morning of August 24, 1896, Bridges drove to Commerce, accompanied by a student, whom he used to lure Mayo over by having the boy pretend to be a prospective student whose father was in the buggy (Goodwin 64). Pulling a gun on Mayo, Bridges then demanded he sign a written apology, which Mayo refused: "The clause, 'Professor Bridges is a perfect gentleman,' could not have been signed in the face of such conduct as was being exhibited," Mayo later wrote (qtd. in Massey 62). Accounts differ as to whether Bridges actually fired his pistol, but he repeatedly lashed Mayo with his whip at gunpoint until some of his students intervened. "Of course Mayo was helpless and took the whipping like a man" (Massey 59). The citizens of Commerce were outraged, but Mayo, after writing an article about the incident in the school's *Normal Guide*, decided to let the matter slide. Henry College, as Mayo likely expected, fizzled out of business a few years later.

Literary Societies, Oratory, and Debate

Mayo saw speaking and writing as equally important skills. To understand how Mayo attempted to integrate his pedagogical practices, therefore, it is essential to look beyond the English classroom. Under Mayo's direction, students at East Texas participated in a rich rhetorical environment, in which literature, drama, oratory, debate, and writing were woven into the daily fabric of campus life. As Ralph Goodwin notes in his history of the college, "In a private institution [such as Mayo's], there was no need at all for sharp divisions between curricular and extracurricular activities; the two areas simply merged" (99). In the earliest years of the school, Mayo and his wife, Etta Booth Mayo, organized readings of Shakespeare each Sunday. "Entire afternoons were given over to the discussions and interpretations of the various characters in the plays," recalled their daughter Gladys, a faculty member at the Juilliard School. "It was intensely interesting to note the developing confidence in the voices of those who, before coming to Commerce, were unacquainted with the works of the great English" (Mayo del Busto 176). On Sunday and Monday afternoons, faculty commonly held reading circles for students in the parlors of their homes (Goodwin 100). While still in Cooper, Mayo had established at least one literary society, and by 1894 the school had three—the Philomathean and Lightfoot for men, and the Amothenian for women—all of which remained active and popular throughout his tenure. As the college expanded, other societies were formed to meet students' interests in art, music, drama, teaching, religion, debate, and politics. Etta Mayo founded at least two societies, the Philharmonic, formed for the study of music and musical theory, and, in 1916, the Frances E. Willard Literary Society, devoted to promoting suffrage and women's rights.[10] In 1913, the school even established a chapter of the Intercollegiate Socialist Society, sponsored by the outspoken Reverend Morgan Smith (Goodwin 102–3), with Mayo's own son Marion serving as secretary.[11] The Classic-Scientific Society, made up largely of students from the classic and scientific tracks, was devoted to the "discovery and development of the writing and speaking ability of its members. It had as its objectives the development of poise, carriage, self-control before an audience, pleasing method of delivery, a clear enunciation, and a well modulated voice suited to the work in hand, and, in addition, experience in various types of writing" (Moore 183).

These literary societies were the center of student life on campus, sponsoring social, athletic, and service activities while remaining "largely devoted to 'literary' effort—to some form of writing, talking, and interpreting" (Moore 182). Each Friday or Saturday evening, students met to discuss literary and political topics, present orations, speeches, essays, poetry, and drama, and hold debates and parliamentary activities. Debate topics ranged from the whimsical ("Affirmed, That Moses was a greater leader than Napoleon") to the more commonly topical ("Affirmed, That we should have mutual ownership of all public utilities") and were regularly reported on in the *Commerce Journal*. At least once per year, the campus would host public debates and oratorical contests among the clubs, which attracted great local interest. James Marcus Bledsoe, a student under Mayo and later president of the college, was especially taken with the annual schoolwide debates and saw them as a stepping-stone to students' later success. "Such intellectual matching of facts, wit, humor, and brilliance of developed and poised personalities helped to mould the ideals, broaden the vision, deepen the determinations, and fire the ambitions of many young men who have since become stalwart leaders in the civic, educational, religious, medical, and legal affairs of state and nation" (107). Not only men but women, too, participated in debate and oratory and delivered commencement and alumni addresses. "[O]ur young ladies are wide awake to the situation of affairs and are grasping the opportunities before them," reported the *Commerce Journal* in 1904. "And from this observation we may say with Judge Gearhart, that 'The coming man may be a woman'" (qtd. in Goodwin 185).

It is difficult, of course, to determine the exact degree of gender equality at East Texas. Even at contemporary normal colleges that promoted women's public participation, institutional and societal gender barriers limited women's opportunities or complicated these efforts. But conditions at East Texas appear to have been quite equitable for the day. Mayo was educated in a proudly coeducational school, and his wife, Etta Booth, was a powerful and independent figure. Texas in the early twentieth century also had a strong tradition of activist women's clubs that promoted women's education and provided models for white Texas women of active, public citizenship. As Mayo founded his school at a time when Victorian models of gendered spheres were losing their hold on both educational institutions and society at large, he and his students did not have to overcome the systemic divisions that schools founded a generation earlier had to negotiate. All of these influences likely combined to promote if not gender equality then at least a shared sense of intellectual life and perhaps opportunity.

Regardless of gender, for many students, especially those coming from small family farms, public-speaking activities represented an important transformation in their lives. Mayo, always seeking to build his students' skills and confidence in them, recognized that the ability to speak well in public was critical not only to their future professional lives but their personal development. Remembered Claude Crawford:

> For this reason he encouraged all of us to be active in the literary societies, debates, and oratorical sprees that he loved so well. How I thrilled at the hope of pleasing him with my profoundly sophomore oration on "The All Sufficiency of Nature!" Who wouldn't have hunted through the whole library for arguments on woman suffrage or compulsory education, if there were the slightest hope that he would be there when the debate came off? He knew very well that one of the best ways of helping a shy greenhorn to look the world squarely in the eye was to give him a chance to come to grips with that world in a situation where brains had a chance and where there was recognition for a job well done. (qtd. in Bledsoe 243)

As a normal school educator, Mayo was not alone in emphasizing public performance. While extracurricular activities, such as speech, drama, and debate, were also becoming common features at liberal arts colleges and state universities in the last quarter of the nineteenth century, at normal schools they were increasingly thought of as not merely extracurricular but part of basic teacher training. As normal school historian Charles A. Harper suggests, a teacher "who could 'read,' direct plays, lead singing, play a musical instrument, and the like, was in greater demand as a teacher than one who could do none of these things" (119). At a number of normal schools, the public nature of these activities was emphasized through the name they were given—"rhetoricals"—and they were often included as part of the required curriculum.

Building on his experiences at Central Normal College, Mayo used the concept of the rhetorical in establishing what he called a "miscellaneous" program, a series of required short courses and extracurricular activities in addition to regular coursework. These activities rotated throughout the year—a typical week's schedule might include a reading circle on contemporary or Southern authors, a seminar on Pestalozzi or Froebel, and a parliamentary session—but some form of debating or public speaking was always required. Mayo saw this work as a cornerstone of democratic education and felt that its neglect by other schools was a "great mistake":

> In our country, where every matter affecting the public is considered
> by a meeting of the people, no citizen ought to be without a knowledge
> of parliamentary usage and practice. . . . In all town meetings, conven-
> tions, literary and religious societies, debating clubs, etc., a knowledge
> of this subject is indispensable. (East Texas Normal College, *Catalogue
> 1903* 32)

Indeed, "so essential did [Mayo] consider it necessary to be able to appear
before an audience, free from embarrassment or apology, to discuss important questions in an effective and becoming manner" (Bledsoe 107), that for
many years students were required to write and deliver an original oration
at the end of each term. Mayo incorporated some of these in *College Orations*, a book of model declamations he published as a teaching guide, along
with a few "feeble efforts" from his own school days: "It will appear to the
matured mind that accuracy is sometimes sacrificed to oratorical effect; but
this is common with buoyant, hopeful youth, and is thought to be excus-
able" (2). In 1910, when the school at last grew too large to accommodate
everyone, Mayo reluctantly made commencement deliveries competitive
but still required that the orations be written (Goodwin 129).

Mayo and his instructors expected students to speak in unscripted settings as well. Recalled Sam Rayburn, "He encouraged class discussion and
debate. . . . And each of us, while we were talking, had to stay alert every
minute, because if we made one mistake another student would say, 'No,
you're not right,' and a debate would be under way again" (25). This lively
atmosphere seemed to pervade the campus. Two visiting students sitting
in on a literature course by English professor Bronly L. Phipps in 1904 were
thrilled by the animated discussion he sparked on a seemingly simple quote
from Tennyson. "We spent the hour on the question and left it undecided
. . . inasmuch as there were about as many answers as pupils in the room"
(qtd. in Goodwin 120–21). The emphasis on oral production remained
strong at East Texas, even after Mayo's death, grounded in the belief that
students—and future teachers—needed to be able "to get up and talk" in
public. Said English professor Mary Bowman, "I stressed oral English so
much over the years because I thought they'd talk much more than they'd
write" (8).

Mayo further emphasized public speaking by incorporating it into the
social life of the school and modeling performance for his students. A key
element in his pedagogy was to "draw his whole school daily into a unified
activity, designed to be both informational and inspirational" (M. Mayo
171). In his earliest teaching assignments, Mayo would begin the day with a

song followed by a brief prayer and end the day with a free-form question-and-answer period, in which he would quiz students on various subjects. "The zest and snappiness with which questions were propounded and answered were proof enough of the value of this activity. It closed the day with a happy, animated mood, and perhaps gave a convincing sense of the value of school life," remembered his brother (M. Mayo 167).

At East Texas, Mayo fostered community with daily chapel exercises each morning before class. A mix of church sermon, revival meeting, Chautauqua, morning assembly, and pep rally, chapel served as a "common meeting ground for the whole school," attended by both students and faculty. Although chapel was not compulsory, "[e]very one felt that he had really missed a great treat if he did not attend" (Moore 186). The morning usually began with an opening hymn, followed by a brief Bible reading or inspirational poem, a devotional prayer, and more song. These were often quite eclectic: "patriotic songs, national songs of other lands, fine old southern melodies, war songs, sea songs, airs from operas, well-known semi-popular songs, and others which the students loved to sing" (Moore 187). The main program of the day was often a surprise, ranging from lectures by Mayo, East Texas faculty, or visiting speakers to visits by successful alumni offering "advice and encouragement to the students who were struggling to get an education" to performances by itinerant entertainers, including magicians, actors, and ventriloquists (Moore 186). Most commonly, however, Mayo would give an inspiring talk, which was always popular. Recalled alumnus W. A. Jackson, "[T]he students especially didn't want to miss chapel when Mr. Mayo conducted it" (Jackson 16).

Many of Mayo's students later testified that chapel was one of the highlights of their educational experience and a key element in encouraging and inspiring them to achievement (Moore; Bledsoe; Massey; Goodwin). Walter Lee Tittle later became a lawyer and Methodist minister:

> Mayo's spirit convinced me that I could get an education. Up to this time it had never occurred to me that it was possible. . . . His consuming passion to have us succeed called into play every power of his being that he might arouse within us the 'will to win' and the spirit 'to carry on.' . . . [I]f he had never appeared in the classroom, his chapel ministrations were enough to forever give him high rank in his chosen field, as well as a warm place in the hearts of thousands who drank in his every word, and became partakers of his conquering spirit. (qtd. in Bledsoe 266)

James Marcus Bledsoe also found encouragement and inspiration in Mayo's words: "Many a time have I filed out of the Chapel Hall, after listening to one of these masterful addresses of Mayo, boiling over with enthusiasm and determination . . . with a feeling that there was absolutely nothing impossible for me to attempt and accomplish, and no high or honorable position beyond my power or merit to attain," he recalled in 1946 (67).

Learning by Doing

As part of his emphasis on learning through practical experience, Mayo eschewed textbooks to teach writing, preferring to use model orations on cultural and political topics. This is an important point for historiographical inquiry, as historians of rhetoric and composition have often looked to textbooks as touchstones for pedagogical practice (Connors, *Composition-Rhetoric*; Berlin, *Rhetoric, Writing*; Kitzhaber). Yet as scholars have recently shown, textbooks do not always accurately reflect or represent classroom activity and are probably most limited in "reveal[ing] the thinking of teachers" (Fitzgerald, "Rediscovered" 244). Progressive-minded teachers in the normal school movement were also troubled by textbooks. On the one hand, the spread of universal primary and secondary education and the explosion of teachers colleges in the late nineteenth century created a demand for age-, grade-, and community-appropriate textbooks, especially in regions in which books of any sort were often scarce. At the same time, instructors objected to the drill-and-grill methods and the one-size-fits-all approach to reading and writing that textbooks engendered. Educational leaders in particular were often ambivalent or hostile to the reliance on textbooks to teach English. "Most of our teachers college teachers, consciously or unconsciously, have become victims of the textbook writers," Thomas Alexander, Columbia Teachers College professor, told his graduate students in 1928 (qtd. in Meadows 27). In rural schools especially, instructors were wary of what they saw as a distinct urban bias. Asked by Harcourt Brace to review a proposed textbook for Texas, Mary Bowman "blasted them sky high":

> You can't possibly mean you considered putting this textbook up in Texas. It reminds me of the *New Yorker*'s map of the United States. There is nothing in this book that shows the authors know there is anything south and west of St. Louis. How do you expect to sell it out in this country if you deny its existence? (Bowman 16)

In his pedagogical guide for teachers in rural schools, *English in the Country School*, Walter Barnes not only takes this bias as a given but sees it as contributing to the rural brain drain. "It has often been pointed out in the last few years that the text-books used in country schools are full of material for city children, thus unconsciously but forcibly directing the mind of country boys and girls away from the farm to urban life" (15).

I find little evidence linking the choice of textbooks chosen by normal colleges to Berlin's traditional rhetorical taxonomy. First, no one textbook dominated normal school curricula. Leon Meadows's 1928 survey of sixty-eight state teachers colleges in the United States found them using thirty-one different rhetoric and composition textbooks. Of the pervasive "big four" authors cited by Kitzhaber,[12] only one, Barrett Wendell, makes the list. Furthermore, normal colleges in the early twentieth century tended to use textbooks primarily as usage guides rather than writing guides. Although the typical textbook devoted 51% of its content to the four "modes" of writing (narration, description, exposition, and argument), instructors devoted only 23% of their page assignments to these sections, preferring to use the textbook as a reference for grammar, usage, and mechanics. Even in this regard, textbooks were often considered inadequate, and 87% of schools supplemented them with handbooks, grammar drills, newspapers, literature, and other texts. It is impossible to tell how much of overall class time was devoted to grammar, but it was clearly an important subject. Ninety percent of term exams covered the "fundamentals—words, sentences, paragraphs, letter-writing, punctuation, grammar, and the 'common errors'" (Meadows 27–35). At the same time, instructors placed great emphasis on the use of outside readings to illustrate lectures, model writing assignments, and inspire classroom discussion. Eighty-two percent of schools required outside reading material for students in composition, such as novels, essays, nonfiction, short stories, poetry, and drama, commonly totaling several hundred pages per semester. Instructors assigned articles from seventy-one different periodicals, most commonly the *Literary Digest*, *School Facts*, *Current History*, the *New Republic*, the *Bookman*, and *National Geographic*. Also popular was a wide range of scholarly journals in English, speech, and education, suggesting the special orientation of teachers colleges (30–35).

Invention and Experience in Normal School Composition

Although argumentative writing was only one of the modes instructors taught, through the first part of the twentieth century, English teachers at many colleges and high schools were increasingly assigning arguments that were rhetorically situated, addressing narrow, contemporary, local topics that in many ways resemble the argument-based, rhetorically situated assignments of contemporary practice. Indeed, in the first two decades of the twentieth century, writing instructors rebelled against what they perceived as the reductive rhetoric and writing instruction of previous generations. By the time Adams Sherman Hill began establishing the new composition program at Harvard in the early 1870s,[13] students elsewhere were already grumbling about the tedious rhetorical instruction they were receiving. As part of his 1928 study, Meadows interviewed pre-1875 graduates of sixteen state normal schools about the composition instruction they had received in college. Their answers almost unanimously reveal a rule-based, philologically oriented system in which actual writing took a backseat to rote memorization.

- "We stressed grammar more than we did writing compositions."
- "Among other things, I was required to analyze, parse, and diagram the whole of *Paradise Lost*. Our compositions were usually on abstract subjects that we knew little about."
- "My teacher was more particular about the form than about the thought."
- "We were required to memorize the rules of the textbook and illustrate these rules in writing."
- "The course in rhetoric was really a course in grammar."
- "We paid little or no attention to the actual practice of writing in the true sense."
- "We wrote little that was of interest to the students or to anyone else."
- "Most of the compositions were dry and insipid."
- "We were seldom given the privilege of writing on subjects that we knew most about." (Meadows 7–8)

At the same time these students were in school, even grammarians were complaining about reductive, rule-obsessed writing instruction. Said textbook author Simon Kerl in 1869:

[I]t is absurd to suppose that the teaching of a little syntax can develop sufficient ability in regard to either language or thought. Yet in most of our schools the direct study of the English language is confined almost entirely to the study of English grammar; and because this science fails to make able speakers and writers, it is severely but unjustly denounced. Analysis is very different from invention; and to know always promptly what should be said is of much greater importance than to know how to say it correctly. . . . I have not given every conceivable variety of error in style, simply because it does not seem necessary that a person should pass through every contagious disease of human nature before he can enjoy good health. There are many errors presented in books, that well-bred children would probably never think of, did they not first see them in their lessons. It seems better to teach style directly by presenting good models, than indirectly by showing how we must avoid bad specimens. (3–4)

Like Kerl, many normal school rhetoric and writing instructors in the early twentieth century consciously rejected what they saw as the reductive formalism of the past, seeking instead to encourage naturalness in expression. "All teachers of English, as well as school executives, are awakening to a realization that the English language can no longer be taught in the traditional way, which gives the student a knowledge of the grammar and the rhetorical principles of the language . . . but leaves him without the power to utilize for social purposes any knowledge he may have," wrote Elizabeth Baker, a longtime Dallas high school teacher and summer faculty member at George Peabody College for Teachers (9–10). Walter Barnes was even more emphatic.

The one who uses natural English does not say "quantities of persons" instead of "lots of people," or "to whom are you talking"? instead of "who (or "whom) are you talking to"? . . . Certainly of all the habits of speech and writing the use of stiff, awkward, half-erudite pretentious, elegant English is the most contemptible. (218–19)

Students before 1875 were asked to write—on the few occasions they were asked to write—on generic topics such as love, courage, sincerity, and sin. Their textbooks suggested such examples as "Submission to Teachers," Resignation under Affliction," and "A Pleasing Disposition." "Practically all the subjects [were] abstract," notes Meadows, "as opposed to the more concrete and practical subjects of today." Rejecting scholars of the previous century, such as Adams Sherman Hill, who "stressed the proper choice and right use of words," contemporary normal school instructors put greater stress "upon ideas and the opportunities for securing new ideas" (Meadows 10–13)—in other words, invention.

The idea of writing as a process had not yet been fully articulated, of course. Instructors still felt that the starting point was for students to have "something to say," but they also felt that their job was to help students *find* something to say. They did so with methods that would not be out of place today: model examples taken from contemporary published writing, revision with attention to rhetorical concerns, peer review, and classroom feedback. These methods even filtered up to state educational agencies. Declared the Texas Department of Education in 1932:

> [I]t is during the process of revision that the pupil learns to apply what he has been taught about the art of writing. Furthermore, teaching a pupil to criticise his own work is of more educational importance than any amount of teacher criticism. Indeed, the greatest help we can be to pupils is to teach them to help themselves. (Lunday 38)

In 1925, at the NCTE meeting in Indianapolis, Dora Smith outlined the new direction composition instructors were taking: "Personal topics are better than impersonal; reality is an improvement on imagination; the immediate experience is superior to the recollected one" (qtd. in Meadows 52). Assigned themes now reflected topics closer to home, often based on student interests: "A Fall Fad," "A Shattered High School Ideal," "Seen on the Bus (or Train)," "Those Shower Baths," "Tractor Plowing," "Sensational Fiction," and "Identifying a Breed of Stock." Other popular assignments included editorials, essays modeled after magazine articles, book reviews, and research papers assigned by other departments (Meadows 52–53).

One of the most exciting and "extensively used" new development in normal schools was the project theme, which developed out of the project method, a "wholehearted purposeful activity proceeding in a social environment" (Kilpatrick, *Project Method* 4). Based upon the normal school ideal of instructing through object lessons and learning by doing, the goal of the project method was to have students engage in a real-world, experiential, knowledge-creating process that would have value outside the classroom. Proponents saw such activity as helping to develop thoughtful citizens who could exercise their own judgment rather than passively follow "plans handed down to them from above. . . . As the purposeful act is thus the typical unit of the worthy life in a democratic society, so also should it be made the typical unit of school procedure," declared progressive educator William Kilpatrick in a popular guide to the method (*Project Method* 6).[14] In their methodology and pedagogical intent, project themes closely resemble the rhetorically situated proposal arguments found in contemporary college rhetorics. "The pupils face a situation, form a purpose, lay plans for executing that purpose, carry out their plans with tongue or pen, and finally judge their own performance. Thus the pupils are the chief actors: they will, they choose, they judge, at every step in the process" (Hatfield 607). Typical subjects included "Preparation for helping junior high school pupils learn to debate," "Why all farmers in North Carolina should grow pecans," "Why students fail in college," and "Suggestions for beautifying our campus." The project theme also allowed for the critique of composition classes themselves: "The advisability of eliminating English I from the curriculum" and "The advisability of sectioning composition students according to their ability" (Meadows 56–57). Of course, projects were only as good as their teachers but the move from individual daily themes to topics of public concern was an important step in reintroducing rhetorical depth into writing assignments. Such assignments fit neatly into the curriculum at East Texas, where Mayo's learning-by-doing ethic struck a chord with students who had likely obtained much of their knowledge and skills through a similar process working on the family farm or doing chores at home. If a father wants to make a son a carpenter, noted Mayo, he does not sit him down and lecture him about carpentering; instead, "he gives him tools and puts him to work on a definite plan" (East Texas Normal College, *Catalogue 1896* 71–72).

Classroom Discipline

According to Mayo, education was within anyone's grasp; all it took was hard work, discipline, and practice. But hand-in-hand with his belief in experiential learning was his demand that students take responsibility for their learning. Despite his often progressive, student-attuned "Normalite" methods, Mayo insisted on strict discipline, both inside the classroom and out. The times seemed to demand it. At the turn of the twentieth century, Commerce, the home of the school, was a rough railroad and cotton-ginning frontier town, with "more saloons . . . than there were grocery and drygoods stores combined" (Bledsoe 46). Students on their way to pick up their mail in town frequently had to dodge drunks in the street, and alcohol was readily available to students, courtesy of a certain convivial but broken-down doctor willing to write questionable prescriptions (Button 41–42). For many families in East Texas, the decision whether to send a child to school was a difficult one; parents fretful over the corrupting influences of town life fully expected the college to provide a wholesome environment.[15] "Be assured that your sons and daughters will not be allowed, even if inclined so to do, to spend your hard earned money and their valuable time, in mischief and frivolity," Mayo promised them (East Texas Normal College, *Catalogue 1905* 38). At schools throughout the region, administrative officials commonly physically disciplined students. Jackson Massey's history of education in Hunt County, for example, is filled with the reminiscences of graduates who, years later, cheerily related the punishments they had received or witnessed as students and that they fully regarded as being well deserved.

> Professor Bridges [of Henry College] . . . was unusually successful by reason of his personal touch with the students and his sympathetic attitude

> toward them generally. . . . However, the occasion demanding, he was not
> averse to the use of drastic methods, because I recall having seen him on
> one occasion take a boy by the neck and kick him out of his office and
> down the stairway. The boy probably weighed about one hundred eighty
> pounds. It is probably unnecessary to say it, but it is a fact, he never had
> any trouble with that boy thereafter. (qtd. in Massey 178)

While Mayo was no fan of frontier justice, he was not afraid to resort to
physically disciplining a student when, as one student put it, "appealing to
their better self" failed (qtd. in Massey 73). One student had been habitu-
ally going through the dorms at night "whooping" and cursing; Mayo hid
in the stairwell and hit him with a rolled-up magazine (Jackson 8–9). On
another occasion, when two students who were disrupting chapel ignored
his request that they take their seats, Mayo "leaped down from the rostrum,
ran down the aisle, boxed their faces right and left until they were red as
beets, grabbed each one by the ear," and dragged them to the front. "Professor Mayo then returned to the rostrum and finished his morning lecture as
though nothing had happened" (Bledsoe 70).

In the classroom, Mayo insisted on nothing less than maximum effort.
He himself set the example for the campus, working harder than anyone else
at a variety of academic and physical tasks. Recalled Sam Rayburn, "Professor Mayo had the knack of creating the impression that any student was
almost a criminal if he wasted time" (25). "The drones and lazy ones soon
were forced out as the pace was set that they could not keep and there was
an atmosphere that was not congenial for them," recalled another student.
"Laziness was a crime," said another. "Nothing was much worse" (qtd. in
Massey 73). Mayo's methods worked, in part, because students were simply
used to hard work. Most had grown up on farms doing daily physical labor
as a matter of course; if anything, the classroom may have represented a
respite from the tasks of their home life. Indeed, to a rural student hungry to
learn and eager, like Mayo had been, to escape "the simple and monotonous
tasks of agricultural life" (M. Mayo 172), the opportunities to be found at
East Texas likely seemed a blessing. "[T]hey wanted that education and that
chance so bad," said English professor Mary Bowman (26). That Mayo's
students breezily dismissed his own temper may be partially because they
were, as alumnus and Regent Garland Button observed, simply "so appre-
ciative" of the opportunity to study that they did not pay much attention
to authority issues: "Our generation. . . . We were awestruck. Just setting
foot upon the campus of a college you immediately were awestruck. Oh, of
course, it didn't feel good when somebody worked you over, but we didn't
rebel against it. . . . Well, we were so thankful for being there" (13).

Grammar in the Classroom and Beyond

Mayo's discipline naturally extended to language instruction. As James Marcus Bledsoe recalled, he was "a stickler for pure and elegant English, both spoken and written, and his enthusiasm seemed to be contagious" (143). Although he emphasized prescription, he was more concerned with practical production than teaching grammar as an exercise in logic or mental faculty building. Like Alfred Holbrook, whose textbooks he employed, Mayo and his instructors took great pains to ensure the interest of students. Mayo himself wrote a manuscript for a practical grammar textbook, which was unfortunately lost in one of the school's early fires. Other English instructors at East Texas were also inspired to generate classroom materials that would spark student interest. Mary Bowman's dissatisfaction with literary readers led her to later help edit two popular works, *Adventures for Readers* and *Adventures in American Literature*, based on students' reading preferences. "I tried everything on them and if they didn't like it, no matter how much I liked it, it didn't go in. If methods of handling a piece of literature didn't work on the kids, out it went. Everything. They had passed on everything I ever published in that book and that's why it was good" (18). Henry Parker Eastman's well-received *Eastman's English Grammar* is admittedly a dry read today. But his goal was to create an easy-to-use reference work for students and teachers. "Many teachers complain, and justly too, we think, that for years the texts on English grammar have been so obscure in their terms, so promiscuous in their arrangement, and so incomplete in their development of the various subjects, that they have been very unsatisfactory to both teacher and pupil" (i).

In the days before the spread of radio, film, and television, little-traveled rural students had few opportunities to hear—and thus acquire—dialects outside of that of their home communities. As such, the language usage of faculty members and other educated citizens became a model for students. At East Texas, English was everyone's responsibility. Even an informal activity, such as men visiting the women's dormitory,[16] was an occasion for instruction.

> Sometimes Dean [of Women Julia] Hubbell would be there herself and, of course, that sent chills through you. . . . We would go in for some minor item like a dance permit or something and if you used the wrong grammar—which a great many of us boys, of course, did in those days—she'd correct you right on the spot. . . . I have one or two words in my vocabulary today that I have no trouble with because Dean Hubbell assisted me along that line. (18)

Debate over points of grammar and usage could often occupy the campus. When "discussion had gone on for some time as to the correct pronunciation of such words as 'revolution,' 'evolution,' 'solution,' [and] 'convolution,'" professor (and alumnus) Seth E. Green finally settled the matter "once and for all time" one morning at chapel.

> He left no doubt in any body's mind, and the dispute was completely ended, by his citation of specific and overwhelming evidence and proof from a number of the leading lexicographers of the English language. He went into the complete history and a scientific study of the English language, and left no one in doubt that the correct pronunciation of such words is to give the syllable "lu," the sound of long double-o . . . with the primary accent on the third syllable, and the secondary accent on the first. (Bledsoe 71)

Such a performance might strike us now as humorously pedantic. But that it was remembered in such detail by Bledsoe some thirty years later suggests that to both faculty and students, language mattered. Indeed, correct usage was a matter of no small pride. On one occasion, Mayo got into a disagreement at chapel with fellow grammarian and English professor Henry Parker Eastman. "As is generally true with the authors of textbooks, especially in English Grammar," Bledsoe dryly noted, "they differed on certain technical points of the subject." Convinced he had been insulted, Eastman exploded, "Don't accuse me of being ignorant; you may accuse me of anything else in the world, even of larceny or of dishonesty, but never accuse me of ignorance" (Bledsoe 71).

Mayo immediately gave in, and the two men laughed it off. But his passion for precision in language was deep seated. His brother Marion recalled:

> The language and manners of the home were largely those of the contemporary rural America. . . . Our vocabulary was no doubt limited; many words had deteriorated in form; many in use were said to be antiquated or obsolete in other sections; and common usage was so ungrammatical that anyone with scholarly inclinations had to learn his mother tongue all over again. Such an overhauling and reconstruction of one's speech requires a sound knowledge of the structure of our language. It becomes obvious, then, how it happened that W. L. Mayo came to appreciate so highly the value of the study of English grammar and why it was that he taught this subject with such earnestness and zeal. He felt this to be necessary to give his students a conscious command of correct English in spoken and written discourse. (162)

Liberal or progressive educators today, of course, would likely not suggest that a student's home dialect was "ungrammatical." Indeed, many scholars consider the disciplinary effects of instruction in standardized dialects an affront to students' dignity and agency. But I find little sense of shame in East Texas students' description of their language use before they came to college; rather, they express a matter-of-fact acknowledgment that they were often fairly well ignorant when they arrived. "For the most part, we were a bunch of poor boys and girls, mostly from farms, and badly in need of polish, social grace, self-confidence, and leadership attributes," said Claude Crawford (qtd. in Bledsoe 243).

If students found their language use lacking, they did not get the message that they were lacking themselves. In Mayo's era, it was not unusual for normal school faculty to feel that they had an even greater responsibility than the faculty at liberal arts colleges to teach the mechanics and structure of English—after all, it was their students who would be teaching in primary and secondary schools (Meadows; Jewett). And of course, the stakes were high. Standards for educated usage were much less forgiving than now, and the junior clerk or elementary schoolteacher who conflated *will* and *shall* or *who* and *whom* could find herself in trouble. Texas's 1896 state grammar exam, required of all those seeking teaching certificates, asked prospective teachers to parse and diagram sentences, identify the various classes of adjectives, clauses, and pronouns, and "state what principles of grammar are violated" in sentences such as "I will not be satisfied"; 50% of the grade for the composition exam, meanwhile, was for "correctness and propriety of language," punctuation, spelling, and capitalization ("State Examination Questions" 168). In 1918, responding to criticism from faculty that courses at North Texas State Normal College contained too much "technical" grammar, English chair (and soon-to-be state superintendent of public instruction) Annie Webb Blanton wrote, "If we are to prepare teachers for high schools, what will be the result, if we turn out teachers of English who do not know the ordinary constructions of the sentence."[17]

Mayo encouraged both student and faculty alike to "develop and improve their ability and skill in the use of better language" (Bledsoe 143). "Every lesson learned in the school is more or less a lesson in English," he said (East Texas Normal College, *Catalogue 1899* 64). In introducing his students to a wider world than could be found on the farm, however, Mayo did not disparage rural life or values. He could be found performing hard manual labor as often as he could be found walking across campus with a book in his hands. Instructors at the school lived in the same small community as the students, often in the college dormitory, and commonly came from normal school backgrounds themselves. Indeed, those who could not adjust to small-town life or rural values sometimes had trouble fitting in. One short-lived German professor with "strong-minded European attitudes toward teaching" found himself castigated in the local newspaper: "The Professor, as every other German, has great contempt for America and American ways" (Goodwin 115). Such close community attention, of course, has the potential for creating conformity. But the teachers at East Texas were not well-meaning outsiders who were teaching—in Lisa Delpit's apt words—"other people's children"; they were teaching their own. And, as at most schools at the time, they had full sanction from parents who not only accepted the school's enactment of in loco parentis but demanded it.

In short, such instruction was locally appropriate. But most importantly—and most valuable to instructors today—underlying Mayo's highly disciplined approach to language instruction was the tacit assumption that it *could be learned*. In the view of Mayo and his faculty, the acquisition of "good English" was not a matter of class, morality, native intelligence, family background, or breeding but rather a matter of simple hard work and discipline and therefore available to all who cared to apply themselves. Indeed, rural students, who were thought to be more practical and serious than their "city cousins" (Barnes 14), might even have been expected to have had an advantage in this regard. Behind the corrections were a fundamental respect for the ability of students and a desire to push them to do their best. As Mary Bowman described her practice, "I taught language good and hard and taught them the English language" (18).

The Normal School Legacy in Rhetoric and Composition

Mayo represents an important, overlooked legacy in rhetorical education. The history of normal schools has been neglected due, in part, to their success. The radical changes they initiated in American education—linking democratic action with education, developing student-centered classrooms and curricula, responding to community needs, opening educational and professional opportunities to students without regard for sex or class—have become such a basic part of the vocabulary of professional educators that we have lost sight of their historical origins. Progressive-minded, democratic education did not begin with the social upheavals of the 1960s nor the Deweyan revolution in the early twentieth century nor even the establishment of land-grant colleges following the Civil War. In each of these cases, normal schools had laid the groundwork. As Jurgen Herbst notes in his history of teacher education and professionalization in America, *And Sadly Teach*,[18] while state universities created a centrally located space for working-class parents to send their children, normal schools "took public colleges and universities out to where they were most needed—into the hinterlands and small towns where the people lived and worked. With the normal schools, true democracy began in higher education" (142).

The success of normal schools was not lost on traditional colleges and universities, which increasingly began to incorporate teacher training into their own institutions through schools of education in the late nineteenth and early twentieth centuries. Teachers College, founded in 1887 as the New York College for the Training of Teachers, became part of Columbia University in 1898. Harvard, somewhat late on the scene, established its graduate school of education in 1920. Unfortunately, as teacher training became more specialized, especially at the administrative and research levels, the split between classroom practitioner and scholar also increased, contributing to the lingering lack of professional status for teachers.

Further contributing to the dilution of the original mission of normal schools was their eclectic, democratic emphasis. Many students did not expect to remain teachers all their lives, nor were they necessarily interested in narrowly defined professional education. Notes Herbst: "Instead of pedagogical vocational schools they wanted 'people's colleges,' which would allow their graduates easy transfer into liberal arts colleges and universities and which would open the door for them to any occupation or profession. . . . [S]tudents, parents, and legislators saw the normal schools and later the teachers colleges as true community colleges or people's colleges" (5–6). Mayo himself promoted this comprehensive vision of normal colleges, insisting that his methods were of value not only for teachers but for anyone seeking to better themselves through higher education.

> Normalism is admitted to be best for the teacher. But some, especially those interested in running schools under the old regime and designing thus to deceive the people, "preach" over all the country that Normal schools are suitable only for those who aim to teach. Now if Normals are best for those who aim to teach, why are they not best for those who are to be taught? (East Texas Normal College, *Catalogue 1896* 70)

By the middle of the twentieth century, the teacher-training duties of normal schools had been largely subsumed by state colleges and universities. In Wisconsin, for example, state teachers colleges became liberal arts colleges in 1951 and state universities in 1964 before finally being incorporated into the University of Wisconsin system in 1971 (Herbst 160). In Texas, a similar pattern occurred. North Texas Normal (1890) became North Texas State Normal in 1901 and eventually the University of North Texas; Southwest

Texas Normal (1903) became Southwest Texas State University; East Texas Normal College, which became East Texas State Normal College after Mayo's death in 1917, is now Texas A&M University–Commerce.

As Herbst suggests, however, the true legacy of the normal school movement might be found not in teacher training programs but in community colleges, which took on the normal school's traditional commitment to educating the children of the poor and working class and those ill-served by state primary and secondary education. Unfortunately, community colleges have been ghettoized in histories of higher education just as primary and secondary schools have been in treatments of English and rhetoric education. Normal schools represent not only an important, influential, and neglected locus in the history of rhetorical education in American colleges, they also serve as the missing link between secondary and higher education, especially public education. In the early twentieth century, normal school educators had great influence in the NCTE. The pages of the *English Journal* contain lively discussion and debate on classroom practices not just by scholars working at colleges but by elementary and secondary schoolteachers and administrators. Indeed, the turn-of-the-twentieth-century debates over the efficacy of grammar instruction were led in large measure by *elementary* school English instructors who doubted the value of the old yet persistent scholastic method of teaching decontextualized rules and vocabulary before students needed to acquire them.

By examining the history of normal schools such as East Texas Normal College, we can also better address contemporary concerns about how to negotiate differences of power and authority in the classroom, especially in regard to standards of usage. While liberal or leftist educators often advocate respect for home dialects against the hegemony of standardized ones or promote a critical, confrontational stance toward capitalist ideologies, quite often it is the parents of working-class or minority students who insist upon rigorous instruction in Standard English, question the value of bilingual or bidialectical education, or insist on measurable economic returns on their investment in higher education. If we wish to truly liberate or empower students, we need to respectfully address these concerns. Mayo did not neglect the traditional goals of liberal arts education, but he believed that education must be practical as well as cultural and of immediate economic use to students for whom attending college was a significant financial and emotional undertaking. Believing his students needed broad communications skills for both civic and professional life, he attempted to integrate reading, writing, and speaking instruction by encouraging classroom discussion and public discourse, making public speaking and oratory essential parts of the curriculum, assigning only a peripheral role to textbooks in English instruction, and—despite his often disciplinary approach—sparking student interest in language. Mayo thus offers lessons for contemporary classrooms by suggesting that, depending on the context, seemingly conservative practices might not necessarily serve conservative or reductive ends. Although he would not likely have agreed that students had a "right to their own language," he insisted that students had a right to their own *lives*; instructing them in the language of power, he believed, was one way to ensure them control over their future. Judging by the large number of students over the years who paid tribute to his legacy, he largely succeeded in his mission.

CONCLUSION

History Matters

At the turn of the twentieth century, there were over a thousand institutions of higher learning in America;[1] this study details just three of them. These histories are necessarily incomplete. But they are necessary. Indeed, in a country with such a decentralized educational system as the United States, national educational histories cannot be understood but in relation to the local communities in which trends both emerge and play out. For African American students and educators at Wiley College, the classical liberal arts tradition represented the pinnacle of academic achievement, while vocational education symbolized continued racial oppression. For rural white women at Texas Woman's University, the situation was reversed; liberal arts education carried the weight of a circumscribed past, while vocational education symbolized a new era of expanded political and economic participation. At East Texas Normal College, meanwhile, William Mayo promised students an education superior to that of the traditional liberal arts college, which he mocked as hidebound and elitist. At Wiley, Melvin Tolson used race pride and the black oratorical tradition to inspire his students. At TWU, students and educators looked to the women's movement and local women's clubs for solidarity and support. At East Texas, Mayo played upon the pioneering, pragmatist spirit of his rural students to spur them to achievement. Such histories matter and not merely to historians but to teachers, administrators, policymakers, and the public. The perceived pedagogical failures and successes of the past and present shape the pedagogy of the future. If we, as instructors and scholars of rhetoric and writing, are to have a say in that future, we must be able to articulate a nuanced interpretation of our past.

Our histories also tell us who we are. As John Brereton notes, scholars in rhetoric and composition commonly "defin[e] themselves by their relationship to their origins" (xi). In overlooking the wide-ranging practices at diverse sites of rhetorical education, we have missed an important chance to reconnect with the often-progressive roots of our field. On both the left and the right, observers of higher education have often been fixed on the ideological flashpoint of the late 1960s. Both conservatives and liberals, reactionaries and radicals, frequently look to this era as either the beginning of significant educational reform or the beginning of the end. In rhetoric and composition studies, this period marks the revitalization of the rhetorical tradition and the revolt against overauthoritarian and positivist pedagogies. But the reform tradition in American education—and rhetoric and composition pedagogy—goes much further back. A fuller understanding of previous waves of activist, populist, and reformist pedagogy better prepares us to set our current debates in their proper historical context. Just as any thoughtful contemporary writing instructor makes use of a variety of theories and practices, from expressivist to cognitivist, from positivist to postmodern, so did previous generations also have a rich repertoire of pedagogies to choose from. Long before writing process theory and postmodern critiques of the construction of knowledge, college English instructors in America sought to empower students through language instruction, link rhetorical instruction to democratic action, and develop locally responsive pedagogies that took into account the needs and desires of diverse communities.

It is true that students and faculty in the late nineteenth and early twentieth centuries were less troubled about the negotiation of power and the imposition of dominant-class ideology through language instruction than we are. But they were not naive. Melvin Tolson and William Mayo, severe, disciplinary grammarians both, saw their work as radical. For Tolson, language instruction gave his students the tools to actively resist the pressures of racism, conservatism, and capitalism. The question of whether the master's tools could be used to tear down or rebuild the master's house never came up, as it never would have occurred to him that the tools belonged to the master in the first place. For Mayo, the teaching of writing, speaking, and grammar opened up a world of cultural and economic possibilities that would have otherwise been denied his students. As a normal school educator, he hoped to break the monopoly on cultural capital claimed by traditional—and often exclusionary and elitist—liberal arts colleges. At Texas Woman's University, instructors sought to help students develop the communicative skills they would need in a society that was both still shaped by and breaking away from traditional roles for women. In order to do justice to past practices, we must interpret them in the contexts in which they developed.

The tasks faced by instructors at Wiley, TWU, East Texas, and other black, women's, and normal colleges were, of course, in some ways easier than those we face today. The traditional work of rhetoric is now done at multiple sites within the contemporary university, in departments of speech, communication, journalism, and theater, as well as English. In the late nineteenth and early twentieth centuries, the small size of many alternative sites of rhetorical education prevented disciplinary fragmentation by default. But these schools often also saw these subjects as inherently integrated and all part of the proper domain of language instruction. At Wiley, TWU, and East Texas, oratory and speaking were important parts of the English curriculum through the 1930s, and public writing was taught in composition as well as journalism classes. Our current degree of disciplinary specialization may work against the kind of comprehensive instruction these schools offered, but that does not mean we cannot promote the integration of these subjects. We can speak to scholars in other departments. We can work to make it easier for students in our departments to take cross-disciplinary courses in communication, reading, writing, speaking, and rhetoric. We can continue to push for a greater integration of rhetoric into the curricula of English departments and a vision of the field in which literacy studies is as important as literary studies. In these endeavors, the past is on our side.

If we are interested in recovering the full richness of the rhetorical tradition, then we must not only look beyond departments of English and the freshman English classroom for evidence of historical rhetorical practices but also go beyond the traditional practices of the freshman English classroom in our own classrooms. The recovery of argument and invention and renewed attention to the composing process are among the most important achievements of contemporary rhetoric and composition pedagogy. Yet we can go further. We can do a better job of acknowledging and exploring other rhetorical traditions and strategies. We can renew scholarly attention on the canon of style. Though we acknowledge the teaching of critical reading, few of us are schooled in teaching reading strategies. While our students frequently report the importance of English and other liberal arts classes in developing their writing skills, they also report being less satisfied with our contribution to the oral communication and group-work skills their jobs require (State University of New York at Albany; Kourenina and McGhee). As Krista Ratcliffe observes, "[I]n the 20th century recovery of rhetoric within composition studies, reading and writing reign as the dominant tropes for interpretive invention; speaking places a respectable third; listening runs a poor, poor fourth" (195). A freshman English classroom may be too full already to cram in yet another rhetorical *topos*, but we can continue to develop courses that treat visual, oral, and professional rhetorics and link these to public life. If our histories teach us anything, it is that rhetorical instruction need not be limited to first-year writing.

Perhaps our most effective pedagogical strategy may simply be closer contact with our students' lives. The meeting ground may have moved from professors' parlors to their offices and from their offices to e-mail exchanges, but our communications are no less important. The personal attention students received at Wiley, TWU, and East Texas went a long way toward ensuring their success. Instructors there sought to educate not just individual students but communities. Not only did they often live in proximity to their students, the small size of their campuses and focused institutional missions promoted contact. These professors knew precisely why their students were attending college—and what they suffered to attend.

Today, especially if we teach in large state universities or at commuter campuses, we may not be able to replicate or even approximate the close-knit environments of these schools. But we can seek ways to create legitimate classroom communities. Such innovations as service learning, online discussion forums, or using the classroom as the audience for assignments may help spark some of the sense of community and purpose that schools such as Wiley, TWU, and East Texas fostered. Attending to our students' needs may also require giving up some of our own agendas. Many of us in the humanities with liberal or radical sentiments are suspicious of anything that smacks of professional or vocational training, seeing it as a compromise with a market-driven value system that already devalues our own work. This is not a position we can afford, nor is it one that progressive educators a century ago necessarily held. Even in the 1870s, Henry Adams had to defer to the judgment of one of his students, who declared bluntly, "The degree of Harvard College is worth money to me in Chicago" (305–6). By 1910, observes Frederick Rudolph, "the vast majority" of American college students "were enrolled in courses of study shaped by utilitarian and vocational values" (210). We must acknowledge that the main reason students attend college— then as well as now—is for the purpose of professional advancement.[2] The difference is that a century ago, students saw a clearer path between language instruction and their own professional goals. Paying attention to students' economic concerns does not entail that we abandon the traditional goals of rhetoric and the liberal arts but that we demonstrate their practical value. After all, rhetoric in the West, from its inception amongst the Sophists in Ancient Greece, has always been at its core a pragmatic art. If we wish to effect any change upon the consciousnesses of our students, we must seek to accommodate them as well as liberate them.

In addition to encouraging a more nuanced view of our history and methods of historiography, I hope this work will promote a more easy relationship with the origins of our field. Our inheritance as rhetoric, writing, and language instructors in the American academy is a rich one, and the late nineteenth and early twentieth centuries are a vital part of that inheritance. Then, as now, writing instructors worked to expand educational opportunities for new constituencies of students, fought against what they saw as the reductive rhetoric of previous generations, and sought to promote citizenship through rhetorical instruction. This is a past that not only deserves to be remembered but might also bear some repeating.

CHRONOLOGY
NOTES
BIBLIOGRAPHY
INDEX

CHRONOLOGY

1801   Johann Heinrich Pestalozzi publishes *How Gertrude Teaches Her Children*.

1823   First normal school in America is established in Concord, Vermont.

1861   William Mayo is born.

1862   First Morrill Act establishes land-grant colleges.

1865   Civil War ends.

1866   Freedmen's Aid Society is founded by members of the Methodist Episcopal Church to establish black schools and colleges.

1869   Harvard President Charles Eliot insists, in *Atlantic Monthly* article, on maintaining split between liberal arts colleges and professional, technical, and normal schools.

1871   Texas A&M University is established by legislature; classes begin in 1876.

1872   First black college in Texas, Paul Quinn, is founded by the African Methodist Episcopal Church.

1872   Adams Sherman Hill is appointed to Harvard.

1873   Harvard introduces freshman entrance exam in composition; Wiley College is founded by the Methodist Episcopal Church.

1876   Central Normal College is founded in Lagoda, Indiana, and moved to Danville in 1878.

1878   Hill publishes *Principles of Rhetoric*.

1881   University of Texas is established by legislature; classes begin in 1883.

1883   Mayo graduates from Central Normal College.

1884   Barrett Wendell introduces "daily themes" at Harvard.

1885   Harvard moves sophomore composition course, English A, to freshman year, initiating establishment of freshman composition nationwide.

1889   Texas State Grange proposes establishment of public women's college; Texas women's organizations take up campaign. Mayo founds East Texas Normal College in Cooper; moves school to Commerce in 1894.

1890   General Federation of Women's Clubs is formed.

1892   First *Report of the Committee on Composition and Rhetoric* is produced at Harvard University.

1897   Texas Federation of Women's Clubs is formed.

1898   Melvin Tolson is born.

1899   School of Oratory is founded at UT; English department eliminates argumentation from rhetoric and composition courses.

1901   Texas Woman's University is established by Texas legislature; classes begin in 1903.

1903   W. E. B. Du Bois publishes *The Souls of Black Folk*.

1906   *Daedalian* literary magazine is founded at TWU.

1911   National Council of Teachers of English is formed.

1912   NCTE begins publishing *English Journal*. University of Texas begins offering home economics courses.

1917   Mayo dies; East Texas Normal College is transferred to the state.

1918   William Kilpatrick publishes *The Project Method*. Texas women win right to vote in primaries; Annie Webb Blanton is elected State Superintendent of Schools.

1920   Nineteenth Amendment grants suffrage to women.

1921   UT opens all School of Oratory courses to women.

1922   Southern Association of Colleges for Women is formed.

1923   Tolson graduates from Lincoln University and begins teaching at Wiley College.

1924   Tolson establishes debate team at Wiley.

1930   Wiley participates in first interracial collegiate debate; Henrietta Bell, a female debater, is part of the team.

1933   Carter G. Woodson publishes *The Mis-Education of the Negro.*

1935   Wiley College debate team defeats national champions, the University of Southern California.

1943   UT allows women to compete in intercollegiate debate.

1947   Tolson leaves Wiley College.

1954   *Brown v. Board of Education of Topeka* leads to desegregation of public schools.

1963   Texas A&M University is opened to women on a limited basis; school is opened completely to women in 1971.

1966   Tolson dies.

NOTES

Introduction: Beyond Ideology in Rhetoric and Composition Historiography

1. Daniel Fogarty first proposed the term *current traditional rhetoric* in 1959 in *Roots for a New Rhetoric*. It was adopted by Richard E. Young in 1978 in "Problems and Paradigms: Needed Research in Rhetorical Invention" and then by James A. Berlin, who is perhaps most responsible for its popularization.

1. Integrating Traditions at a Private Black College

1. See chapter 5 of Jacqueline Jones Royster's *Traces of a Stream*, which includes a comparison of the experiences of black female students at Oberlin College and Atlanta University, and Scott Zaluda's "Lost Voices of the Harlem Renaissance: Writing Assigned at Howard University, 1919–31."

2. See S. Michael Halloran, "From Rhetoric to Composition" and "Rhetoric in the American College"; Gregory Clark and Halloran; and Gerald Graff.

3. In writing Tolson's funeral program, his colleague and later biographer Joy Flasch, recalling "his fondness for parallelisms, for irony, for juxtaposition" ("Melvin Beaunoris Tolson" 4), tried to capture these qualities, eulogizing him as "Bootblack and Poet/Dishwasher and Teacher/Cook and Philosopher/Waiter and Lecturer/Meatpacker and Mayor" (*Obsequies*).

4. This follows Michael R. Heintze's count of Thomas Jesse Jones's 1917 report for the Bureau of Education; Jones, dubious of the quality of coursework offered at Texas College, discounts their self-report of three students and officially records 129 in his summary chart.

5. Not to be confused with Sam Houston, the hero of the Texas Revolution and first president of the Republic, Samuel Huston was an Iowa landowner who donated $9,000 to help found the college.

6. The school was named for Bishop Isaac D. Wiley, a leader in the Freed-men's Aid Society and an advocate of black education.

7. Reported then-student Robert E. Brown: "Sunday morning, most of us refused to go to Sunday School or to church. The president prayed that God would strike all of us who were not present, dead in our tracks. His prayer was not answered because none of us died" (45). The ensuing controversy helped lead to the installation of the school's first black president, Isaiah B. Scott, the following fall.

8. Brown later became principal of Marshall's Central High School.

9. Pemberton, who graduated from Wiley in 1888, helped found Central High in 1894. Under his leadership, the school became one of the first accredited black high schools in the state and an important feeder school for Wiley.

10. *Sweatt v. Painter* (1950), along with *Sipuel v. Board of Regents of University of Oklahoma* (1948), which Tolson campaigned for, helped pave the way in 1954 for *Brown v. Board of Education of Topeka*.

11. It may be difficult to establish with complete certainty when the first interracial debate took place. Though Tolson was certainly a pioneer, his was not the only team to meet white colleges, though it was arguably the most active and successful. In an interview, historian John Hope Franklin, who was a member of the Fisk debate team in the early thirties, recalled his team meeting a number of white schools, including the University of Notre Dame and New York University, as early as 1932. Fisk's coach, Theodore S. Currier, who was white, cultivated relationships with these schools in the interest of exposing his students to as many educational opportunities as possible. Says Franklin of the white teams, "They seemed quite willing, and able, and anxious to debate us."

12. The story of female debaters is worth further study. Wiley was not the only college to allow women to debate. In 1930, Virginia Union's first team was composed of two women. As black colleges were traditionally coeducational, it is possible that female participation may have been encouraged by the large presence of women on campus.

13. Tolson, who was notoriously inexact with dates, variously remembered this as 1929 or 1930.

14. Bovard Auditorium's current seating capacity is 1,544. Before the debate, USC's *Daily Trojan* reported, "A large audience is anticipated," because Wiley's alumni association had already presold five hundred tickets at twenty-five cents each ("Debaters to Meet"). Final crowd estimates range from eleven hundred to twenty-two hundred, but all sources agree that the event was packed.

15. Tolson, along with other activists, toured Oklahoma in 1947 with Fisher (then Sipuel) in a fundraising campaign in support of her lawsuit against the University of Oklahoma Law School, which had denied her admission under

the state's Jim Crow laws. *Sipuel v. Board of Regents of University of Oklahoma* (1948), argued by then–NAACP lawyer Thurgood Marshall before the U.S. Supreme Court, led to the law school's desegregation and was an important landmark on the way to *Brown v. Board of Education of Topeka* (1954).

16. This article, written by Edmund Rollins for the *San Antonio Register*, was picked up by the Associated Negro Press and carried in several black newspapers.

17. This is from notes to a speech at Prairie View A&M University in Texas.

2. Balancing Tensions at a Public Women's University

1. Women's enrollment exceeded that of men for the first time in 1979; in 2000, 56.4% of college students were women (United States Census Bureau, "Table A-6").

2. Ida Tarbell (1857–1944) was a muckraking journalist whose investigation of John D. Rockefeller and Standard Oil helped lead to the U.S. Supreme Court's breakup of the Standard Oil Trust in 1911 under the auspices of the Sherman Antitrust Act. Ruth Hale (1887–1934) was a theatrical press agent and journalist; as co-founder of the Lucy Stone League (along with journalist Jane Grant, cofounder of the *New Yorker* with her husband, Harold Ross), she was one of the leaders in the fight to allow women to legally keep their own names when they married.

3. *Coordinate institutions* are female colleges associated with predominantly or exclusively male institutions, such as Radcliffe with Harvard, Barnard with Columbia, and Sophie Newcomb with Tulane.

4. The name was changed to the College of Industrial Arts (C.I.A.) in 1905, as "the original title resembled that of a reform school and provoked letters inquiring about the 'inmates'" (Welch 126). C. I. A. became Texas State College for Women in 1934 and finally Texas Woman's University in 1957. For the purposes of this study, the college is referred to by its current name, Texas Woman's University, or TWU, as it is commonly called.

5. Education was segregated by color at Southern institutions at the time.

6. The motto was suggested by Regent Helen M. Stoddard. Its source was the educational philosopher and reformer Johann Comenius (1592–1670), though the idea has a long history, from Aristotle ("The things we have to learn before we can do them, we learn by doing them, e.g. men become builders by building and lyre players by playing the lyre; so too we become just by doing just acts, temperate by doing temperate acts, brave by doing brave acts" [*Nicomachean Ethics* 2, i]) to John Dewey. Stoddard saw in Comenius an early advocate for women's rights: "In an age when women were kept ignorant, Comenius yet advocated her intellectual capacity; in an age when woman was hardly accorded a soul, he yet believed in her economic independence. He declared: 'Girls as

well as boys should be educated. They are formed in the image of God as well as man; they are endowed with equal sharpness of mind and capacity for learning; often, indeed, with more than the opposite sex'" (Stoddard 192).

7. The Texas Federation of Women's Clubs was formed in 1897 as the Texas Federation of Women's Literary Clubs after a call for a state organization by the Waco Woman's Club. In 1899 the organization joined the General Federation of Women's Clubs and dropped the word *Literary* from its title (Seaholm, "Earnest Women" 339–46).

8. In Texas A&M's early years, a few women were permitted to take classes, but they were not eligible to receive degrees. In 1914, William Bizzell, fresh from TWU, assumed the presidency. Bizzell publicly supported female students at A&M, and by 1925, thirty were attending. His attempt to make the school's unofficial policy official failed, however. In 1925, after his resignation and the mysterious awarding of a degree in the "last days" of his administration to a female student who was only to have received a certificate, women were formally banned from campus (Knippa 25–27), a move that survived three court challenges. In 1963, facing increasing public pressure, declining prestige, stagnant enrollment, and high attrition, the board of directors reluctantly opened its graduate programs to women and its undergraduate program to female staff, the wives and daughters of faculty and staff, and the wives of students. It was not until 1971 that the school was completely opened to women. "The record enrollments of the following decades saved A&M from its position as a small, floundering college and transformed it into a world class university" (Knippa 141).

9. Rosenberry served as president of the Association of Collegiate Alumnae from 1917 to 1921. In 1921, the organization merged with the Southern Association of College Women to form the AAUW (Talbot and Rosenberry).

10. This figure increases to 62.9% if the 123 women who did not report their employment status are excluded from the survey (Bentinck 38).

11. Isadore Callaway, who wrote a column for the *Dallas Morning News* for twenty years under the pen name Pauline Periwinkle, was a strong proponent of suffrage, equal rights for women, progressive political reform, and women's clubs, which she saw as "an ideal vehicle for familiarizing women with the conditions in their communities that needed their attention" (McElhaney xvi).

12. The TFWC's education committee first proposed a home economics program to the UT Board of Regents in 1904 but was told no money was available. The school was eventually established through the "persistence and good connections" of the clubwomen and the donation of the building by UT Regent George Brackenridge, the brother of influential clubwoman Eleanor Brackenridge (McArthur 39).

13. The recipient of eight Academy Awards and thirty-five nominations, Head (1897–1981) worked on numerous films, from *Breakfast at Tiffany's* to *Vertigo* to *The Sting*. She created a number of iconic costumes, including Dorothy Lamour's body-hugging sarong in *The Jungle Princess*, Grace Kelly's lavish and chic evening gowns in *To Catch a Thief*, Bette Davis's off-the-shoulder cocktail dress in *All about Eve*, Elizabeth Taylor's strapless white gown in *A Place in the Sun*, and Audrey Hepburn's casual sets in *Sabrina*.

14. His *Early Romantic Drama at the English Court* (1917) was well regarded.

15. In 1920, at UT, four faculty offered ten courses; at TWU, six faculty offered fifteen distinct courses.

16. UT's School of Oratory was not completely opened up to women until 1921, and they were not permitted to participate in intercollegiate debates until 1943 (Regan 33–35).

17. In 1915, of 545 regularly enrolled students, 296 belonged to either the Mary Eleanor Brackenridge Club or the Chaparral Club.

18. Both the yearbook and the literary magazine were at times called the *Chaparral* or the *Daedalian*. To avoid confusion, I have referred to issues of the *Chaparral Monthly*, the *Daedalian Monthly*, and the *Daedalian Quarterly* simply as the *Daedalian*. When citing the *Chaparral* or *Daedalian* yearbook, I identify it simply as the yearbook.

19. In 1915, Cobb was one of the first three women to obtain a bachelor's degree from the university; she returned as an English professor while pursuing graduate work at the University of California and the University of Chicago.

20. The *Daedalian* editors responded with typical understatement: "[W]e have information from a reliable source that Mr. Skiles knows, or thinks he knows, a great deal concerning the subject in question. . . . Whether he does or does not know co-eds, he certainly left the impression that he has information on all matters concerning them. . . . Mr. Skiles is the possessor of a rare and ready wit which will help him out of many difficulties in times to come" (May 1914 16).

21. Bentinck, surveying married graduates from the 1915 to 1939 class, found 37.5% employed (548 of 1461); Cornell, surveying married graduates from the 1904 to 1921 class, found 43.1% employed (97 of 225).

3. Challenging Orthodoxies at a Rural Normal College

1. Exact summer enrollment figures at East Texas were likely higher than officially recorded, as Mayo did not count continuing students from the fall and spring in his summer totals. In 1909, for example, actual summer attendance was 1,524, while official attendance was 911. In 1916, unique summer enrollment at East Texas was 1,457. Total summer enrollment was probably around 1,700

(Bledsoe 49–50). That same year, total summer enrollment at the University of Texas was 1,477, though only 434 of these students were enrolled in the summer normal program (Benedict 808).

2. The first two editors of the *English Journal*, James Fleming Hosic and W. Wilbur Hatfield, taught at Chicago Normal College.

3. "'Anschauung' is the most difficult of all Pestalozzian terms, even in his own language, because he uses it in so many different ways. . . . [I]t may mean sense-impression, observation, contemplation, perception, apperception, or intuition, as the transition is made from relatively receptive and unconscious processes to full mental awareness and activity" (Silber 138).

4. "Few colleges give even the slightest attention to questions of pedagogy," found the National Educational Association's Committee on Normal Education in 1892 (781).

5. The *Oxford English Dictionary* defines *memoriter* as learning or speaking from memory. Originally, its usage appears to have been predominantly descriptive. By the late nineteenth century, however, the term had taken on a distinctly pejorative cast: "The mere memoriter preacher." For Mayo and other normal school educators, it seemed to serve as shorthand for all the ills represented by traditional rote learning.

6. Though fiercely independent, Mayo maintained relationships with a number of progressive educators who supported his efforts and lectured at the college. These included: Hugh Thomas Musselman, editor of the *Texas School Journal*; Albert Edward Winship, editor of the Boston-based *Journal of Education*, who encouraged Mayo to keep his school independent from any governing bodies; William Seneca Sutton, dean of the University of Texas School of Education and later acting president of the university; and Philander P. Claxton, U.S. Commissioner of Education (1911–21), who visited the campus on several occasions (Bledsoe 261–62).

7. The German educator Friedrich Froebel (1782–1852) argued that young children primarily learned by engaging with the world through play. Like Pestalozzi, Froebel based his pedagogy on children's natural cognitive and social development. He is best known as the founder of the kindergarten (literally "child's garden"), "an institution for self-instruction, self-education, and self-cultivation of mankind, as well as . . . cultivation of the same through play, creative self-activity, and spontaneous self-instruction" (Froebel 6).

8. An early version of what might now be called the phonics method, the A-B-C method began with the letters of the alphabet and their sounds, followed by basic phonemes and monosyllabic words, taught by "tight drill and practice sequences" (Pearson 2).

9. Mayo is reported to have tossed as many books as he could out of the window of the burning building, but the school's records and his own papers, including the manuscript of a grammar and composition textbook he had been writing, were destroyed (Goodwin 24).

10. Etta Mayo had long had an interest in Willard and the temperance movement; she was responsible for naming Frances E. Willard Hall, the new women's dormitory built in 1910 (Linck and Linck 29).

11. The Intercollegiate Socialist Society, founded in 1905 by Upton Sinclair, was reorganized as the League for Industrial Democracy in 1921. Its youth branch developed into Students for a Democratic Society in 1960. Morgan A. Smith, a radical Commerce minister, published a number of pamphlets and songbooks advocating socialism and the social gospel, including *Christ as a Social Reformer* ("Just the thing to hand to that religious neighbor of yours"), *Ownership of Land*, and *Socialism in Song*, which collected popular and original hymns, frequently set to the tune of well-known songs and spirituals. Selections included "Amazing Graft" ("Amazing Grace"), "Murderous Capitalism," and "What a Weapon Is the Ballot" ("What a Friend We Have in Jesus"). Said Smith, "[T]he capitalist system makes a thousand fold better provision for the dogs of rich loafers than it does for working men, their wives and children. Now and then we run across a hypocritical Pharisee who is so exceedingly pious that he claims to be shocked at hearing the songs of freedom in this book sung to the old sacred melodies so familiar to the people" (Smith). Mayo's response to his son's joining the Intercollegiate Socialist Society is, alas, unknown. Though critical of socialism, like many in Commerce he was a friend of Smith. "While I cannot endorse the general bearing of the sentiment," he wrote of *Socialism in Song*, "I must admit that the songs are strikingly interesting and the good old fashioned tunes wonderfully forceful" (qtd. in Goodwin 132).

12. Kitzhaber identified four theorists whose popular textbooks did the most to influence and shape early composition studies: Adams Sherman Hill, John Franklin Genung, Barrett Wendell, and Fred Newton Scott (who coauthored textbooks with Joseph Villiers Denney).

13. Hill was appointed by President Eliot in 1872. One of his first acts was to establish a placement exam in English composition, demanding "correct[ness] in spelling, punctuation, grammar, and expression" (Harvard University, *Catalogue 1873* 53). Though Harvard's sophomore course in composition, English A, was not moved to the freshman year until the mid-1880s, it had long been shaped by Hill, whose 1878 *Principles of Rhetoric* became an influential textbook. Though Hill has recently been treated more sympathetically than in the past, his insistence that rhetoric was an art and not a science, his scant attention to

rhetoric's role in invention, and his attention to mechanical concerns laid the groundwork for what has come to be known as current-traditional rhetoric.

14. Originally published in *Teachers College Record* in 1918, *The Project Method* went through eleven printings through 1929. A prolific writer on education, Kilpatrick was considered the "founder" of the method.

15. The cover of the 1896 *Catalogue* for nearby Henry College advertised, "There has not been a gallon of whisky sold in Campbell for fifteen years."

16. Recalled Garland Button, "I obviously never got beyond the ground floor" (17).

17. Already a well-known author of English textbooks at this point, Blanton soon became an important figure in Texas education and politics. In 1918, with the support of the Texas Equal Suffrage Association and defying the order of North Texas State Normal president William Bruce that no faculty member participate in politics or suffrage activities, Blanton campaigned for state superintendent of public instruction. Although women could not yet participate in general elections, they had won the right to vote in primaries in Texas in 1918; Blanton won the Democratic nomination through the efforts of women voters and then carried the general election, making her the first woman elected to statewide office in Texas. Like many activist white Texan women of her era, Blanton mixed "southern traditionalism, reform feminism, and purposeful Progressivism. . . . Blanton held no startling feminist ideology . . . but rather found her motivation in a naturally developing awareness of gender inequities" (Cottrell xix–xxi). In teaching grammar, she was a traditionalist; politically, she positioned herself as a both an advocate of women's rights and a traditional Southern Democrat; later, as a University of Texas School of Education faculty member, she was instrumental in building the school's rural education department.

18. The title is a play on Chaucer's description of the Clerk in the prologue to the *Canterbury Tales*: "And gladly would he learn, and gladly teach" (And gladly wolde he lerne, and gladly teche).

Conclusion: History Matters

1. The 1900–1901 *Report of the Commissioner of Education* lists 605 traditional colleges and universities, 42 schools of technology, 65 agricultural and mechanical colleges, and 288 public and private normal schools. This figure does not take into account independent professional schools of medicine, law, theology, pharmacy, and nursing.

2. The most commonly cited evidence for the decline of the liberal arts and the concurrent increase in careerism among students is the annual *American Freshman* survey undertaken by the Higher Education Research Institute at UCLA: in 2001, 73.6% of students listed "being very well off financially" as

an essential or very important life goal, while only 43.1% chose "developing a meaningful philosophy of life." In 1967, the situation was reversed: 41.9% and 85.8% respectively (Astin, Oseguera, Sax, and Korn 58–59). "American higher education," argues former Assistant Secretary of Education Diane Ravitch, "has remade itself into a vast job-training program in which the liberal arts are no longer central" (qtd. in Cooke). This is not an entirely fair conclusion. In 1967, a smaller percentage of students attended college than today, and they formed a more homogenous, financially better-off group than today's student body. And even then, 56% of freshmen agreed that the "chief benefit of a college education is that it increases one's earning power" (Astin, Parrot, Korn, and Sax 56).

BIBLIOGRAPHY

Abrahams, Roger D. *Talking Black*. Rowley, MA: Newbury, 1976.

Adams, Charles Francis, Edwin Lawrence Godkin, and Josiah Quincy. *Report of the Committee on Composition and Rhetoric*. Cambridge: Harvard U, 1892.

Adams, Henry. *The Education of Henry Adams*. 1918. New York: Modern Library, 1931.

Adams, Katherine H. *A Group of Their Own: College Writing Courses and American Women Writers, 1880–1940*. Albany: State U of New York P, 2001.

Anderson, James D. *The Education of Blacks in the South, 1860–1935*. Chapel Hill: U of North Carolina P, 1988.

Aptheker, Herbert, ed. *The Education of Black People: Ten Critiques, 1906–1960*. By W. E. B. Du Bois. New York: Monthly Review, 2001.

Arendt, Hannah. "What Is Authority?" *Between Past and Future: Eight Exercises in Political Thought*. New York: Viking, 1968. 91–141.

Aristotle. *Nicomachean Ethics*. Trans. W. D. Ross. Oxford: Clarendon P, 1908. 18 January 2002. Columbia U Library. 4 July 2002 <http://www.ilt.columbia.edu/publications/artistotle.html>.

Astin, Alexander W., Leticia Oseguera, Linda J. Sax, and William S. Korn. *The American Freshman: Thirty-Five Year Trends, 1966–2001*. Los Angeles: Higher Education Research Institute, U of California, Los Angeles, 2002.

Astin, Alexander W., Sarah A. Parrot, William S. Korn, and Linda J. Sax. *The American Freshman: Thirty Year Trends, 1966–1996*. Los Angeles: Higher Education Research Institute, U of California, Los Angeles, 1997.

Avent, Joseph Emory. *The Summer Sessions in State Teachers' Colleges as a Factor in the Professional Education of Teachers*. Richmond, VA: Byrd, 1925.

Bacon, Jacqueline. *The Humblest May Stand Forth: Rhetoric, Empowerment, and Abolition*. Columbia: U of South Carolina P, 2002.

Bagg, Lyman. *Four Years at Yale*. New Haven, CT: Chatfield, 1871.

Baker, Elizabeth Whitemore. *Spoken English and How to Teach It*. Chicago: Rand McNally, 1925.

Balester, Valerie M. *Cultural Divide: A Study of African-American College-Level Writers*. Portsmouth, NH: Boynton/Cook, 1993.

Barnes, Walter. *English in the Country School*. Chicago: Row, 1913.

Beeler, Kent D., and Philip C. Chamberlain. "'Give a Buck to Save a College': The Demise of Central Normal College." *Indiana Magazine of History* 67.2 (June 1971): 117–28.

Beil, Gail K. "Sowing the Seeds of the Civil Rights Movement: Dr. J. Leonard Farmer and Wiley College, Marshall, Texas, as Case Studies of the Educational Influence on the Modern Civil Rights Leaders." M.A. thesis. Stephen F. Austin State U, 1999.

Bellamy, Caroline Barbee. "A Study of the Significant Changes in the Growth and Development of the Texas State College for Women." M.A. thesis. Texas State College for Women, 1939.

Benedict, H. Y. *A Source Book Relating to the History of the University of Texas: Legislative, Legal, Bibliographical, and Statistical*. U of Texas Bulletin 1757 (10 Oct. 1917).

Bentinck, Catherine. "A Statistical Analysis of the Vocations and Earnings of 1,669 Employed TSCW Alumnae, 1915–1939." M.A. thesis. Texas State College for Women, 1941.

Berlin, James A. *Rhetoric and Reality: Writing Instruction in American Colleges, 1900–1985*. Carbondale: Southern Illinois UP, 1987.

———. *Writing Instruction in Nineteenth-Century American Colleges*. Carbondale: Southern Illinois UP, 1984.

Bérubé, Michael. "Avant-Gardes and De-Author-izations: *Harlem Gallery* and the Cultural Contradictions of Modernism." *Callaloo* 12.1 (Winter 1989): 192–215.

———. *Marginal Forces/Cultural Centers: Tolson, Pynchon, and the Politics of the Canon*. Ithaca: Cornell UP, 1992.

Bickham, Jack M. Letter to Ruth Tolson. 9 Sept. 1966. Tolson Papers, Library of Congress.

Biggers, John. Letter to Melvin Tolson. 14 Mar. 1963. Tolson Papers, Library of Congress.

Blanton, Annie Webb. Letter to William H. Bruce. 23 July 1917. Bruce File, Archives, U of North Texas.

Blayney, Lindsey. *C.I.A. The Texas State College for Women, Denton, Texas: Its Ideals, Work and Organization*. College bulletin 115 (1 June 1925).

Bledsoe, James Marcus. *A History of Mayo and His College*. Commerce: East Texas State Teachers College, 1946.

Boswell, Hamilton. Telephone interview. 11 May 2001.

Bowers, William. "All We Read Is Freaks." *Oxford American* Jan./Feb. 2003: 40–54.

Bowler, Mary Mariella. *A History of Catholic Colleges for Women in the United States of America*. Washington: Catholic U of America, 1933.

Bowman, Mary. Interview with Corrinne E. Crow. 20 Feb. 1976. Special Collections, Archives, James G. Gee Library, Texas A&M U–Commerce.

Brackenridge, Mary Eleanor. "Industrial Arts for Women." *Fort Worth Record and Register* 10 Mar. 1907, sec. 3: 10.

Brawley, Benjamin. *History of Morehouse College*. 1917. College Park, MD: McGrath, 1970.

Brereton, John C., ed. *The Origins of Composition Studies in the American College, 1875–1925: A Documentary History*. Pittsburgh: U of Pittsburgh P, 1995.

Briggs, Le Baron Russell. "The Harvard Admission Examination in English." *Twenty Years of School and College English*. Ed. Adams Sherman Hill, Le Baron Russell Briggs, and Byron Satterlee Hurlbut. Cambridge: Harvard U, 1896. 17–32.

Brooks, Gwendolyn. Rev. of *Harlem Gallery*. *Negro Digest* 14.11 (Sept. 1965): 51–52.

Brown, Elsa Barkley. "Womanist Consciousness: Maggie Lena Walker and the Independent Order of Saint Luke." *Signs* 14.3 (Spring 1989): 610–33.

Brown, Robert A. *The Story of Central Normal College, Danville (Hendricks County), Indiana, 1878–1946*. Indiana: self-published, 1984.

Brown, Robert E. "Autobiographical Sketches." 1953. Archives, Wiley College.

Button, Garland. Interview with Corrinne E. Crow. 10 Dec. 1975. Archives, James G. Gee Library, Texas A&M U–Commerce.

Callaway, Isadore [Pauline Periwinkle]. "The Higher Education of Women an Imperative Need of the Time." *Dallas Morning News* 7 June 1896: 15.

Campbell, Doak S. *Problems in the Education of College Women: A Study of Women Graduates of Southern Colleges*. Field Study 6. Nashville: George Peabody College for Teachers, 1933.

Campbell, Helen. "'Problem is Economic, Not Racial,' Negro Says." *Daily Texan* (U of Texas) 12 Mar. 1946: 1–4.

Campbell, JoAnn. "Controlling Voices: The Legacy of English A at Radcliffe College 1883–1917." *CCC* 43.4 (Dec. 1992): 472–85.

———. "Freshman (sic) English: A 1901 Wellesley College 'Girl' Negotiates Authority." *Rhetoric Review* 15.1 (Fall 1996): 110–27.

———. "'A Real Vexation': Student Writing in Mount Holyoke's Culture of Service, 1837–1865." *College English* 59.7 (Nov. 1997): 767–88.

Cansler, Ronald Lee. "'The White and Not-White Dichotomy' of Melvin B. Tolson's Poetry." *Negro American Literature Forum* 7.4 (Winter 1973): 115–18.

Carr, Jean Ferguson, Stephen L. Carr, and Lucille M. Schultz. *Archives of Instruction: Nineteenth-Century Rhetorics, Readers, and Composition Books in the United States.* Carbondale: Southern Illinois UP, 2005.

Central Normal College. *Catalogue.* 1878.

Chamberlain, Mariam K. *Women in Academe: Progress and Prospects.* New York: Russell Sage, 1988.

Charney, Davida, John H. Newman, and Mike Palmquist. "'I'm Just No Good at Writing': Epistemological Style and Attitudes toward Writing." *Written Communication* 12.3 (July 1995): 298–329.

Clark, Elizabeth. "An Evening with Edith Head." *Denton Record-Chronicle* 4 Apr. 1979: 1C–2C.

Clark, Gregory, and S. Michael Halloran, eds. *Oratorical Culture in Nineteenth-Century America: Transformations in the Theory and Practice of Rhetoric.* Carbondale: Southern Illinois UP, 1993.

Cobb, Susan F. "The English Problem at C.I.A." *Daedalian Monthly* May 1914: 10–11.

Connors, Robert J. *Composition-Rhetoric: Backgrounds, Theory, and Pedagogy.* Pittsburgh: U of Pittsburgh P, 1997.

———. "Women's Reclamation of Rhetoric in Nineteenth-Century America." *Feminine Principles and Women's Experience in American Composition and Rhetoric.* Ed. Louise Wetherbee Phelps and Janet Emig. Pittsburgh: U of Pittsburgh P, 1995. 67–90.

———. "Writing the History of Our Discipline." *An Introduction to Composition Studies.* Ed. Erika Lindemann and Gary Tate. New York: Oxford UP, 1991. 49–71.

Conway, Kathryn M. "Woman Suffrage and the History of Rhetoric at the Seven Sisters Colleges, 1865–1919." Lunsford, *Reclaiming* 203–26.

Cooke, Dana. "Life's Ups and Downs." *Pulteney St. Survey* Spring 1997. 8 Aug. 2002 <http://campus.hws.edu/new/pss/Careers.html>.

Cornell, Charlotte. "Survey of Graduate Alumnae of the Texas State College for Women, 1904 to 1921." M.A. thesis. Texas State College for Women, 1941.

Cott, Nancy F. "What's in a Name? The Limits of 'Social Feminism'; or, Expanding the Vocabulary of Women's History." *Journal of American History* 76.3 (Dec. 1989): 809–29.

Cottrell, Debbie Mauldin. *Pioneer Woman Educator: The Progressive Spirit of Annie Webb Blanton.* College Station: Texas A&M UP, 1993.

Cox, Alice Carol. "The Rainey Affair: A History of the Academic Freedom Controversy at the University of Texas, 1938–1946." Diss. U of Denver, 1970.

Cox, Oliver C. *Caste, Class, and Race: A Study in Social Dynamics*. Garden City, NY: Doubleday, 1948.

Crawford, Robert, ed. *The Scottish Invention of English Literature*. Cambridge: Cambridge UP, 1998.

Crowley, Sharon. *Composition in the University: Historical and Polemical Essays*. Pittsburgh: U of Pittsburgh P, 1998.

———. *The Methodical Memory: Invention in Current-Traditional Rhetoric*. Carbondale: Southern Illinois UP, 1990.

Daniels, Elizabeth. *History of Vassar College*. 11 Nov. 1999. Vassar College. 6 Mar. 2002 <http://vassun.vassar.edu/~daniels/>.

"Danville." *Indianapolis Daily Sentinel* 28 Jan. 1881: 5.

Davis, Herschel A. "Wiley Noted for Its Fine Debaters." [*Marshall News Messenger* ?] 11 Oct. 1934: n. pag. Tolson Papers, Library of Congress.

Dawson, George. *Life Is So Good*. New York: Random, 2000.

"Debaters Leave on Annual Trip." *Campus* [Oklahoma City U] 27 Mar. 1931: 1.

"Debaters to Meet Negro Team Today." *Daily Trojan* [U of Southern California] 2 Apr. 1935: 1.

"Debaters Win in Many Contests." *Torch* [Oklahoma City U] May 1930: 1–6.

Delpit, Lisa D. *Other People's Children: Cultural Conflict in the Classroom*. New York: New Press, 1995.

Derks, Scott, ed. *The Value of a Dollar: Prices and Incomes in the United States, 1860–1989*. Detroit: Gale Research, 1994.

Dogan, Matthew W. "The Methodist Episcopal Church and the Education of Its Negro Membership." *Methodism and the Negro*. Ed. Isaac Lemuel Thomas. New York: Eaton, 1910. 81–90.

Du Bois, W. E. Burghardt, and Augustus Granville Dill. *The College-Bred Negro American*. Atlanta University Publications, 15. Atlanta: Atlanta UP, 1910.

Eastman, Henry Parker. *Eastman's English Grammar: A Practical Grammar for Schools and Colleges*. Greenville, TX: Dennis, 1904.

East Texas Normal College. *Catalogue*. [annual publication.] 1896–1917.

Eldred, Janet Carey, and Peter Mortensen. "Coming to Know a Century." *College English* 62.6 (July 2000): 747–55.

Eliot, Charles William. "The New Education. Its Organization." Pt. 1. *Atlantic Monthly* Feb. 1869: 203–20.

"Episcopal Address." *Journal of the Twenty-Fourth Delegated General Conference of the Methodist Episcopal Church, 1904*. Los Angeles, 4–29 May 1904. Ed. Joseph B. Hingeley. New York: Eaton, 1904. 111–50.

Erhardt, Marie. Editorial. *Daedalian Monthly Annual Issue. Daedalian Yearbook 1914*. 189.

Fabio, Sarah Webster. "Who Speaks Negro?" *Negro Digest* 16.2 (Dec. 1966): 54–58.

Farmer, James. *Lay Bare the Heart: An Autobiography of the Civil Rights Movement*. New York: Arbor, 1985.

Farnham, Christie Anne. *The Education of the Southern Belle: Higher Education and Student Socialization in the Antebellum South*. New York: New York UP, 1994.

Farnsworth, Robert M. *Melvin B. Tolson, 1898–1966: Plain Talk and Poetic Prophecy*. Columbia: U of Missouri P, 1984.

Ferreira-Buckley, Linda. "Rescuing the Archives from Foucault." *College English* 61.5 (May 1999): 577–83.

Fisher, Ada Lois Sipuel (with Danney Goble). *A Matter of Black and White: The Autobiography of Ada Lois Sipuel Fisher*. Norman: U of Oklahoma P, 1996.

Fitzgerald, Kathryn. "The Platteville Papers: Inscribing Frontier Ideology and Culture in a Nineteenth-Century Writing Assignment." *College English* 64.3 (Jan. 2002): 273–301.

———. "A Rediscovered Tradition: European Pedagogy and Composition in Nineteenth-Century Midwestern Normal Schools." *CCC* 53.2 (Dec. 2001): 224–50.

Flasch, Joy. "Melvin Beaunoris Tolson—the Man." Black Heritage Week. Oklahoma State U. April 1967. Tolson Papers, Library of Congress.

———. *Melvin B. Tolson*. New York: Twayne, 1972.

———. "Melvin B. Tolson: A Critical Biography." Diss. Oklahoma State U, 1969.

———. *Obsequies of Melvin Beaunoris Tolson, Senior*. 3 Sept. 1966. Tolson Papers, Library of Congress.

Fogarty, Daniel. *Roots for a New Rhetoric*. New York: Teachers College, Columbia U, 1959.

Franklin, John Hope. Telephone interview. 6 May 2001.

Freedmen's Aid Society. *Report of the Freedmen's Aid Society of the Methodist Episcopal Church, 1868*. Cincinnati: Western Methodist Book Concern, 1868.

Fritz, Edna Ingels. Fritz Collection, Archives, Texas Woman's U.

Froebel, Friedrich. *Pedagogics of the Kindergarten*. Trans. Josephine Jarvis. New York: Appleton, 1900.

Fultz, Michael. "'The Morning Cometh': African-American Periodicals, Education, and the Black Middle Class, 1900–1930." *Print Culture in a Diverse America*. Ed. James P. Danky and Wayne A. Wiegand. Urbana: U of Illinois P, 1998. 129–48.

Galyon, Daisy. Interview with Corrinne E. Crow. 4 July 1974. Archives, James G. Gee Library, Texas A&M U–Commerce.

Gammage, Judie Walton. "Quest for Equality: An Historical Overview of Women's Rights Activism in Texas, 1890–1975." Diss. North Texas State U, 1982.

Garbus, Julie. "Riding the Third Wave of Rhetorical Historiography." *Rhetoric Society Quarterly* 31.3 (Summer 2001): 119–29.

Gere, Anne Ruggles. *Intimate Practices: Literacy and Cultural Work in U.S. Women's Clubs, 1880–1920.* Urbana: U of Illinois P, 1997.

Gibbs, Warmoth T. *President Matthew W. Dogan of Wiley College.* Marshall, TX: Firmin Greer, [1933?].

Gillette, Michael L. "Heman Marion Sweatt: Civil Rights Plaintiff." *Black Leaders: Texans for Their Times.* Ed. Alwyn Barr and Robert A. Calvert. Austin: Texas State Historical Assoc., 1981. 157–88.

Gilyard, Keith, and Elaine Richardson. "Students' Right to Possibility: Basic Writing and African American Rhetoric." *Insurrections: Approaches to Resistance in Composition Studies.* Ed. Andrea Greenbaum. Albany: State U of New York P, 2001. 37–51.

Goodwin, Ralph. "A Light Which Cannot Be Hid: The Story of East Texas State University, 1889–1989." Unpublished manuscript. Archives, James G. Gee Library, Texas A&M U–Commerce, 1990.

Gordon, Lynn D. *Gender and Higher Education in the Progressive Era.* New Haven: Yale UP, 1990.

Gotera, Vincente F. "'Lines of Tempered Steel': An Interview with Yusef Komunyakaa." *Callaloo* 13.2 (Spring 1990): 215–29.

Graff, Gerald. *Professing Literature: An Institutional History.* Chicago: U of Chicago P, 1987.

Greer, Jackie Matthews. "Career Preparation Part of the Academic Tradition." *Traditions.* Ed. Mary Evelyn Blagg Huey. Denton: Texas Woman's U, 2001. 30.

Greer, Jane. "'No Smiling Madonna': Marian Wharton and the Struggle to Construct a Critical Pedagogy for the Working Class, 1914–1917." *CCC* 51.2 (Dec. 1999): 248–71.

Halloran, S. Michael. "From Rhetoric to Composition: The Teaching of Writing in America to 1900." *A Short History of Writing Instruction from Ancient Greece to Twentieth-Century America.* Ed. James J. Murphy. Davis, CA: Hermagoras, 1990. 151–82.

———. "Rhetoric in the American College Curriculum: The Decline of Public Discourse." *PRE/TEXT* 3.3 (1982): 245–69. Rpt. in *Pre/Text: The First Decade.* Ed. Victor J. Vitanza. Pittsburgh: U of Pittsburgh P, 1993. 93–115.

Hare, Nathaniel. Letter to Melvin Tolson. 12 May 1958. Tolson Papers, Library of Congress.

Harper, Charles A. *A Century of Public Teacher Education*. Washington: NEA, 1939.

Harvard University. *Catalogue*. [annual publication.] 1873–86.

Hatfield, W. Wilbur. "The Project Method in Composition. 1." *English Journal* 11.10 (Dec. 1922): 599–609.

Heights, Henry. Letter to Melvin Tolson. 9 Sept. 1944. Tolson Papers, Library of Congress.

Heintze, Michael R. *Private Black Colleges in Texas, 1865–1954*. College Station: Texas A&M UP, 1985.

Henry College. *Catalogue*. 1896. [catalogued as Emerson College.] Center for American History, U of Texas at Austin.

Herbst, Jurgen. *And Sadly Teach: Teacher Education and Professionalization in American Culture*. Madison: U of Wisconsin P, 1989.

Holbrook, Alfred. *An English Grammar, Conformed to Present Usage; with an Objective Method of Teaching the Elements of the English Language*. Cincinnati: Van Antwerp, 1873.

———. *A New English Grammar, Conformed to Present Usage; with an Objective Method of Teaching the Elements of the English Language*. Cincinnati: Van Antwerp, 1889.

———. *The Normal: Methods of Teaching the Common Branches*. New York: Barnes, 1874.

———. *Reminiscences of the Happy Life of a Teacher*. Cincinnati: Elm Street, 1885.

Holt, Mildred Pearce. "A History of the College of Industrial Arts." M.A. thesis. U of Texas, 1926.

Hook, Lucyle. Hook Collection, Archives, Texas Woman's U.

Horner, Winifred Bryan. *Nineteenth-Century Scottish Rhetoric: The American Connection*. Carbondale: Southern Illinois UP, 1993.

Horowitz, Helen Lefkowitz. *Alma Mater: Design and Experience in the Women's Colleges from Their Nineteenth-Century Beginnings to the 1930s*. 2nd ed. Amherst: U of Massachusetts P, 1993.

Hubbard, Louis H. "The Place of Vocational Training as an Objective of the Woman's College." Diss. U of Texas, 1929.

———. *Recollections of a Texas Educator*. Salado, TX: self-published, 1964.

———. "'What Young Women Think of Equal Pay for Equal Work,' and 'The Employment of Married Women.'" *Proceedings of the Fourteenth Annual Meeting, Southern Association of Colleges for Women*. Louisville, 4 Dec. 1935. 34–35.

Huey, Mary Evelyn Blagg, ed. *Traditions*. Denton: Texas Woman's U, 2001.

Hughes, Langston. "Here to Yonder." *Chicago Defender* 15 Dec. 1945: n. pag. Tolson Papers, Library of Congress.

Hughes, Opal. "Song of Myself." *Daedalian Yearbook 1911*. 158.

"Is the Higher Education of Girls a Good Use for War Profits?" *Evening Sun* [New York] 26 Apr. 1916: 10.

Jackson, W. A. Interview with Corrinne E. Crow. 5 Mar. 1974. Archives, James G. Gee Library, Texas A&M U–Commerce.

Jarrett, Hobart. "Adventures in Interracial Debates." *Crisis* Aug. 1935: 240.

———. Letter to Robert Farnsworth. 15 Mar. 1982. Tolson Papers, Library of Congress.

Jenkins, Martin D. "Enrollment in Negro Colleges and Universities, 1937–38." *Journal of Negro Education* 7.2 (Apr. 1938): 118–23.

Jewett, Ida. A. *English in State Teachers Colleges: A Catalogue Study*. New York: Teachers College, Columbia U, 1927.

Johnson, Nan. *Nineteenth-Century Rhetoric in North America*. Carbondale: Southern Illinois UP, 1991.

Jones, Edward A. *A Candle in the Dark: A History of Morehouse College*. Valley Forge, PA: Judson, 1967.

Jones, Thomas Jesse. *Negro Education: A Study of the Private and Higher Schools for Colored People in the United States*. Bulletin (Office of Education) 38–39. Washington, DC: GPO, 1917.

Justin, Margaret M. "Background for Home Economists." *Journal of Home Economics* 38.4 (Apr. 1946): 196–98.

Kansas State Agricultural College. *Catalogue*. 1874.

Kates, Susan. *Activist Rhetorics and American Higher Education, 1885–1937*. Carbondale: Southern Illinois UP, 2001.

Kelley, William Melvin. Letter to Melvin Tolson. May 1966. Tolson Papers, Library of Congress.

Kerber, Linda K. "Separate Spheres, Female Worlds, Woman's Place: The Rhetoric of Women's History." *Journal of American History* 75.1 (June 1988): 9–39.

Kerl, Simon. *Elements of Composition and Rhetoric*. New York: Ivison, 1869.

Kilpatrick, William H. Introduction. *The Education of Man: Aphorisms*. By Heinrich Pestalozzi. New York: Philosophical Library, 1951. vii–xii.

———. *The Project Method: The Use of the Purposeful Act in the Educative Process*. New York: Teachers College, Columbia U, 1929.

Kitzhaber, Albert R. *Rhetoric in American Colleges, 1850–1900*. Dallas: Southern Methodist UP, 1990.

Knippa, Heidi Ann. "Salvation of a University: The Admission of Women to Texas A&M." M.A. thesis. U of Texas at Austin, 1995.

Kourenina, Lyudmila, and Debbie E. McGhee. "Graduate Survey Results: English—Seattle Campus." *1999 University of Washington Graduates, One Year after Graduation.* U of Washington. Office of Educational Assessment Report 00-7 (Oct. 2000). 15 Feb. 2003 <http://www.washington.edu/oea/0007.htm>.

Kynell, Teresa C. *Writing in a Milieu of Utility: The Move to Technical Communication in American Engineering Programs, 1850–1950.* 2nd ed. Stamford, CT: Ablex, 2000.

Lacy, Etta M. "English as She Is Spoke at C.I.A." *Daedalian Monthly* Mar. 1912: 4–6.

"Launching of College Was Big News Here: How Denton Record 'Covered' Opening." *Denton Record-Chronicle* 5 Nov. 1952, sec. 2: 1–10.

Levi, Giovanni. "On Microhistory." *New Perspectives on Historical Writing.* Ed. Peter Burke. University Park: Pennsylvania State UP, 1992. 93–113.

Lewis, Bertram. Letter to Melvin Tolson. 29 Mar. 1950. Tolson Papers, Library of Congress.

Linck, Ernestine Sewell, and Charles E. Linck Jr. *The Amazing Etta Booth Mayo.* Commerce, TX: Cow Hill, 1995.

Lincoln University. *Catalogue.* [annual publication.] 1922–23.

———. Transcript of Melvin Tolson. 1923.

Little, Monroe H. "The Extra-Curricular Activities of Black College Students 1868–1940." *Journal of Negro History* 65.2 (Spring 1980): 135–48.

Llorens, David. "Seeking a New Image: Writers Converge at Fisk University." *Negro Digest* 15.8 (June 1966): 54–68.

Logan, Shirley Wilson. *"We Are Coming": The Persuasive Discourse of Nineteenth-Century Black Women.* Carbondale: Southern Illinois UP, 1999.

Lowe, Ramona. "Poem 'Rendezvous with America' Wins Fame for Melvin Tolson." *Chicago Defender* 24 Feb. 1945: n.pag. Tolson Papers, Library of Congress.

Lucas, Christopher J. *Teacher Education in America: Reform Agendas for the Twenty-First Century.* New York: St. Martin's, 1997.

Lunday, Ella. *The Teaching of High School English.* Texas State Department of Education. Bulletin 312 (Dec. 1932).

Lunsford, Andrea A. "On Reclaiming Rhetorica." Lunsford, *Reclaiming* 3–8.

———, ed. *Reclaiming Rhetorica: Women in the Rhetorical Tradition.* Pittsburgh: U of Pittsburgh P, 1995.

Massey, Jackson. "A History of College Education in Hunt County." M.A. thesis. U of Texas, 1928.

Mayo, Marion J. "Reminiscences of the Early Life of Two Brothers." Bledsoe 159–73.

Mayo, William L. *College Orations: Selected Extracts Arranged for Declamatory Contests.* 2nd ed. Commerce: East Texas Normal College, 1901.

Mayo del Busto, Gladys. "Mrs. Etta Booth Mayo." Bledsoe 175–79.

McArthur, Judith N. *Creating the New Woman: The Rise of Southern Women's Progressive Culture in Texas, 1893–1918.* Urbana: U of Illinois P, 1998.

McCandless, Amy Thompson. *The Past in the Present: Women's Higher Education in the Twentieth-Century American South.* Tuscaloosa: U of Alabama P, 1999.

McCown, Modena. Interview with Opal Williams and Joe Fred Cox. 1972. Archives, James G. Gee Library, Texas A&M U–Commerce.

McElhaney, Jacquelyn Masur. *Pauline Periwinkle and Progressive Reform in Dallas.* College Station: Texas A&M UP, 1998.

McHenry, Elizabeth. *Forgotten Readers: Recovering the Lost History of African American Literary Societies.* Durham, NC: Duke UP, 2002.

Meadows, Leon Renfroe. *A Study of the Teaching of English Composition in Teachers Colleges in the United States.* New York: Teachers College, Columbia U, 1928.

Menger, Johnowene Brackenridge Crutcher. "M. Eleanor Brackenridge, 1837–1924, a Third Generation Advocate of Education." M.A. thesis. Trinity U, 1964.

Miller, Susan. *Assuming the Positions: Cultural Pedagogy and the Politics of Commonplace Writing.* Pittsburgh: U of Pittsburgh P, 1998.

———. *Textual Carnivals: The Politics of Composition.* Carbondale: Southern Illinois UP, 1991.

Miller, Thomas P. *The Formation of College English: Rhetoric and Belles Lettres in the British Cultural Provinces.* Pittsburgh: U of Pittsburgh P, 1997.

———. "Where Did College English Studies Come From?" *Rhetoric Review* 9.1 (Fall 1990): 50–69.

Miller-Bernal, Leslie. *Separate by Degree: Women Students' Experiences in Single-Sex and Coeducational Colleges.* New York: Lang, 2000.

Miller-Bernal, Leslie, and Susan L. Poulson, eds. *Going Coed: Women's Experiences in Formerly Men's Colleges and Universities, 1950–2000.* Nashville: Vanderbilt UP, 2004.

Moore, Minnie. "Reminiscences and Impressive Incidents in East Texas Normal College." Bledsoe 181–91.

National Educational Association. "Report of the Committee on Normal Education." *Journal of Proceedings and Addresses, 1892.* New York: NEA, 1893. 781–88.

Negro Year Book, 1921–22. Ed. Monroe N. Work. Tuskegee, AL: Tuskegee Institute, 1922.

Negro Year Book, 1941–46. Ed. Jessie Parkhurst Guzman. Tuskegee, AL: Tuskegee Institute, 1947.

Newcomer, Mabel. *A Century of Higher Education for American Women*. New York: Harper, 1959.

Nielsen, Aldon L. "Melvin B. Tolson and the Deterritorialization of Modernism." *African American Review* 26.2 (Summer 1992): 241–55.

Norris, Clarence W. *Up from Poverty*. [San Antonio?]: self-published, 1987.

North, Stephen M. *The Making of Knowledge in Composition: Portrait of an Emerging Field*. Upper Montclair, NJ: Boynton/Cook, 1987.

Novick, Peter. *That Noble Dream: The "Objectivity Question" and the American Historical Profession*. Cambridge: Cambridge UP, 1988.

Ogren, Christine A. "Where Coeds Were Coeducated: Normal Schools in Wisconsin, 1870–1920." *History of Education Quarterly* 35.1 (Spring 1995): 1–26.

Olson, Gary A. "Toward a Post-Process Composition: Abandoning the Rhetoric of Assertion." *Post-Process Theory: Beyond the Writing-Process Paradigm*. Ed. Thomas Kent. Carbondale: Southern Illinois UP, 1999. 7–15.

———. "Writing, Literacy and Technology: Toward a Cyborg Writing." (Interview with Donna Haraway). *Women Writing Culture*. Ed. Gary A. Olson and Elizabeth Hirsh. Albany: State U of New York P, 1995. 45–77.

"One Harlem Poet Who Writes Language of the 'Blacks.'" *Muhammad Speaks* 13 Aug. 1965: 17.

Paine, Charles. *The Resistant Writer: Rhetoric as Immunity, 1850 to the Present*. Albany: State U of New York P, 1999.

Palmer, Joyce Cornette, and Deb Martin. "A Brief History of the Department of English, Speech, and Foreign Languages at Texas Woman's University, 1901–2000." Archives, Texas Woman's U.

Pangburn, Jessie M. *The Evolution of the American Teachers College*. New York: Teachers College, Columbia U, 1932.

Parker, John W. "Current Debate Practices in Thirty Negro Colleges." *Journal of Negro Education* 9.1 (Jan. 1940): 32–38.

———. "The Status of Debate in the Negro College." *Journal of Negro Education* 24.2 (Spring 1955): 146–53.

Parr, James Harvey. "The History of Central Normal College." M.A. thesis. Indiana U, 1927.

Payne, Bruce R. "The Probable Future of the Higher Education for Women." *Proceedings of the Thirteenth Annual Meeting, Southern Association of Colleges for Women*. Atlanta, 5 Dec. 1934. 56–61.

Pearson, P. David. "Reading in the Twentieth Century." CIERA Report 01–08. 9 August 2001. Center for the Improvement of Early Reading Achievement, U of Michigan School of Education. 3 July 2006 <http://www.ciera.org/library/archive/index.html>.

Pestalozzi, Johann Heinrich. *How Gertrude Teaches Her Children: An Attempt to Help Mothers Teach Their Own Children and an Account of the Method.* Trans. Lucy E. Holland and Frances C. Turner. Ed. Ebenezer Cooke. Syracuse, NY: Bardeen, 1898.

"Poet Thieves by Listening, Tolson Says." *Daily Oklahoman* 15 Feb. 1966: n. pag. Tolson Papers, Library of Congress.

Potter, David. "The Debate Tradition." *Argumentation and Debate: Principles and Practices.* Rev. ed. Ed. James H. McBath. New York: Holt, 1963. 14–32.

Randall, Dudley. "Portrait of a Poet as Raconteur." *Negro Digest* 15.3 (Jan. 1966): 54–57.

Ratcliffe, Krista. "Rhetorical Listening: A Trope for Interpretive Invention and a 'Code of Cross-Cultural Conduct.'" *CCC* 51.2 (Dec. 1999): 195–224.

Rayburn, Sam. "A Teacher Who Seized Time by the Forelock." *NEA Journal* 49.3 (Mar. 1960): 25.

Readers' Guide to Periodical Literature. Vol. 7 (Jan. 1929–June 1932). Ed. Alice M. Dougan and Bertha Joel. New York: Wilson, 1932.

Regan, Alison Elizabeth. "Promises, Problems, and Politics: The History of Rhetoric, English Studies, and Writing Instruction at the University of Texas at Austin, 1883–1994." Diss. U of Texas at Austin, 1996.

Roberts-Miller, Patricia. *Deliberate Conflict: Argument, Political Theory, and Composition Classes.* Carbondale: Southern Illinois UP, 2004.

Roebuck, Julian B., and Komanduri S. Murty. *Historically Black Colleges and Universities: Their Place in American Higher Education.* Westport, CT: Praeger, 1993.

Rollins, Edmund. "Texas U. Hears Racism Blasted by Negro Speaker." *San Antonio Register* 15 Nov. 1946: 1–5.

Rothermel, Beth Ann. "A Sphere of Noble Action: Gender, Rhetoric, and Influence at a Nineteenth-Century Massachusetts State Normal School." *Rhetoric Society Quarterly* 33.1 (Winter 2003): 35–64.

Royster, Jacqueline Jones. *Traces of a Stream: Literacy and Social Change among African American Women.* Pittsburgh: U of Pittsburgh P, 2000.

Royster, Jacqueline Jones, and Jean C. Williams. "History in the Spaces Left: African American Presence and Narratives of Composition Studies." *CCC* 50.4 (June 1999): 563–84.

Rudolph, Frederick. *Curriculum: A History of the American Undergraduate Course of Study since 1636.* San Francisco: Jossey-Bass, 1977.

Salvatori, Mariolina Rizzi, ed. *Pedagogy: Disturbing History, 1819–1829.* Pittsburgh: U of Pittsburgh P, 1996.

Samuel Huston College. *Catalogue.* [annual publication.] 1900–21.

Sánchez, Raúl. "Composition's Ideology Apparatus: A Critique." *JAC* 21.4 (Fall 2001): 741–59.

Schemo, Diana Jean. "Black Colleges Lobby Hard to Lure the Best and Brightest." *New York Times* 8 Mar. 2001. Lexis-Nexis.

Scherman, Tony. "The Great Debaters." *American Legacy* Spring 1997: 40–42.

Schultz, Lucille M. *The Young Composers: Composition's Beginnings in Nineteenth-Century Schools.* Carbondale: Southern Illinois UP, 1999.

Scott, Fred Newton, and Joseph Villiers Denney. *Elementary English Composition.* Boston: Allyn, 1900.

———. *The New Composition-Rhetoric.* Boston: Allyn, 1911.

———. *Paragraph-Writing: A Rhetoric for Colleges.* Boston: Allyn, 1909.

Seaholm, Megan. "Earnest Women: The White Woman's Club Movement in Progressive Era Texas, 1880–1920." Diss. Rice U, 1988.

———. "Texas Federation of Women's Clubs." *Handbook of Texas Online.* 4 Dec. 2002. Texas State Historical Assoc. 9 Jan. 2003 <http://www.tsha.utexas.edu/handbook/online/articles/view/TT/vnt1.html>.

Shapiro, Karl. Introduction. *Harlem Gallery: Book 1, the Curator.* By Melvin B. Tolson. New York: Twayne, 1965. 11–15.

———. Letter to Melvin Tolson. 15 Apr. 1965. Tolson Papers, Library of Congress.

Sharer, Wendy B. *Vote and Voice: Women's Organizations and Political Literacy, 1915–1930.* Carbondale: Southern Illinois UP, 2004.

Shepard, Aline. "The Work of Women's Clubs in America." *Daedalian Quarterly* Spring 1917: 34–37.

Shurtleff, Nathaniel B., ed. *Records of the Governor and Company of the Massachusetts Bay in New England.* Vol. 2. Boston: William White, 1853. 5 vols.

Silber, Kate. *Pestalozzi.* 3rd ed. London: Routledge, 1973.

Simmons, Sue Carter. "Radcliffe Responses to Harvard Rhetoric: 'An Absurdly Stiff Way of Thinking.'" *Nineteenth-Century Women Learn to Write.* Ed. Catherine Hobbs. Charlottesville: UP of Virginia, 1995. 264–92.

Sloss, Minerva A. "A Tribute to Melvin Tolson." *Oklahoma Today* 26.3 (Summer 1976): 13–15.

Smith, Morgan A. *Socialism in Song.* Commerce, Texas: self-published, 1911.

Smitherman, Geneva. "'The Blacker the Berry, the Sweeter the Juice': African American Student Writers." *The Need for Story: Cultural Diversity in Classroom and Community.* Ed. Anne Haas Dyson and Celia Genishi. Urbana, IL: NCTE, 1994. 80–101.

———. *Talkin and Testifyin: The Language of Black America.* Boston: Houghton, 1977.

Smith-Rosenberg, Carroll. *Disorderly Conduct: Visions of Gender in Victorian America.* New York: Knopf, 1985.

Somerville, John Alexander. *Man of Colour.* Kingston, Jamaica: Pioneer, 1951.

"State Examination Questions." *Texas School Journal* 14.5 (May 1896): 168–71.

State University of New York at Albany, Office of Institutional Research. *A Study of Albany Alumni Who Graduated from Sixteen of the Largest Undergraduate Majors.* Assessment Report 11 (Apr. 1992).

Stoddard, Helen M. *To the Noon Rest: The Life, Work and Addresses of Mrs. Helen M. Stoddard.* Ed. Fanny L. Armstrong. Butler, IN: Higley, 1909.

Storms, Albert Boynton. "Democracy and Education." *Journal of Proceedings and Addresses of the Forty-Fifth Annual Meeting.* NEA. Winona, MN: NEA, 1907. 62–70.

Talbot, Marion, and Lois Kimball Mathews Rosenberry. *The History of the American Association of University Women, 1881–1931.* Boston: Houghton, 1931.

Taylor, A. Elizabeth. "A Summary History of Texas Woman's University, 1901–1971." Archives, Texas Woman's U.

Taylor, Douglas Barnes. "Negro Education in Texas." M.A. thesis. U of Texas, 1927.

Taylor, Howard. "Euthenics 1—Human Adjustment: An Orientation Course Offered at Oklahoma College for Women." *Proceedings of the Tenth Annual Meeting, Southern Association of Colleges for Women.* Montgomery, 2 Dec. 1931. 21–23.

Texas Almanac and State Industrial Guide for 1912. Dallas: Belo, 1912.

Texas Woman's University. *Catalogue.* [annual publication.] 1903–39.

———. *Chaparral*; *Daedalian.* [annual yearbooks]. 1906–39.

———. *Daedalian Monthly*; *Daedalian Quarterly.* [monthly or quarterly publications.] 1911–39.

———. *Fall Announcement.* 1904.

———. *Sixth Biennial Report of the Board of Regents.* 1913–14.

Thatcher, Rebecca. "106-year-old Huston-Tillotson Alumna Honored." *Austin American-Statesman* 29 July 1999. Lexis Nexis.

Thompson, Joyce. *Marking a Trail: A History of the Texas Woman's University.* Denton: Texas Woman's UP, 1982.

Threlkeld, Hilda. [printed as "Thelkeld."] "What the South Expects of the Education of Its College Women." *Proceedings of the Twenty-Fourth Annual Meeting, Southern Association of Colleges for Women.* Louisville, 1 Dec. 1947. 35–40.

Todd, William Clyde. "The Attitudes of the Negroes of Texas toward Higher Education." M.A. thesis. U of Texas, 1929.

Toler, Velta Pardue. "Educational Activities of Texas Federation of Women's Clubs—1897–1937." M.A. thesis. U of Texas, 1938.

Tolson, Melvin B. *Caviar and Cabbage: Selected Columns by Melvin B. Tolson from the* Washington Tribune, *1937–1944.* Ed. Robert M. Farnsworth. Columbia: U of Missouri P, 1982.

———. "The Foreground of Negro Poetry." *Kansas Quarterly* 7.3 (Summer 1975): 30–35.

———. *"Harlem Gallery" and Other Poems of Melvin B. Tolson.* Ed. Raymond Nelson. Charlottesville: UP of Virginia, 1999.

———. *The Harlem Group of Negro Writers.* Ed. Edward J. Mullen. Westport, CT: Greenwood, 2001.

———. "Langston Hughes' Goodbye Christ a Challenge and Warning." *Pittsburgh Courier* 28 Jan. 1933: sec. 2: 10.

———. Letter to Benjamin and Kate Bell. 28 Dec. 1961. Tolson Papers, Library of Congress.

———. Letter to *Partisan Review.* 3 Dec. 1956. Tolson Papers, Library of Congress.

———. "A Man against the Idols of the Tribe." *Modern Quarterly* 11.7 (Fall 1940): 29–32.

———. Melvin Beaunoris Tolson Papers, Library of Congress.

———. "The Odyssey of a Manuscript." *New Letters* 48.1 (Fall 1981): 5–15.

———. "A Poet's Odyssey." *Anger, and Beyond: The Negro Writer in the United States.* Ed. Herbert Hill. New York: Harper, 1966. 181–95.

———. "Recipes for the Success of Black Men." *Oracle* [1938?]: 15–16. Tolson Papers, Library of Congress.

———. "Richard Wright: Native Son." *Modern Quarterly* 11.5 (Winter 1939): 19–24.

———. "She Can't Take It." *Flash* 31 Aug. 1939: 6. Tolson Papers, Library of Congress.

———. "Some Problems of the Writer as Artist." Tolson Papers, Library of Congress.

———. "Wanted: A New Negro Leadership." *Oracle* Sept. 1937: 10–11.

Tolson, Melvin B., Jr. Telephone interview. 25 Feb. 2001.

"Two Officials of A.A.U.W. Speak at Colleges Here." *Denton Record-Chronicle* 29 Mar. 1928: 6.

United States. Bureau of the Census. *Fifteenth Census of the United States: 1930.* Vol. 3, pt. 2. Washington, DC: GPO, 1932.

———. Bureau of the Census. "Table A-6. Age Distribution of College Students 14 Years Old and Over, by Sex; October 1947 to 2000." 1 June 2001. U.S. Census Bureau. 1 Jan. 2003 <http://www.census.gov/population/socdemo/school/tabA-6.pdf>.

———. Bureau of the Census. *Twelfth Census of the United States, Taken in the Year 1900.* Vol. 2, pt. 2. Washington, DC: GPO, 1902.

———. Bureau of Education. *Report of the Commissioner of Education for the Year 1890–91.* Vol. 2. Washington, DC: GPO, 1894.

———. Bureau of Education. *Report of the Commissioner of Education for the Year 1900–01.* Vol. 2. Washington, DC: GPO, 1902.

———. Bureau of Education. *Report of the Commissioner of Education for the Year Ending June 30, 1905.* Vol. 1. Washington, DC: GPO, 1907.

University of Texas. *Catalogue.* [annual publication.] 1900–21.

Urquhart, George R. "The Status of Secondary and Higher Education of Negroes in Texas." M.A. thesis. U of Texas, 1931.

Vanwinkle, Betsy. "Home Sewing Saves Half of Ready-Made Cost." *Denton Record-Chronicle* 4 Apr. 1979: 2C.

Varnum, Robin. *Fencing with Words: A History of Writing Instruction at Amherst College during the Era of Theodore Baird, 1938–1966.* Urbana, IL: NCTE, 1996.

Vaughn, Lola Mae. "Teacher Training in Texas State College for Women." M.A. thesis. Texas State College for Women, 1939.

Wagner, Joanne. "'Intelligent Members or Restless Disturbers': Women's Rhetorical Styles, 1880–1920." Lunsford, *Reclaiming* 185–202.

Welch, June Rayfield. *The Colleges of Texas.* Dallas: GLA, 1981.

Wells, Guy H. "How Youth Looks at Social and Political Questions." *Proceedings of the Fourteenth Annual Meeting, Southern Association of Colleges for Women.* Louisville, 4 Dec. 1935. 32–34.

Wells, Henrietta Pauline Bell. Personal interview. 1 May 2001.

Whitbread, Thomas. "In Praise of M. B. Tolson." *Whomp and Moonshiver.* Brockport, NY: BOA, 1982. 45–46.

White, Edmund Valentine. *Historical Record of the State College for Women: The First Forty-Five Years, 1903–48.* College bulletin 364 (1 Dec. 1948).

———. *Lengthening Shadows, or, From Country School to College Campus.* Denton: self-published, [1948?].

White, Hayden V. *Metahistory: The Historical Imagination in Nineteenth-Century Europe.* Baltimore: Johns Hopkins UP, 1973.

———. *Tropics of Discourse: Essays in Cultural Criticism.* Baltimore: John Hopkins UP, 1978.

Wilds, Deborah J. *Minorities in Higher Education, 1999–2000.* Washington: American Council on Education, 2000.

Wiley, Autrey Nell. Wiley Collection, Archives, Texas Woman's U.

Wiley College. *Catalogue.* [annual publication.] 1920–45.

"Wiley College and University of Kansas Debate April 20." *Kansas City Call* 6 Apr. 1934: 1.

Williams, William Carlos. *Paterson.* New York: New Directions, 1963.

Woodson, Carter G. *The Mis-Education of the Negro.* 1933. Washington: Africa World, 1990.

Work, Mary B. *Biographical Sketch of Cree T. Work.* Denton: Texas Woman's U, [195-?].

———. "The Home Economics Movement in Texas." *Dallas Morning News* 29 Mar. 1909: 12.

Young, Richard E. "Paradigms and Problems: Needed Research in Rhetorical Invention." *Research on Composing: Points of Departure.* Ed. Charles R. Cooper and Lee Odell. Urbana, IL: NCTE, 1978. 29–47.

Zaluda, Scott. "Lost Voices of the Harlem Renaissance: Writing Assigned at Howard University, 1919–31." *CCC* 50.2 (Dec. 1998): 232–57.

INDEX

Abney, Teresa, 104
Abrahams, Roger D., 36
Adams, Franklin, 126
Adams, Henry, 155
Adams, John Quincy, 119
Adams, Katherine H., 64
African American discourse, 36, 40, 51, 55–56
African American Vernacular English (AAVE), 36
African Americans: and black newspapers, 52, 57; and civil rights movement, 42; in Denton County, 106; intellect of, 47; literacy of, 22; lynching and other violence against, 28, 37, 46, 50–51, 128; suffrage for, 81, 106. *See also* black colleges; desegregation; segregation
Alexander, Thomas, 138
American Association of University Women (AAUW), 78, 80, 166*n*9
Anderson, John A., 82
anschauung (sense impression), 118, 168*n*3
Aptheker, Herbert, 51
Arendt, Hannah, 38
Aristotle, 49, 165*n*6
Armstrong, Samuel Chapman, 18
audience, 48, 57, 98–99
authority, 37–43
Avent, Joseph Emory, 122

Bacon, Jacqueline, 15
Bagg, Lyman, 20
Baker, Elizabeth, 141
Balester, Valerie M., 36
Barnes, Walter, 138–39
Bates College, 44
Beil, Gail K., 28
Bell, Benjamin, 42, 49, 51
Bentinck, Catherine, 83, 86, 167*n*21
Berlin, James A., 1, 6, 8, 17, 21, 139
Bérubé, Michael, 16, 58
Bible, 36, 55–56, 110
Biggers, John, 58
Bishop College, 23, 44
Bizzell, William B., 73, 97–98, 166*n*8
Black Arts Movement, 53, 54
black colleges: and academic "whitewashing," 51–52; classical liberal arts tradition at, 15, 19–20, 22, 24, 32, 59–60, 68, 110, 152; competition among, 23; differences among, 22–23; enrollment statistics of, ix, 19, 22, 60–61; faculty and presidents of, 24; institutional features of, 61; mission of, 15–16, 21; private versus public, 18–23; and black communities, 21–22; rhetorical education at, 15, 20–21, 43–44, 59–60; role of, 60–61; in Texas, 18; women students at, 61. *See also* Wiley College
Black Consciousness Movement, 53

Black English Vernacular (BEV), 36
blacks. *See* African Americans
Blanton, Annie Webb, 147, 170*n*17
Blayney, Lindsey, 109
Bledsoe, James Marcus, 134, 137–38, 145
Boswell, Hamilton, 28, 30, 39–40, 42
Bowden, Artemisia, 23
Bowers, William, 61
Bowman, Mary, 136, 138, 144, 145, 148
Bozeman, Jessie, 98
Brackenridge, Eleanor, 71, 77–78, 94–95, 166*n*12
Brackenridge, George, 166*n*12
Bralley, Francis Marion, 73–74, 95–96
Branch, Mary Elizabeth, 23
Brereton, John C., ix, 153
Bridges, Henry T., 132–33, 143–44
Briggs, Le Baron Russell, 3
Brooks, Charles, 118
Brooks, Gwendolyn, 16, 53
Brooks, Maybelle, 98
Brown, Hallie Quinn, 17, 116
Brown, Robert E., 23, 27, 164*nn*7–8
Brown v. Board of Education of Topeka, 164*n*10, 165*n*15
Bruce, William, 170*n*17
Button, Garland, 144, 170*n*16

Callaway, Isadore, 84, 85, 166*n*11
Calverton, V. F., 34
Campbell, Doak Sheridan, 85
Campbell, JoAnn, 65
Cansler, Ronald Lee, 54, 57–58
Carr, Jean Ferguson, 1
Carr, Stephen L., 1
Central Normal College, 122–27, 131–32, 135
Channing, Edward T., 4
Chaucer, Geoffrey, 170*n*18
Ciardi, John, 57
Clark, Evert Mordecai, 121–22
Clark, Lindsay, 127
classical liberal arts tradition, 15, 19–20, 22, 24, 32, 59–60, 68, 110, 152
Claxton, Philander P., 168*n*6
Cobb, Susan F., 63, 101, 167*n*19
Cole, Thomas, 42
Coleridge, Samuel Taylor, 56

colleges. *See* higher education; *specific colleges and universities*
Collins, Margaret, 108
Columbia Teachers College, 138, 149
Columbia University, 29, 33, 84, 165*n*3
Comenius, Johann, 165–66*n*6
community colleges, 150
composition. *See* rhetorical education
Connors, Robert J., 1, 5, 8
Cornell, Charlotte, 167*n*21
Cott, Nancy F., 80–81
Cox, Oliver Cromwell, 15, 28–29, 33
Crawford, Claude, 129, 135, 147
Crawford, Robert, 7
Crowley, Sharon, 1, 6, 8, 51, 110
Cummings, E. E., 103
Cunningham, Minnie Fisher, 81
current-traditional rhetoric, 1–3, 6, 8, 17, 31, 66, 163*n*1, 169–70*n*13
Currier, Theodore S., 164*n*11

Daedalian, 68, 85, 89–90, 92, 94–110, 167*nn*18, 20
Darst, Warren, 122
debate: and audience, 48; at black colleges, 43–44; dress and appearance of debate team, 49; at East Texas Normal College, 134; interracial debates, 44–46, 164*n*11; and logical fallacies, 48–49; at Texas Woman's University (TWU), 93; at University of Texas, 107–8; at Wiley College, 20–21, 25, 43–49, 164*n*14; and women, 44–45, 164*n*12. *See also* rhetorical education
Decker, Sarah Platt, 83
Delpit, Lisa, 148
Denney, Joseph Villiers, 26, 32, 169*n*12
desegregation, 42, 50, 164*n*10, 164–65*n*15. *See also* segregation
Dewey, John, 75, 165*n*6
Dickinson, Emily, 61
Dill, Augustus Granville, 22
Dogan, Matthew, 18, 23, 27, 29–31, 45, 50
Dos Passos, John, 14
Dove, Rita, 16
Du Bois, W. E. B., 22, 49, 51
Duncan, Edna, 87

Eastman, Henry Parker, 145, 146
East Texas Normal College: administration of, 114; buildings of, 169*n*11; chapel exercises at, 137–38, 144, 146; classroom discipline at, 143–44; current name of, 150; debate and oratory at, 134–38; and education for community, 128–33; enrollment statistics of, 114, 167–68*n*1; faculty of, 127–28, 136, 145, 147–48; fires at, 11, 128, 145, 169*n*9; flexible schedule of, 129–30; founding date of, x, 10, 113, 127; gender equality at, 134–35; goals of, xi, 10; grammar instruction at, 113, 145–48; influence of Central Normal College on, 126, 135; and learning by doing, 128–29, 138, 143; literary and musical societies at, 127–28, 133–34; Mayo as founder of, xi, 10, 113; Mayo's pedagogy at, 113–17, 135–38, 150–54; original location of, 127–28; preparatory year at, 131; rhetorical instruction at, 116–17, 135–38, 145–48; student costs at, 131; and textbooks, 123, 124, 138, 145; visiting performers at, 128. *See also* normal schools
Eldred, Janet Carey, 7
Eliot, Charles, 120–21, 169*n*13
Eliot, T. S., 35, 37, 54
Ellison, Lee Monroe, 91
embodied rhetoric, 17
Emerson, Charles Wesley, 93
Emerson, Ralph Waldo, 32
employment of women, 69, 79, 83, 86–87, 112, 167*n*21
English Journal, 115, 150, 168*n*2
Erhardt, Marie, 63, 101

Fabio, Sarah Webster, 54
Farmer, James, 28, 29–30, 38–39, 42
Farmer, James Leonard, 15, 28–30, 34, 55
Farnham, Christine Anne, 82
Farnsworth, Robert M., 42
Fay, Lucy, 89, 95
Ferber, Edna, 103
Ferreira-Buckley, Linda, 11
Fisher, Ada Lois Sipuel, 50, 164–65*n*15
Fisk College, 43, 44, 46, 49, 164*n*11

Fitzgerald, Kathryn, 115, 122
Flasch, Joy, 35, 40, 41, 50, 54, 163*n*2
Fogarty, Daniel, 163*n*1
Franklin, John Hope, 164*n*11
Freedmen's Aid Society, 15, 23, 24, 164*n*6
Fritz, Edna Ingels, 80, 84–85
Froebel, Friedrich, 119, 126, 135, 168*n*7
Frost, Robert, 55, 96, 102
Fultz, Michael, 52

Garbus, Julie, 6
Gearhart, Judge, 134
gender. *See* women
General Federation of Women's Clubs (GFWC), 76, 83, 166*n*7
Genung, John Franklin, 32, 169*n*12
George Peabody College, 69, 141
Gere, Anne Ruggles, 65
Gibbs, Mrs. W. D., 70
Gilyard, Keith, 36
Goodwin, Ralph, 133
Gordon, Lynn D., 12–13, 65, 97
grammar. *See* rhetorical education
Grant, Jane, 165*n*2
Grant, Jason, 25–26
Green, Seth E., 146
Greer, Jackie Matthews, 86
Greer, Jane, 66
Grubbs, Vincent W., 77

Hale, Ruth, 65, 107, 165*n*2
Hall, Samuel Read, 118
Haraway, Donna, 8
Harlem Gallery (Tolson), 16, 53, 54, 58
Harper, Charles A., 135
Harper, William F., 122
Harvard University: debate at, 43; Eliot as president of, 120–21, 169*n*13; graduate school of education at, 149; music and drama clubs of, 128; newspaper at, 98; and Paine, 7; Radcliffe as coordinate institution of, 165*n*3; rhetorical education at, 66, 92; utilitarian value of education at, 155; writing skills at, 3, 169–70*n*13
Hatfield, W. Wilbur, 168*n*2
Hayden, Robert, 56

Hayes, Robert E., 42
Head, Edith, 86–87, 167n13
Heights, Henry, 43
Heintze, Michael R., 163n4
Henderson, Rev. J. R., 49
Henry College, 132–33, 143–44, 170n15
Herbart, Friedrich, 119
Herbst, Jurgen, 148–49, 150
higher education: careerism among students in, 170–71n2; statistics on, 152, 170n1. *See also* black colleges; normal schools; rhetorical education; *specific colleges and universities*
Hill, Adams Sherman, 4, 140, 141, 169–70nn12–13
Holbrook, Alfred, 119, 122–24, 126, 145
home demonstration agents, 86
home economics, 68, 70, 79, 83–87, 88, 111
Hook, Lucyle, 102
Horn, Paul Whitfield, 63–64
Horner, Winifred, 7
Horowitz, Helen Lefkowitz, 65
Hosic, James Fleming, 168n2
Howard University, 49, 51, 61
Hubbard, Louis H., 74–76, 79, 96, 107
Hubbell, Julia, 145
Hughes, Langston, 49
Hughes, Opal, 104–8
Humphries, Jessie, 95
Hurston, Zora Neale, 53
Hutchinson, A. S. M., 103

integration. *See* desegregation

Jackson, W. A., 137
Jarrett, Hobart, 31, 42, 46–47, 48
Jefferson, Thomas, 49
Johnson, Eliza Sophia, 77–78
Johnson, Nan, 5
Jones, Elinor, 106
Jones, Thomas Jesse, 163n4
journalism, 98, 107. *See also Daedalian*
Justin, Margaret M., 84

Kaestle, Carl, 6
Kates, Susan, 4, 5, 17, 115–16

Kelley, William Melvin, 41
Kerl, Simon, 140–41
Kilpatrick, William, 142, 170n14
King, Martin Luther, Jr., 55
Kitzhaber, Albert R., 1, 139, 169n12
Komunyakaa, Yusef, 57, 58

Lacy, Etta M., 89–90
Langston University, 31, 37, 42, 45
Levi, Giovanni, 7
Lewis, Bertram, 42–43
Lincoln, Abraham, 32
Lincoln University, 26, 32, 33, 34
literacy, 6, 22, 154
Logan, Shirley Wilson, 15, 65
L'Ouverture, Toussaint, 32
lynching, 28, 37, 46, 50–51, 128

Malone, Margaret, 100–101
Mann, Horace, 118
Marshall, Thurgood, 42, 165n15
Marshall, Tex., 28–30. *See also* Wiley College
Marx, Karl, 34, 39
Massey, Jackson, 131, 132, 143–44
Mayes, Will H., 107
Mayo, Etta Booth, 127–28, 133, 134, 169n10
Mayo, Gladys, 133
Mayo, Marion, 126, 137, 146
Mayo, William Leonidas: and accreditation, 114; and chapel exercises, 137–38, 144, 146; childhood of, 126; children of, 127; and classroom discipline, 143–44; death of, 10, 114, 150; early jobs of, 127; and education for community, 128–33; education of, 122, 126–27, 134; as founder of East Texas Normal College, xi, 10, 127; and grammar, 145–48; and learning by doing, 128–29, 138, 143; and literary societies, debates, and oratory at East Texas Normal College, 133–38; on "normalism," 128–29, 149; on normal schools, 120, 121; pedagogy of, at East Texas Normal College, 113–17, 135–38, 150–54; personal papers of, 11; and textbooks, 123, 124, 138, 145; whipping of, by Bridges, 132–33

McArthur, Judith N., 81, 83–84

McCandless, Amy Thompson, 65, 69, 105

McCleary, Johnnie Marie Van Zandt, 42

McHenry, Elizabeth, 15

McLeod, Egbert C., 23, 31

Meadows, Leon, 139, 140, 141

memoriter, 124, 168n5

Methodist Episcopal Church (MEC), 15, 18, 23, 24

Meyers, Bessie, 87

Miller, Kelly, 49

Miller, Susan, 8, 65

Miller, Thomas P., 3, 7

Miller-Bernal, Leslie, 65

Milton, John, 32

Mirick, Dorris, 106

Montessori, Maria, 119

Morgan, Nadine, 109

Mortensen, Peter, 7

Mount Holyoke College, 65, 86

Mullen, Edward J., 16

Musselman, Hugh Thomas, 168n6

Nash, Walter, 130

Nation, Carry, 128

National Association for the Advancement of Colored People (NAACP), 29, 42, 46, 165n15

National Council of Teachers of English (NCTE), 113, 115, 142

National Education Association, 168n4

National Normal University, 119, 122, 126

Nelson, Raymond, 16

Nielsen, Aldon L., 58, 59

Nixon, Richard M., 42

normal schools: and American ideal, 119–22; composition instruction at, 139–43; contributions of, 148–50; curriculum of, 135; Eastern versus Western, 117–18; enrollment statistics of, 122; and grammar instruction, 147; history of, 118–19, 122–24; mission of, 121, 122; origin of term, 118; pedagogy of, 117–22, 124–26, 138–43; and project method, 142–43, 170n14; rhetorical instruction at, 4, 124–25, 148–51; and "rhetoricals," 135; statistics on, 170n1; students of, 115,

122; summer sessions of, 122; in Texas, 149–50; and textbooks, 138–39; versus universities and liberal arts colleges, 115, 120–22. *See also* East Texas Normal College

Norris, Clarence, 23

North, Stephen M., 5

North Texas State Normal College, 147, 149, 170n17

Novick, Peter, 12

Oberlin College, 163n1

Oklahoma City University (OCU), 45–46

Oliver, Mattie Booth, 127

Olson, Gary A., 8, 110

O'Neill, Tip, ix

oratory. *See* debate; rhetorical education

Ousley, Clarence, 70, 76, 79

Paine, Charles, 4, 5, 6, 7, 8, 17

Parker, John W., 20

Paul Quinn College, 18

Payne, Bruce R., 69

pedagogy: at East Texas Normal College, 113–17, 135–38, 150–54; Charles Eliot on, 121; mainstream versus activist, 116; of normal schools, 117–22, 124–26, 138–43; at Wiley College, xi, 9, 15, 16, 17, 31–43, 59–62, 152, 153. *See also* rhetorical education

Pemberton, H. B., 29–30, 164n9

Pestalozzi, Johann Heinrich, 118–19, 124, 125, 135, 168n3

Phipps, Bronly L., 136

phonics method, 168n8

Platteville Normal School, 66

poetry: *Daedalian* articles on, 101, 102, 103; by Tolson, 16, 34, 36–37, 43, 54–59

Poulson, Susan L., 65

Pound, Ezra, 54

Prairie View A&M, 18, 19

project method, 142–43, 170n14

public speaking. *See* debate; rhetorical education

Radcliffe College, 65–66, 109, 165n3

Rainey, Homer, 14, 50

Ratcliffe, Krista, 155
Ravitch, Diane, 171n2
Rayburn, Sam, 131, 136, 144
reading instruction. *See* rhetorical education
Regan, Alison Elizabeth, 11
Rendezvous with America (Tolson), 16, 43
rhetorical education: and academic "whitewashing," 51–52; activist rhetoric, 5, 16; archival sources on, 11–12; assumptions on historiography of, 7–8; at Central Normal College, 124–25; chronology on, 159–61; composition instruction, 139–43; current-traditional rhetoric, 1–3, 6, 8, 17, 31, 66, 163n1; grammar instruction, 35–36, 89–90, 101–2, 113, 123–25, 139, 140–41, 145–48; at Harvard University, 66, 92; at normal schools, 4, 124–25, 148–51; oratory, 20–21, 25, 59–60, 93, 134–38; outside readings for, 139; recommendations on, 154–56; reform tradition in, 153; revisionist turn in historiography on, 4–6; roots of reductive rhetoric, 2–3; textbooks for, 25–26, 32, 138–39, 145, 169n12; for women, 65–66. *See also* debate; East Texas Normal College; Texas Woman's University; Wiley College
rhetoric of assertion, 8
Richards, Ellen Swallow, 85
Richardson, Elaine, 36
Roberts-Miller, Patricia, 38
Rogers, J. E., 124
Rollins, Edmund, 165n16
Rosenberry, Lois Mathews, 80, 166n9
Rothermel, Beth Ann, 115
Royster, Jacqueline Jones, 15, 51, 163n1
Rudolph, Frederick, 155

Sackville, Margaret, 99–100, 108
Samuel Huston College, 20, 21, 22, 23, 24, 26, 29, 163n5
Sánchez, Raúl, 8
Sandburg, Carl, 32–33, 96, 101
Schultz, Lucille M., 1, 4, 5, 115
Scott, Emmett, 30
Scott, Fred Newton, 26, 32, 116, 169n12

Scott, Rev. Isaiah B., 24, 164n7
Seaholm, Megan, 76
segregation: and interracial debates, 45–47; of Marshall, Tex., 26–31; of Texas Woman's University (TWU), 106–7; Tolson on, 39. *See also* desegregation
Shakespeare, William, 32, 56, 57, 95, 133
Shapiro, Karl, 41, 54
Sharer, Wendy, 65
Shurter, Edwin DuBois, 11
signifying, signification, 36, 49
Sinclair, Upton, 169n11
Sipuel v. Board of Regents of University of Oklahoma, 164n10, 165n15
Skiles, Robert, 108, 167n20
Sloss, Minerva A., 40–41
Slosson, Edwin E., 98
Smith, Morgan A., 133, 169n11
Smitherman, Geneva, 36, 51
Smith-Lever Act (1914), 79
Smith-Rosenberg, Carroll, 110
Snow, W. H., 130
socialism, 133, 169n11
Somerville, John Alexander, 56
Sophie Newcomb College, 65, 165n3
Southern Association of Colleges for Women (SACW), 69, 75
Standard American English (SAE), 36, 60, 110, 113, 150
Stoddard, Helen M., 77–78, 84, 165–66n6
Storms, Albert, 120
Sutton, William Seneca, 168n6
Sweatt, Heman, 42
Sweatt v. Painter, 164n10
Swygert, H. Patrick, 61

Talladega College, 43, 44
Tanner, Mary, 102–3
Tarbell, Ida, 65, 165n2
Taylor, Howard, 69
teaching: certification, 73, 87, 130; and other careers, 130–31; popularity of, as career for women, 86, 87; salaries, 86, 130. *See also* East Texas Normal College; normal schools
temperance movement, 20, 76, 77, 79, 128, 169n10

Tennyson, Alfred Lord, 32

Texas A&M, 73, 77, 78, 79, 107, 109, 166n8

Texas A&M University–Commerce. *See* East Texas Normal College

Texas Federation of Women's Clubs (TFWC), 67, 76–79, 84, 166nn7, 12

Texas Intercollegiate Press Association (TIPA), 99, 100, 107–9

Texas Southern University, 18, 42

Texas Woman's University (TWU): archives of, 9–10, 11, 92; board of regents for, 77–78; buildings of, 78; compared with women's colleges in East, 72, 111–12; creation of, 68–76; curriculum of, 67, 68, 70, 73–76, 87–93; and *Daedalian*, 68, 85, 89–90, 92, 94–110, 167nn18, 20; debate at, 93; dress code at, 104–5; English department at, 89–92; enrollment statistics of, 70; founding date of, x, 9, 64, 70; funds for, 78, 106; goals and mission of, xi, 9–10, 64, 66–67, 68, 70–71, 88, 112; grammar instruction at, 89–90, 101–2; home economics at, 68, 70, 79, 83–87, 88, 111; *Lass-O* newspaper at, 96, 97; as liberal arts institution, 74–75, 81–82, 90–91; literary clubs and cultural life at, 68, 93–96, 167n17; literary merit of *Daedalian* writing, 108–9; names of, 165n4; political writings at, 105–7; presidents of, 70–71, 73–76, 109; pride of students at, 107–9; prizes won by *Daedalian*, 109; and progressive politics, 79–81; public speaking at, 93, 167n15; racial stereotypes at, 107; and resistance to women's rights, 63–64; rhetorical instruction at, 68, 75, 87–96, 110–11, 154; satires of, in *Daedalian*, 103–5; segregation of, 106–7; statistics on, 64; student costs at, 72; student demographics of, 71–73, 109; student English papers from, 92; student-run publications at, 96–109; and teacher certification, 73, 87; variety of writings and writing styles in *Daedalian*, 110; visiting speakers and performers at, 95–96; vocational education at, 68, 70–71, 74, 81–82, 83, 86, 88, 152; and women's social networks, 67, 76–81, 106, 109; writing courses at, 91–92; yearbook of, 96, 97, 109, 167n18. *See also* women

textbooks: and East Texas Normal College, 123, 124, 138; Holbrook's use of, 123; literary readers edited by Bowman, 145; and normal schools, 138–39; in rhetorical education, 25–26, 32, 138–39, 145, 169n12; for rural schools, 138–39; at Wiley College, 25–26

Threlkeld, Hilda, 82

Tillotson Institute, 21, 22, 23

Tittle, Walter Lee, 137

Tolson, Melvin Beaunoris: African American discourse used by, 36, 40, 56; on bourgeois, conservative values, 53; childhood of, 32; on Christianity and Jesus, 34; contradictions embraced by, 16, 31–32, 49–59, 163n3; criticisms of, 40–41, 53, 54; and debate team, 20–21, 43–49; departure of, from Wiley College, 23, 31; as dramatics coach, 45; education of, 26, 29, 32–33; father of, 33–34; and grammar, 35–36; and guns on campus, 28; influence of, on students, 42–43; at Langston University, 31, 37; learning from practices of, 59–62; oratorical teaching style of, 34–35; pedagogy of, xi, 9, 15, 16, 17, 31–43, 59–62, 152, 153; poetry by, 16, 34, 36–37, 43, 54–59; political activism of, 29, 37, 42, 50–51, 164–65n15; power and authority of, in classroom, 37–43; public writing by, 31, 37, 53, 56–57; on race and class, 33, 37, 53, 56–57; students' relationships with, 17; *Washington Tribune* newspaper column by, 31, 57, 58. *See also* Wiley College

Tolson, Melvin, Jr., 35–36, 42, 44, 51, 56

Tolson, Ruth, 51

Tuskegee Institute, 18, 44

Tuttle, Mary Louise, 84

UCLA Higher Education Research Institute, 170–71n2

universities. *See* higher education; *specific colleges and universities*

University of Michigan, 44

University of Oklahoma, 45, 50, 164–65*n*15
University of Southern California (USC), 47, 48, 56, 164*n*14
University of Texas: academic freedom at, 14, 15; debate at, 107–8; desegregation of law school at, 42, 164*n*10; education school at, 170; home economics program at, 166*n*12; Rainey's firing by, 14, 50; speech program at, 20, 167*nn*15, 16; summer enrollment of, 114; and Texas Intercollegiate Press Association (TIPA), 107; and Texas Woman's University (TWU), 71, 73, 74, 109
University of Wisconsin, 149

Varnum, Robin, 4, 5
Vassar College, 72, 75, 86, 112
Virginia Union, 164*n*12
vocational education, 68, 70–71, 74, 81–82, 83, 86, 88, 152. *See also* home economics; normal schools

Wagner, Joanne, 66
Walker, Corrie, 108
Walker, Mamie, 92
Ware, E. E., 44
Washington, Booker T., 18, 30
Washington Tribune, 31, 57, 58
Watson, Andrew Polk, 29
Wellesley College, 65, 83, 109
Wells, Henrietta Bell, 35, 37, 38, 40, 44–45, 48, 49
Wendell, Barrett, 139, 169*n*12
West, Mae, 47
West, Ruth, 65, 105–6
Wharton, Marian, 66
Whitbread, Thomas, 14, 50
White, Edmund Valentine, 73, 74, 107
White, Hayden V., 12
Whitman, Walt, 49
Wilberforce University, 116
Wiley, Autry Nell, 89, 91, 92
Wiley, Bishop Isaac D., 164*n*6
Wiley College: and archives, 11; classical liberal arts education at, 24, 152; competition between Bishop College

and, 23; debate at, 20–21, 25, 43–49, 164*n*14; Dogan as president of, 18, 23, 27, 29–31, 45, 50; drama at, 45; faculty of, 14–15, 24, 25–26, 28, 29; founding date of, x, 9, 23; goals and mission of, xi, 15, 24, 30–31; grammar instruction at, 35–36; and guns on campus, 27–28; history of, 18, 23–24; learning from Tolson's practices at, 59–62; library for, 30; literary societies at, 20–21, 25; and Methodist Episcopal Church, 15, 18, 23, 24; NAACP chapter at, 29, 42; naming of, 164*n*6; and negotiation with white community, 29–31; oratory at, 25; power and authority of Tolson in classroom at, 37–43; presidents following Dogan at, 23, 24, 31, 42, 164*n*7; religious rules and restrictions at, 26–27; and segregation, 26–31; student strike at, 27; textbooks used at, 25–26; Tolson's departure from, 23, 31; Tolson's pedagogy at, xi, 9, 15, 16, 17, 31–43, 59–62, 152, 153. *See also* black colleges
Willard, Frances E., 133, 169*n*10
Williams, Jean C., 51
Williams, Lenora, 25–26
Williams, William Carlos, 16
Wilson, Mary, 82
Winship, Albert Edward, 168*n*6
women: antebellum ideal of Southern lady, 82–83; at black colleges, 61; businesswomen in fiction, 102–3; and debate teams, 44–45, 164*n*12; employment of, 69, 79, 83, 86–87, 112, 167*n*21; and female consciousness versus feminist consciousness, 80–81; gender equality at East Texas Normal College, 134–35; higher education for, 64–69, 82, 165*n*1; as journalists, 107; New Woman, 111; and progressive politics and Southern identity, 79–81; resistance to rights of, 63–64, 69–70, 80–81; rhetorical education of, 65–66; social role of, 63–64, 68–70, 111; rights and suffrage for, 81, 106, 111, 133; and women's clubs, 67, 76–83, 89, 106, 109, 111, 134. *See also* Texas Woman's University

Women's Christian Temperance Union
(WCTU), 20, 76, 77, 79, 128
Woodson, Carter G., 52
Woolf, Virginia, 65
Wordsworth, William, 102, 103
Work, Cree T., 70–71, 73, 78
Work, Mary Brown, 71, 79, 80
Wright, Ilah, 21

Wright, Richard, 50
writing instruction. *See* rhetorical education

Yale University, 20, 43, 98, 121–23
Young, Richard E., 163*n*1

Zaluda, Scott, 51–52, 163*n*1

David Gold is an assistant professor of English and composition coordinator at California State University, Los Angeles, where he teaches undergraduate and graduate courses in rhetoric, writing, and language and literacy. He is particularly interested in the voices of marginalized rhetors and the intersections between literacy and civic action. His work has appeared in *College Composition and Communication*, *College English*, *English Journal*, *Rhetoric Review*, and the *Writing Instructor* as well as in edited collections.